THE PROMISE OF BAPTISM

THE BOOKSTORE

THE PROMISE OF BAPTISM

An Introduction to Baptism in Scripture and the Reformed Tradition

James V. Brownson

WILLIAM B. EERDMANS PUBLISHING COMPANY
GRAND RAPIDS, MICHIGAN / CAMBRIDGE, U.K.

Wm. B. Eerdmans Publishing Co.

2140 Oak Industrial Drive N.E., Grand Rapids, Michigan 49505 /

P.O. Box 163, Cambridge CB3 9PU U.K.

Printed in the United States of America

11 10 09 08 07   7 6 5 4 3 2 1

Library of Congress Cataloging-in-Publication Data

Brownson, James V.

   The promise of baptism: an introduction to baptism in Scripture and the
Reformed tradition / James V. Brownson.

      p.   cm.

   Includes bibliographical references and index.

   ISBN 978-0-8028-3307-5 (pbk.: alk. paper)

   1. Baptism — Biblical teaching.   2. Reformed Church — Doctrines.   I. Title.

BS2545.B36B76 2007

234'.161 — dc22

                                       2006022844

www.eerdmans.com

Contents

Preface

Although writing is a solitary act, it is never done in isolation from others. I am grateful for the many people who have assisted me in writing this book. I am deeply grateful to Western Theological Seminary for providing the sabbatical leave that enabled this book to be written, and to the seminary library staff for their assistance with many requests. I am also grateful for a number of friends and colleagues who read drafts of portions of this book and provided invaluable feedback and critique. I say thank you to J. Todd Billings, George Brown, Timothy Brown, Kathryn Brownson, William C. Brownson, Bill De Boer, David Landegent, David Stubbs, Dennis Voskuil, and Leanne Van Dyk. Although their insights have greatly improved the book, the responsibility for its weaknesses must remain entirely with me.

This book is dedicated to my daughters and son, Rachel, Anna, and Will, with the prayer that they may continue more and more to discover the meaning, hope, and promise of their baptisms.

Introduction

This is a book about baptism. It addresses itself to people at those points in their lives when baptism becomes an issue of interest or importance: A teenager has recently decided to become a Christian, and wants to know what the next step might be. A couple are about to give birth to their first child, and now they are thinking about what it might mean to have the baby baptized. A woman in her fifties was baptized as an infant, but was not raised as a Christian. She finds herself coming to faith later in life, and wonders whether she should be baptized again, or what her earlier baptism as an infant meant. A Christian family moves into a community, and joins a church whose understanding of baptism is different from the view in their former congregation, and they wonder who is right, and whether this disagreement is something worth worrying about. Parents in their forties agonize over their son, baptized as an infant, who now wants nothing to do with the church. What does that baptism from years ago mean now? A church board pauses to reflect on their life together as a congregation, and wonders if the practice of baptism in the congregation is all it could and should be. A seminary student puzzles over the technical theological literature on baptism, and looks for ways to communicate the essentials of the doctrine in ways that are simple and accessible. All of these people, and more besides, are envisioned as audiences for this book.

At one level, baptism is astonishingly simple. Christians gather in worship. A new Christian is brought forward. Questions are asked, and affirmations are given. Water is applied to this person (by sprinkling, pouring, or immersion). The leader repeats the age-old formula of Matthew 28:19, saying, "I baptize you in the name of the Father, and of the Son, and of the Holy Spirit." That's it!

Yet there is much going on in this deceptively simple rite. Through baptism, a person is marked as a Christian and recognized as a member of the covenant community, the church. Although most Christians agree broadly about what it means to be a Christian and a member of the church, this apparent agreement begins to become less clear and consistent as the questions and issues become more specific and concrete. It is these complexities that this book will explore.

For much of their lives, many Christians hardly think about these more complex questions. But circumstances usually will raise them at some point for many of us. One of those points arises when a couple has their first child. What does Scripture teach about young children and their relationship to the church? Should they be considered Christians (and therefore be baptized) because they are members of God's covenant, as most paedobaptists believe? (Paedobaptists are those who hold that the infants of Christian parents are eligible for baptism.) Or should baptism be withheld until these young children are able to confess their own faith, as believer baptists hold? (I use the term "believer baptist" to refer to those who believe that baptism should be administered only to those who confess their own faith in Christ.) And if baptism is withheld, does that mean that these young children are then to be considered as if they are not Christians at all until they are baptized? If these young children die in infancy before they are baptized, are they therefore consigned by God to eternal judgment? If these unbaptized children of believers are *not* consigned to eternal judgment, on what basis are they considered to be saved? Are they saved by Christ's death and resurrection, even while unbaptized, or are they saved because God regards them as innocent until they reach the "age of discretion"? If they are saved by Christ's death and resurrection, why not recognize this by baptizing them into Christ's death and resurrection? If they are saved by virtue of their innocence, then perhaps sin — especially what theologians call *original sin* — is not as serious a problem as some Christians think it is.

The paedobaptist position is loaded with similar conundrums. Suppose that children baptized as infants grow up and never embrace Christian faith as their own. Does this mean that their baptism was invalid? If the answer is that the baptism is still valid, does this understanding of baptism undercut the importance of repentance and faith? If we say that the persistent unbelief of a baptized person nullifies the significance of their baptism, then we are left uncertain about when baptism is and is not "effective." Does the rite express anything beyond the hopes and prayers of the parents and congregation for the infant being baptized?

But the puzzles do not end with questions regarding the baptism of infants. What are we to make of the woman baptized in her teens, who later rejects her faith and dies alienated from the church? What was the significance of her baptism, and what does it mean now at her funeral? Does baptism, whether applied to infants or to believers, give us *anything* in itself, on which we can attach our hopes and confidence? Or is it merely a ritual, the meaning of which is entirely dependent on our ongoing faith in God and our faithfulness to the promises we make at our baptism?

Or consider the case of someone who is baptized as a Roman Catholic, but rejects the faith in his teens. He subsequently returns to an evangelical Protestant church in his forties after many years of life full of brokenness and sin. Should he be *re*-baptized? If so, is the new baptism done because the Catholic baptism is not recognized as valid, or because this person, like the Prodigal Son, was lost, and now is found? Should baptism then be repeated *whenever* someone is "lost," and becomes "found"? If the Catholic baptism is not recognized as valid, what makes it invalid? What in general is the difference between a valid and invalid baptism? Does a perceived theological error in the church performing a baptism mean that all baptisms performed by that church are invalid? If so, perhaps anyone who switches denominations out of a change in theological conviction should be re-baptized. But that would seem to suggest that all those other denominations cannot even be regarded as Christian at all.

We could fill many more pages with such dilemmas. There are many complicated and interrelated questions that arise when we talk about baptism. This book will not answer all of them, but will provide a "road map" through some of the more common problems and questions. Because part of the challenge in understanding baptism is simply learning what the questions are, this book is organized in brief chapters, each of which attempts to address a single question. This has two advantages: you always know "where you are," and what the topic under consideration is. You also are able to move quickly to the topics that interest you most. The use of brief chapters also gives the reader time and opportunity to reflect and to consolidate thinking after each question is discussed, before moving on.

The order in which the questions in this book are arranged has its own logic and assumptions. It will be important to read at least the first six chapters (chapters 1-6) in order, so that the foundational theological and biblical questions are clearly in view. After that, it will be easier to skip around to the topics that are of most interest, though if the entire book is to be read, it is still best done in its normal sequence. The rest of the book is structured into thematic sections, each of which has a brief introduction. Some chapters presuppose the discussion in other places, and that fact will be indicated at the relevant place.

Each chapter is tightly focused on a specific question, and many of them are rather densely packed with information. Especially if someone is new to the theological questions surrounding baptism, this book will be more profitably read in small doses of one or two chapters over a period of time, rather than in long readings at a single sitting. After reading a chapter, you may wish to review the major points of the chapter in the summary entitled "To Sum Up." This summary is followed by some questions for further reflection and discussion, and then a suggestion for further research, which often can be done on the Internet. You may also wish to explore some of the biblical references in more detail, and to jot down what seems convincing or questionable to you in the topic at hand.

Before diving into the discussion, let me say some things about myself and my approach that may be helpful in orienting the reader to what is said here. I am a minister in the Reformed Church in America, a small denomination in North America that traces its roots back to the Reformation, especially to the teaching of John Calvin. This theological tradition in which I am located is commonly referred to as the Reformed tradition, emphasizing that the church must always *reform* its faith and practice so that it is more deeply in accordance with the Word of God. This tradition practices infant baptism, and has placed great emphasis on the centrality of Scripture and on the importance of faith in Christ as the sole means of our salvation.

I am also installed into an ecclesiastical office known as Professor of Theology in my denomination. This is a fairly little-known church office that still exists in only a few denominations. This office means that the church has asked me to take a particular responsibility for training candidates for ordination, and for the teaching ministry of the church as a whole. In that capacity, I teach New Testament studies (and some other topics as well) in a theological seminary devoted primarily to preparing candidates for ordained ministry. I see myself as a biblical theologian in service to the church.

I write this book out of a desire to be of service to the church. Though my primary area of interest is not in systematic or practical theology —

the normal academic areas dealing with the doctrine of baptism — it is my concern for the church that leads me to write this book. I find much confusion on various topics related to baptism in many parts of the church, and an absence of clear and accessible materials that illumine this important practice of the church. In this book I will argue as vigorously as I can for the practice of infant baptism, but I also will seek to set this discussion within an overall doctrine of baptism that has the depth and richness to speak to many of the questions arising in the church today.

In the discussion that follows, some recurring themes will emerge. I am convinced that the church is called to be in mission, not just as one activity among many others, but rather as the church's central vocation. Baptism into the church means baptism into God's mission in the world. I also believe that the church is a *body* — that it has a corporate identity that is larger and richer than merely a sum of the individual members who belong to it. In the face of an increasingly individualistic society, being baptized into the church as a *body* is a theme that needs to be rediscovered.

I also believe that the church is a gathering of *disciples*, who are always learning and growing as they follow Jesus Christ. Disciples often fail. Disciples don't have it all together. We need to think about baptism not as the end of the salvation road, but as the beginning of the discipleship road. This means that we need to think about Christian faith itself as a kind of *process*. We look back to Jesus and to the Christians who have gone before us. We live today in communion with the Holy Spirit and each other, seeking to be obedient to God's call in our time, and we look forward to what God has promised to do in our world, but which we do not yet see. We must always think about baptism in this larger context and process.

Finally, in keeping with the Reformed tradition, I believe that the proclamation of Scripture and the administration of the sacraments are absolutely central to the life of the church. The Reformers — both Luther and Calvin — regarded these as the central "marks" of the church, and as absolutely foundational for everything else in the life of the church. If these are well, the church's core identity will be intact, and it will have the resources it needs to engage the ongoing problems that arise in seeking to follow Jesus. If these are obscured, it will be hard to be clear or strong on anything else. It is out of that conviction that I write this book, with the prayer that the church's practice of baptism may, through this book, be made more deeply biblical, and that the church will consequently be empowered for a more confident and faithful mission in Christ's name.

SECTION I

BASIC QUESTIONS

This first section, made up of chapters 1-6, sets an overall context for thinking about baptism, beginning with basic Christian identity, then turning to some foundational assumptions about the church, and finally looking at some larger questions surrounding sacraments in general. Because these chapters deal with issues at a fairly high level of generality, the language may at times seem abstract and a little more difficult to grasp. Despite this higher level of abstraction, it is important to begin this way, and I believe it is worth the extra effort to explore these questions. Baptism is an area of significant controversy among Christians. Much of the controversy arises from differing assumptions at a very basic level: What does it mean to be a Christian, what is the church, and what is *happening*, in the most basic sense, when we baptize someone? All of the rest of this book will simply elaborate and make more specific the framework laid out in these first six chapters.

1 What Does It Mean to Be a Christian?

To be baptized is, quite simply, to become a Christian. But even a simple statement like this raises a host of questions: Can one become a Christian without being baptized? Can one be baptized without being a true Christian? Does being baptized *make* you a Christian, or are you baptized *because* you have already become a Christian? We will explore all these questions, and many more, as this book unfolds. But before we even begin to talk about baptism itself, we first need to explore what it means to be a Christian.

If we take our cue from the Gospel According to Matthew and the book of Acts, Christians are *disciples* of Jesus. Matthew ends his gospel with the Great Commission, in which Jesus commands his followers to "make disciples of all the nations, baptizing them in the name of the Father, and of the Son, and of the Holy Spirit, and teaching them to obey everything that I have commanded you" (Matt. 28:19-20). The very grammar of this command makes it clear that the central command is to make disciples, and that this is accomplished through baptizing and teaching. We see the same language of discipleship picked up repeatedly in the book of Acts, which describes the emergence of the early Christian movement. Here as well, the standard term used for Christians is "disciples" (Acts 6:1-2; 9:1, 26; 11:26, etc.). Note particularly Acts 11:26, which indicates how the original name "disciples" gradually became "Christians." So a Christian is a disciple of Jesus.

What is a disciple, and what do disciples do? Disciples are essentially *learners* and *followers*. The word "disciple" literally means "learner." Disciples are people who follow someone from whom they hope to learn. Following means being with someone, sharing experiences, sharing common tasks. It also means submitting to someone else's direction and guidance.

Disciples follow in order to learn, in order to grow. To be a disciple is to be a learner and follower on a path of growth, submitting to the guidance and instruction of a teacher.

But being a Christian does not mean being a disciple of just anyone; it means being a follower of Jesus Christ. Christians are people who have become captivated, often in ways they cannot entirely explain, by Jesus Christ. They find themselves drawn to him, challenged by the honesty and graciousness of his life, encouraged by his concern for outsiders and "sinners," grieved by his horrible death, and drawn to a deeper hopefulness by his resurrection. They see their own sinfulness exposed and forgiven by his death on their behalf. Christians are those who believe that Jesus is the source of the deepest wisdom and the truest power available in this world. They believe that God is uniquely present in this vivid and compelling human person. Furthermore, they believe that he is alive, that he has defeated death, and that he continues to be present to them. Therefore when Jesus says to a Christian, "Follow me," that person understands this not merely as a human suggestion, but as the call of God. This is why Christians are learners who follow Jesus as Savior and Lord, friends who hope to be transformed by their relationship with him, and witnesses of his power who are sent by him to share this good news in the world.

But there is one peculiar characteristic of disciples of Jesus that we should note, at least if we take the gospel stories of Jesus' life as our starting point. None of Jesus' disciples volunteered for the job. There is an interesting story in the gospels where one person volunteered to be a disciple (Matt. 8:19-20), but Jesus didn't respond too positively to the offer. Disciples do not choose their masters; masters choose their disciples (cf. John 15:16).

This continues to be true in the experience of Christians today. It's not that Christians don't consciously choose to become disciples. It's just that when Christians look back on that choice after they have made it, they discern that God's action to choose them preceded their choosing, not just in a general way, but in a way that was very particular to their own life. Often they can identify very specific events or experiences which, in hindsight, they recognize as the loving hand of God, steering them toward discipleship. God was at work in their life long before they knew it, preparing them to make the choice to become a disciple (cf. Jer. 1:5). Christians recognize that it was this prior choice of God to work in their lives that brought them to the point where they could and did choose to become a disciple. We choose to become disciples because God first chose us (cf. 1 John 4:19).

The priority of God's call to us to become disciples also brings with it another critical part of what it means to be a Christian. To be a Christian is to live by grace (Eph. 2:8). God's call on us *precedes* our response of obedience and faith; indeed, it is God's prior call that makes any obedience and faith on our part even possible. "While we were still sinners," Paul says, "Christ died for us" (Rom. 5:8). Christians follow Jesus not merely because of his wisdom, but because they believe his death and resurrection was, in some mysterious way, done *for* them. It is because of his suffering that they have new life; because of his self-offering that they are reconciled to God. It is his resurrection that gives them the hope of their participation in a new creation still to come. Christians believe that in Jesus' death and resurrection they have received a most extraordinary love which they could never deserve, and can never repay.

This means that Christians are not people who "have it all together." Being a Christian is not a badge of spiritual accomplishment. Rather, being a Christian means standing in the grace of Jesus Christ, who chose disciples who were completely ignorant of, and often even resistant to, what he had in mind (e.g., Mark 8:31-33). Being a Christian means at times being like the disciples, who all deserted Jesus and fled when he needed them the most, just before his death. Being a Christian means living in the knowledge that one's discipleship is radically dependent on the forgiving grace of God shown in Jesus' life, death, and resurrection. To be a disciple is to know that, at the core of one's life, one still has much to learn, and that the first step in our discipleship is always the step of receiving forgiveness. All our obedience, all our attempts at faithfulness and responsibility to God's call, thus flow from an even more basic posture of gratitude that we have been given a life which, in the most basic sense, we do not deserve and did not earn.

This is what the New Testament means by the word "faith." Faith is a matter of trusting, first of all, that Jesus will accept us as his disciples even if we are far from perfect. It's a matter of trusting that God's grace, given to the world in Jesus, extends all the way to us. And it's a matter of trusting that, as disciples of Jesus, we can learn and grow, and be transformed and used for God's good purposes, through the wisdom, love, and power of Jesus.

So Christians are disciples, followers of Jesus who seek to learn and to grow, and who live their lives trusting that God has called and chosen them before they even made their own choice to become disciples. They are thus deeply aware of God's kindness and grace which precedes and empowers their own commitment to Christ. Disciples live by faith, trusting in this grace as the foundation for their lives.

But God not only *chooses* Christians; God also *joins Christians to Jesus* in a powerful bond. This is what theologians call "union with Christ," and we will not fully understand what it means to be a Christian without including this vital element. Jesus tells his disciples, after giving them the Great Commission in Matthew 28:19-20, "I am with you always, to the end of the age." Christians are those who experience the risen Jesus as *present* to them in an ongoing way. But the way in which Jesus is present to Christians goes far deeper than the way in which we may be "present" to each other. Jesus is present in and with us by the power of the Holy Spirit. Note how, for example, Jesus says in John 14:18, "I will not leave your orphaned; I am coming to you." Immediately after this, Jesus goes on to speak of the sending of the Holy Spirit (14:26). We are united to Jesus by the Holy Spirit.

This presence of Jesus through the Holy Spirit to Christians is similar to the way we are present to each other when we know each other best and are most available to each other — physically, emotionally, and spiritually. But this experience of interpersonal presence is only a faint echo of the way in which Jesus is united with and present to Christians. Jesus is distinct from Christians and "other" than Christians (we do not literally "become" Jesus), and yet Jesus is deeply within and united to Christians.

Early Christians were so conscious of this reality that they spoke of the events and experiences of Jesus' life as if they had also happened to them. So the New Testament speaks of how Christians have been "crucified with Christ" (Gal. 2:19), how Christians have been "raised with Christ" (Col. 3:1), how Christians are "heirs" of God's grace along with Jesus (Rom. 8:17). Indeed, one gets the strong sense that for the New Testament, everything that happens to Jesus or is true of Jesus also applies, in some sense, to Christians. Christians believe that Jesus embodies a new way of being human within God's favor. And those who are joined to Jesus experience this new form of humanity, by the power of the Spirit.

Of course, Christians don't experience this new reality perfectly. A very large part of the "learning" of discipleship is learning how to leave behind the old patterns of life which are part of our old identity, and to take on more and more the new patterns of life that are part of our new identity in Christ. But Christians believe that the only reason they can engage in such growth at all is because God has already *given* them a new identity, a new way of being human, by uniting them to Jesus. Christians are always learning and growing toward *becoming* in their daily lives the kind of persons that they already *are* in their union with Christ.

Up to this point, we have been discussing what it means to be *a* Christian. But in a very real sense, there is no such thing as an individual Christian. When God joins Christians to Jesus, God also joins them to something bigger than themselves; they become incorporated into the church, the "body of Christ." In the New Testament, it is inconceivable for Christians to think of themselves as united to Christ without also thinking about the ways they are united to other Christians. This was true even in Jesus' own ministry. He didn't have one disciple; he had twelve, and many more beyond his "inner circle." Almost all of the learning of Jesus' disciples took place as a group, rather than in one-on-one interactions with Jesus. This same pattern continued in the early church, as Christians gathered in groups called *ekklesiai* (the Greek word for "churches," which can also be translated "meetings" or "assemblies"). From the beginning, it was unimaginable that someone might become a Christian without also becoming part of a church, a local gathering of disciples of Jesus. The union with Christ experienced by Christians also unites them to each other.

But the body of Christ to which Christians are united is not a social club of like-minded people; it is not a self-help organization for people trying to make spiritual progress. It is a body of people who are gifted by the Holy Spirit and sent on a mission (Eph. 4:7-13; John 20:21). In their life of discipleship, growth, and learning, Christians experience a transformative power that comes from beyond themselves. But that power is not just for their own self-improvement; it is given in order for them to love and serve others, and to bear witness to the one whom they follow as Lord. And the church of Jesus Christ as a whole exists, not for itself, but to love and serve the whole world in Jesus' name, inviting all to become his disciples, beginning with the people in the church's own neighborhoods and cities. Jesus *sends* the church into the world, so that the reconciling and healing power of God is available, not only to those who are already part of the fellowship, but finally, to the whole world.

Obviously, much more can and will be said on almost all these points. But in this chapter, we have looked with a wide-angle lens at the question of basic Christian identity. In a sense, the remainder of this book will only expand on what we have already raised here. Many disagreements and uncertainties among Christians regarding baptism can be traced back to differing understandings of what basic Christian life is all about. That is why we begin here, with these basic questions.

To Sum Up

> To be a Christian is to be
>   – a disciple of Jesus,
>   – called by God,
>   – living by grace through faith,
>   – joined to Christ and to fellow Christians by the power of the Holy Spirit,
>   – gifted and sent on God's mission to the world.

For Further Reflection and Discussion

> Do you think of Christians primarily as disciples of Jesus? What other core metaphors are you familiar with that express what it means to be a Christian? What speaks most powerfully to you about being a disciple?

> How have you experienced the reality discussed in this chapter, that God's choosing us takes place *before* we choose to follow Jesus? Some Christians fear that this emphasis on God's first choosing us makes human beings into robots who have no free will. What do you think?

> Do you think of Christian life primarily in terms of your own salvation and spiritual growth, or do you see Christian life primarily focused on following Jesus in mission? What difference might these two different approaches make to one's understanding of baptism?

For Further Study

> A clear and accessible discussion of basic Christian life can be found in C. S. Lewis's book *Mere Christianity,* available through several publishers.

2 What Is the Church?

The last chapter ended with the affirmation that there is really no such thing as an individual Christian. As a Christian, being joined to Christ necessarily means being joined to other Christians in the church. But what exactly is this "church" to which Christians are joined? We will never understand baptism if we do not understand the nature of the church.

What is the church? For some, it is the building up on Twelfth Street, just off River Avenue. A more discerning response might speak of the people who gather for worship in that building on Sunday mornings: they are the church. Someone else might speak of all Christians in all times and places, who are united with each other in Christ. There is truth in all these answers. Although the New Testament never speaks of "church" as a *building,* many New Testament writers will speak, for example, of "the church of God that is in Corinth" (1 Cor. 1:2). In most of the New Testament usage, "church" refers to a specific group of people gathered in a particular place. In this sense, speaking of "the group that gathers for worship on Twelfth Street" is very much in keeping with the way the New Testament speaks of "church."

There are also a few passages in the New Testament that speak of the church in a way that goes beyond the local congregation to encompass all Christians (e.g., Gal. 1:13; Eph. 1:22-23). In the broadest sense, the church is made up of all those who have been joined to Christ and make up his body in the world. But the most common sense of the word in the New Testament is somewhat more local and specific, referring normally to a group of Christians living close enough to one another to gather regularly as disciples of Jesus.

This gathering of God's people has a long, long history. In fact, the whole Bible is a story about the way God has been gathering and calling a *people* to be in a special relationship with him. God calls Abraham, and promises to enter into a special relationship with him and his descendants (Gen. 15). Later, God rescues Abraham's descendants, the Hebrew people, from slavery in Egypt, and promises to be their God in a special way (Exod. 19:4-7). The same promise is extended to David during the period of the monarchy (Isa. 55:3-4). Even after the people of God are sent into exile, the hope still remains that God will again re-gather this scattered people (Ezek. 37:21-28).

The Christian church is the continuation and extension of this purpose of God, begun with Israel long ago. The inclusion of Gentiles within the church is a new thing in the New Testament, but it is the same tree into which these Gentiles are now grafted (Rom. 11:17-24). God's consistent purpose throughout all of history, as revealed in the Old and New Testaments, has been to gather a people, with whom God enters into a special relationship.

God achieves this purpose through the making of *covenants*. God's covenants follow a consistent pattern throughout the Bible. They begin with God acting to show generosity, mercy, and kindness to people. God makes a covenant with Noah by rescuing him from the flood in Genesis 6:18. God comes to Abraham, and promises that he will be the father of nations in Genesis 12. God rescues the Hebrew people from slavery in Egypt. God singles out David to be king when he is an obscure shepherd boy in the backwater town of Bethlehem. In each of these cases of covenant-making, God initiates the covenant by his own gracious and generous action. In each case, God expects, in response to this expression of generosity, for the other party to show allegiance and faithfulness to God. Noah must build an ark. Abraham must leave his home country and travel to a new land. The Hebrew people must receive and keep the commandments given at Mt. Sinai. David must be faithful to God as king over Israel.

Of course, the sad history of the people of God throughout the Bible is that human beings rarely and only for brief periods of time respond in grateful allegiance to God's generosity. Time and again, the people of God fail to be faithful, fail to show true allegiance in response to God's kindness. But the wonder of the biblical story is that God doesn't give up, but responds to human faithlessness — with judgment, to be sure, but also with even greater kindness and generosity. "Where sin increased," says Paul, "grace abounded all the more" (Rom. 5:20). It is this surprising action of God that lies at the very heart of the church's identity and calling.

The church knows that its ultimate security and identity is not wrapped up in its ability to be faithful to God, but rather in God's tenacious determination to be faithful and gracious. The church is the community of people who are continually surprised by God's kindness and generosity, which always comes to us as a gift, far beyond what we deserve or have any right to expect. The covenant given to the church is summed up in the cup offered to us in the Lord's Supper as the "new covenant" in Jesus' blood (Luke 22:20; 1 Cor. 11:25), the sign of Jesus' self-offering in the face of human resistance and rebellion. Over and over, the church, overcome by this goodness, finds itself called again to new allegiance and obedience to God.

So the church is a *covenant community* that receives the good news of God's forgiving grace in Jesus Christ, and responds by offering itself to God in grateful discipleship, obedience, and allegiance. But this calling of the people of God throughout history has never been for its own benefit, but always in service to God's concern for the whole world. Abraham is promised that in his descendants, all the families of the earth will be blessed (Gen. 12:1-3). This promise is expanded upon in Exodus 19:6, in which God declares that Israel will be "for me a priestly kingdom and a holy nation." This same language is echoed in 1 Peter 2:9-10:

> But you are a chosen race, a royal priesthood, a holy nation, God's own people, in order that you may proclaim the mighty acts of him who called you out of darkness into his marvelous light. Once you were not a people, but now you are God's people; once you had not received mercy, but now you have received mercy.

God blesses a people so they will be a blessing to others. God calls a people to be close to him and to be holy so that they in turn can be priests to others, bringing God's holy presence and blessing to others. The church is blessed in order to be a blessing (Gen. 12:2).

What does it mean that the church is "blessed to be a blessing"? It does not mean that the church has more wisdom than others, which it cheerfully dispenses to the ignorant. It does not mean that the church has great economic and political power, which it wields benevolently in the service of others. Nor does it mean that the church is made up of people who are highly respected by others, who can therefore use their influence for the common good. In fact, Paul specifically rejects the notion that the blessing the church offers to others is based on its own wisdom, status, or power:

Consider your own call, brothers and sisters: not many of you were wise by human standards, not many were powerful, not many were of noble birth. But God chose what is foolish in the world to shame the wise; God chose what is weak in the world to shame the strong; God chose what is low and despised in the world, things that are not, to reduce to nothing things that are, so that no one might boast in the presence of God. (1 Cor. 1:26-29)

The blessing the church offers to the world consists entirely in this, that the church points people's attention not to itself, but to the gracious and faithful presence and activity of God in the world. This presence and activity manifested itself most powerfully in Jesus Christ, who revealed God's power and love in the face of human resistance and indifference. It is precisely this presence and activity of God of which Jesus speaks when, in his preaching, he announces that "the Kingdom of God is at hand." The Kingdom of God is not primarily a place, nor is it merely to be identified with the church. Rather the phrase (which could also be translated "reign of God") refers primarily to God's *action* as the sovereign of the world, extending divine generosity to the world, and asking for faithful allegiance in return. This is what Jesus announces in his proclamation of the Kingdom of God — that God is offering to the world, through Christ's ministry, a new and transformed way of living, empowered by God's love and kindness. What God expects in return is faith — human trust, gratitude, and allegiance.

This relationship between the church and the Kingdom of God needs further exploration. We have said that the Kingdom of God focuses our attention not on the church, but on God's activity as sovereign in the world. But if the church is not to be *identified* with the Kingdom of God, what is the relationship between the church and the Kingdom of God? Or to put it differently, if the church is indeed "blessed to be a blessing," how exactly does God's blessing flow out to the world through the church? Many theologians have put the matter this way: *the church is the sign, foretaste, and instrument of the Kingdom of God.*

The church is first of all the *sign* of the kingdom or reign of God. Isaiah 42:6 declares to the people of God, "I have given you as a covenant to the people, a light to the nations." God *gives* the people of God to the world, as a beacon summoning the world to himself. Jesus picks up the same theme when he declares to his disciples, "You are my witnesses" (Acts

1:8). This means that the church is always pointing beyond itself to God's gracious presence and activity in the world, a presence and activity that manifested itself most powerfully and truly in the life, death, and resurrection of Jesus. In this sense, the church is a herald, an announcer, if you will, who directs the attention of all who will listen to Jesus Christ, crucified, risen, alive and present in the world. It directs people's attention to what Jesus Christ has done and continues to do in the world.

But the church not only points beyond itself. It also embodies, though in a limited way, something of the new life spoken about by Jesus in his proclamation of the Kingdom of God. In this sense, the church is a *foretaste* of the Kingdom of God, which God intends for the whole creation. This experience of the church as foretaste of the Kingdom is not always present, and is not always present in the same degree. Indeed, there are many times when the church's dominant experience lies in sharing the sufferings of Christ. Despite this, however, the church also experiences moments when people are reconciled with each other, when they experience the forgiveness of sins and the power of a new kind of life flowing into them. There are times when healing, joy, and newness of life break into the ordinary course of life in surprising ways.

In reflecting upon such moments, the New Testament speaks of how the Holy Spirit has been given to the church as a "deposit" or "down payment" (2 Cor. 1:22; Eph. 1:14) of the full blessing and grace which God intends to pour out when all of God's purposes for the whole creation have come to their completion. The church never experiences these blessings perfectly or in their completeness in this life, and never in a way that is not mixed also with failure and grief. But nevertheless, the church bears witness that it has been drawn into a new way of being human, and life in the Kingdom of God is a new and transformed existence. It not only *says* this, but it actually, at least in some sense, *experiences* this. The Kingdom of God, says Paul, is "righteousness, peace, and joy in the Holy Spirit" (Rom. 14:17). Life in the church provides glimpses of what life will be like for the whole of creation when all God's gracious purposes for the world have come to their completion.

But there is one further aspect of the church's relationship to the Kingdom of God: the church is the *instrument* of the Kingdom of God. Jesus not only calls disciples and trains them; he sends them out to be the salt of the earth and the light of the world (Matt. 5:13). This is in keeping with the great prophecy of Isaiah cited earlier:

> I am the LORD, I have called you in righteousness, I have taken you by the hand and kept you; I have given you as a covenant to the people, a light to the nations, to open the eyes that are blind, to bring out the prisoners from the dungeon, from the prison those who sit in darkness. (Isa. 42:6-7)

God gives the church to the world in order to "open the eyes that are blind, to bring out the prisoners from the dungeon, from the prison those who sit in darkness." It is through the people of God that God shows compassion and mercy to the world. It is through the witness of the church, in both its words and its actions, that the world is (or is not) persuaded that God really is gracious and kind, and worthy of human allegiance and faithfulness in return.

As a sign, foretaste, and instrument of the Kingdom of God, the church believes that it can be used by God for God's good purposes. Yet this can be a heady and intoxicating belief, which can far too easily seduce the church into arrogance and pride. This is part of the reason why the church always gathers under the sign of the cross, the symbol of God's enduring love in the face of the evil, violence, and rebellion of even the most religiously devout. The church must continually remind itself that whatever power, righteousness, or witness it may offer to the world originates not from itself but from its union with Jesus Christ. Even when used by God, the church never ceases to be the community of redeemed sinners, surprised by God's grace. At the moment the church loses sight of this, its witness utterly collapses.

So what is the church? It is the covenant people of God, a specific gathering of those who have been recipients of God's kindness and mercy, who are seeking to respond in faithful discipleship to that call — a call expressed preeminently in the summons to become disciples of Jesus Christ. God's call to the church is to be the sign, foretaste, and instrument of the Kingdom of God; to be "the salt of the earth" and "the light of the world."

To Sum Up

> In the New Testament, the church is assumed most commonly to be the local body of disciples who gather in a specific place. More generally, the church can also be understood in some New Testament passages to be all Christians who have been united to Jesus Christ.

➤ The church is a covenant community, called into existence by God's grace, and summoned to faithful allegiance. It never ceases to need God's grace.

➤ The church is "blessed to be a blessing." The church becomes a blessing to the world by being the sign, foretaste, and instrument of the Kingdom of God.

For Further Reflection and Discussion

➤ How might our understanding and practice of baptism change if we emphasize the church either as a local fellowship or as the worldwide communion of all Christians?

➤ How would your congregation articulate its basic sense of purpose? How is this purpose similar to or different from the thesis of this chapter that the church is called to be the sign, foretaste, and instrument of the Kingdom of God?

➤ When you think of baptism, does it speak to you primarily of the blessing we receive, or of the summons we receive in baptism to *be* a blessing?

For Further Study

➤ For a helpful and more in-depth discussion of the issues raised in this chapter, see Darrell L. Guder, ed., *Missional Church: A Vision for the Sending of the Church in North America* (Grand Rapids: Eerdmans, 1998).

3 What Does It Mean to Be a *Member* of the Church?

It is one thing to think about the church in general; it is another to think about how individuals are related to the church. Christians cannot think about the church without also thinking about themselves, and their relationship to the church. Since baptism is the rite that marks the beginning of membership in the church, we need to reflect on what it means to be a member of the church.

This task is made more difficult by the complexities of language as it develops over time. When the New Testament was written, the word which we translate "member" (in Greek, *melos*) had only one clear and simple meaning: it referred to a part of the human body, most commonly an arm or leg. Prior to the emergence of Christianity, the Greek word was never used in a metaphorical sense to describe persons who were part of an organization or group.[1] It was in no small part the influence of the writings of the apostle Paul that led to the now commonly accepted idea that the word "member" can refer to persons who are part of some larger organization or group. In Paul's day, "member" simply meant "body part," and when Ephesians 5:30 says "we are members of [Christ's] body," the original readers would most naturally have contemplated the picture of themselves as arms, legs, noses, and other various appendages on the physical body of Jesus Christ. What was for them a metaphor is for us merely unadorned organizational language. So if today we want to consider what it means to be a member of the church, we too might ask our-

---

1. The Latin word *membrum* did, on occasion, refer to persons who were part of a group, but this usage does not appear in Greek until well after the New Testament was written. It is probable that the postbiblical Greek usage was influenced by the New Testament.

16

selves what it might mean to be the legs, hands, noses, ears, tongue, and so forth, of Christ's body.

This will require a significant reorienting of our imagination. Our thinking about what it means to be part of a social group is deeply shaped by our North American political and social context, which has a way of thinking about participation in groups that differs dramatically from the biblical image of being members of Christ's body.

In order to clarify how different this New Testament notion of membership in Christ's body is, it may be useful to contrast it with the notion of social life implicit in the American Declaration of Independence, a document whose words and values are deeply ingrained in the modern psyche. The Declaration begins as follows:

> We hold these truths to be self-evident, that all men are created equal, that they are endowed by their Creator with certain unalienable Rights, that among these are Life, Liberty and the pursuit of Happiness. — That to secure these rights, Governments are instituted among Men, deriving their just powers from the consent of the governed. — That whenever any Form of Government becomes destructive of these ends, it is the Right of the People to alter or to abolish it, and to institute new Government, laying its foundation on such principles and organizing its powers in such form, as to them shall seem most likely to effect their Safety and Happiness.

There are three underlying assumptions in these words, all of which differ markedly from the biblical image of the body of Christ. First, if we are members of a body, we must recognize that different body parts are not "created equal." Of course, each body part is of inestimable value, and Paul in 1 Corinthians 12 states that even the seemingly less important body parts deserve the greater honor. But different body parts are most assuredly not identical or interchangeable — so at least in this sense, they are not "equal." God does indeed place a radically high value on each human life, and God also shows no favoritism or partiality (Rom. 2:11). Even so, if the essential image of the church is that its makeup is to be compared to the composition of the human body, we can hardly say that the church is made up of people who are to be regarded as equal in the sense of being interchangeable. Rather, the church is *diverse,* and that diversity is part of God's basic intention for the church.

Secondly, the Declaration assumes that human organizations are essentially *free* and *voluntary*. It asserts that governments derive "their just powers from the consent of the governed." Humans ought not to be coerced into being part of organizations or governments to which they do not give their consent. North Americans therefore place a high value on the idea that participation in organizations should be voluntary, rather than coerced. Yet this notion that organizations are voluntary is not without its limitations, even apart from considering the church. We are all part of a family, yet few of us have had the privilege of choosing our families, or of granting our consent to the authority of our parents. Unless we are immigrants, we did not choose (or consent to be born into) the country of which we are citizens.

What is true for our families and our native countries is also true of membership in the church. The church is not like the PTA, which seeks to attract the voluntary commitment of parents whose children attend a school. Nor is it even like the Rotary Club, which periodically decides to invite new members to join its ranks. One does not become part of Christ's body by deciding to do so. Nor does one become part of Christ's body by the approval of the existing parts of Christ's body, any more than my two hands could decide that my body needed a third hand to help out with a difficult problem. We become part of Christ's body because God joins us to Jesus Christ and *makes* us part of Christ's body. Being part of Christ's body is not a human option; it is a divine act.

Of course, we must consent to this act of God, just as children need to accept the authority of their parents, and citizens must consent to the rules of the society in which they find themselves. Yet membership in the body of Christ does not *spring from* my consent, any more than membership in my family springs from my consent to be part of my family. It is simply a reality that is given to me, and I can choose either to resist it or to consent to it, but neither my resistance nor my consent alters the givenness of my family or my country of origin. This is why C. S. Lewis, for example, can describe himself as "the most reluctant convert in all of England."[2] Lewis narrates his entire conversion to Christianity not so much as his discovery of and choosing to be united to Christ, but rather God's relentless pursuit — and finally capture — of him. We do not become members of Christ's body by our choice; we instead respond in trust and obedience to what *God* does in joining us to Jesus Christ.

2. *Surprised by Joy: The Shape of My Early Life* (London: Geoffrey Bles, 1955), p. 215.

Thirdly, membership in the church is directed toward very different *ends* and *purposes* from those normally associated with human organizations and groups. Returning again to the Declaration of Independence, we note that it asserts the rights of people "to institute new Government, laying its foundation on such principles and organizing its powers in such form, as to them shall seem most likely to effect their Safety and Happiness." Here we see another basic assumption: human associations exist to pursue the ends and goals of the individuals who make up the group. Groups form in order to effect their own "Safety and Happiness." Yet this is certainly not the most important goal or purpose of the church, which is blessed to be a blessing, called by God to be the "salt of the earth and the light of the world." Membership in the church is not for our benefit; it is an obedient response to the call of God — more like being drafted into the military or being summoned to jury duty than like joining the local country club or neighborhood association.

This analysis is not in any way intended to disparage the values found in the Declaration of Independence. There is much of enormous value in it. But while the governments of which the Declaration speaks are human creations, the church of Jesus Christ is not; it is the body of Christ, a work of God. We cannot therefore simply or directly apply the values we attach to normal human associations and groups to the church, without recognizing its unique place in human life. The church is not, as we too easily assume, a voluntary association of like-minded individuals. It is much more the community of those who have been called by God and joined to Jesus Christ. It is made up not so much of like-minded individuals as of a diversity of members (body parts), who may often find it hard to understand each other because they are *not* always like-minded on many topics. It is not a gathering of individuals who share a common pursuit of safety and happiness, but rather a community of disciples who find themselves together challenged to take up their crosses and follow Jesus Christ, knowing that paradoxically, it is precisely in giving up the pursuit of their own safety and happiness that they will find true life. To be a member of the church is to be part of this living body of Christ in the world, directed and empowered by God through the Holy Spirit, in the service of God's great and gracious mission to the world.

What difference does our notion of church membership make in the way we think about baptism? Our discussion in this chapter suggests that baptism is not so much our volunteering to be part of the church, but it is instead an expression of God's claim upon us. We shall explore this idea further in the next chapter, when we ask whether baptism focuses primarily on what *we* do, or on what *God* does. But our notions about church membership touch on other issues as well. We see in various churches two different understandings of the *basis* for church membership, which correspond to the differences we have been exploring in this chapter. Some Christians see the church as defined and shaped ultimately by the confession of faith shared by its members. In this view, the church is united because its members all believe the same thing, and find themselves committed to the same ends and purposes. To these Christians, the church *is,* in essence, a voluntary association of like-minded individuals. Accordingly, baptism, which publicly marks the beginning of membership in the church, is essentially a voluntary confession of faith.

Other Christians choose a different starting point for thinking about church membership. For them, the church is defined at its core by God's *calling.*[3] The church is made up of those whom God has called and joined to Jesus Christ. This more God-centered way of thinking about the church is the approach taken in this book. In this view, baptism expresses not primarily our shared faith, but rather God's call and claim upon us. In this view, our membership in the body of Christ does not begin with our agreement, in every detail, about what it means to be a Christian. Nor does it originate with our voluntary commitment to each other and to our shared ideals or goals. Rather, membership in the church springs from the fact that we all find ourselves to be called by the same God in Jesus Christ. Because we belong to God in Jesus Christ, we also belong to each other.

When we define membership in terms of God's calling, rather than by shared confession, we are *not* saying that a shared confession of faith is unimportant. Nor are we saying that it does not matter whether or not people give themselves voluntarily in response to God's call. Quite to the contrary, it is *because* the same God has called us that we must work hard to articulate our shared confession. It is *because* God has called us that we can and must give ourselves freely to God's service. But church membership *begins,* not with shared convictions, nor with our voluntary commitment, but with God's call.

---

3. For a more in-depth discussion of *calling* as the basis for church membership, see chapter 22.

To Sum Up

➤ Church membership means not uniformity, but the rich interaction of many gifts, perspectives, and functions.

➤ Church membership springs not from our voluntary choice, but from God's call upon us.

➤ Church membership is directed, not toward our safety and happiness, but toward God's mission in the world.

➤ Consequently, our thinking about the church (and our thinking about baptism) needs to begin not with our choices or our confession, but with God's call.

For Further Reflection and Discussion

➤ Do you think your congregation is more inclined to the "voluntary association of like-minded individuals" notion of membership, or to the notion of church membership as divine calling? How does that commitment shape the life and character of the church? What are its strengths and weaknesses?

➤ Given the fact that the Declaration of Independence represents a way of thinking about organizational involvement that is deeply ingrained in our culture, how realistic and viable is it to try to establish church membership on a very different basis and assumption?

➤ How do we reconcile our modern notion of "shopping" for a church that seems to fit us, with the biblical notion that church membership begins with divine calling?

For Further Study

➤ Do a biblical word study on "call" and "called," using a concordance or a Bible search program on a computer, and explore how it is linked with the church and church membership. (You'll have to weed through a lot of ordinary usages to find those where God is the one doing the calling. If you are short on time, limit your search to the Pauline epistles. If you have Internet access, you may try searching at http://www.biblestudytools.net/.

4 What Is a Sacrament, and How Does It Differ from an "Ordinance"?

Before exploring baptism in particular, it will be useful to think about sacraments in general. Most Protestant churches recognize two sacraments: baptism and the Lord's Supper. The Quakers and the Salvation Army have no sacraments; Roman Catholics recognize seven sacraments, including baptism and Eucharist, as well as confirmation, reconciliation, anointing of the sick, marriage, and Holy Orders.

But even the term "sacrament" is disputed among Protestant Christians. Some Christians prefer the word "ordinance" as a general term to describe both baptism and the Lord's Supper. Generally speaking, the word "sacrament" places the focus on baptism or the Lord's Supper as a *means* or *instrument of grace,* a sort of channel through which God's grace comes to us in a unique way. Those who prefer the word "ordinance" emphasize instead that our celebration of baptism and the Lord's Supper is an act of obedience to Christ (because these two rites are commanded or *ordained* by Christ — see Matt. 28:19, Luke 22:19, 1 Cor. 11:23-25). Usually those who prefer the word "ordinance" want to avoid the idea that God's grace comes to us in any unique way in baptism or the Lord's Supper. Instead, this position emphasizes that God's grace comes always and only through faith in the gospel of Jesus Christ. The rites of baptism and the Lord's Supper exist only in the service of this general channel by which God's grace comes to us.

Neither the word "sacrament" nor the word "ordinance" is used in the New Testament to describe either baptism or the Lord's Supper. The New Testament itself does not give us a broader defining category for these rites. This is instead an issue that has emerged in the history of the church, as the church has sought to understand more clearly its own life and practice.

The definition of a sacrament/ordinance has a long and extremely complex history which we cannot explore in detail here, but it will be important to understand some of the major questions and issues, especially as they relate to the distinction between sacrament and ordinance.

The word "sacrament" is a translation of the Greek word *mysterion,* which means "secret" or "that which transcends human understanding." When this Greek word was translated into Latin early in the history of the church, the Latin word *sacramentum* was used. *Sacramentum,* while occasionally referring to something secret, refers most commonly to an oath or promise, and can even refer to a deposit of money made to secure a promise. The two dimensions of these words provide the basic frame for the church's thinking about baptism and the Lord's Supper: these rites refer beyond themselves to the mysterious and transcendent work of God, and are an expression of *promise* or *commitment.*

But *whose* promise or commitment is expressed in baptism or the Lord's Supper? This is where the distinction between a sacrament and an ordinance emerges. For those who prefer the word "ordinance," baptism and the Lord's Supper are like visually enacted sermons, which bring vividly before our mind the mystery of the gospel message that Christ died and rose for us and that his death and resurrection cleanse us from sin and offer us new life. In this view, when we undergo baptism or partake of the Lord's Supper, we are expressing our own commitment to and trust in the truth of that same gospel. We are saying "yes" to the gospel, and enacting *our* commitment to live by its truth. In this ordinance view, God has acted long ago in Jesus Christ to offer grace to the world. God has also acted prior to our undergoing baptism or partaking of the Lord's Supper to bring us to a saving understanding of the gospel. God does nothing essentially new or in addition to these prior acts when we baptize or celebrate the Lord's Supper. Rather, it is *we* who make a promise; we express our faith and grateful response to God's graciousness, and in that faithful response, we experience the transformation that comes whenever God's gracious kindness is met with allegiance and trust. In the ordinances, we complete our covenant with God by *our promise* to receive God's grace and to respond to God's grace with our allegiance. Our practices of baptism and the Lord's Supper are thus part of our obedience to Christ, part of the grateful allegiance we express to God's grace offered to us in the proclamation of the gospel.

Others take a different view, preferring the word "sacrament." This view focuses attention primarily not on what *we* do and promise in baptism and the Lord's Supper, but on what *God* does and promises. In the sacramental view, God makes a specific promise to those who receive baptism or the Lord's Supper. In the sacraments, God makes covenant with us, extending his generosity to us in particular, and calling forth from us our grateful trust and allegiance. But the primary focus, in this view, is not on our grateful allegiance, but rather on God's promise, God's generosity. Our faith and allegiance is not so much *expressed in* the sacraments as it is *called forth by* the sacraments. In baptism and the Lord's Supper, God shows himself as gracious, not just to the world in general, but to us in particular. Now it is incumbent upon us, nourished and sustained by this kindness, to live lives of grateful obedience, in response to this more specific and focused promise and kindness of God which has been given to us.

It is important to recognize that both the "sacrament" and "ordinance" views share much in common. Both recognize the basic biblical pattern of covenant, in which God comes to the world in gracious generosity, and calls for a response of faith and allegiance. Both recognize that this response of faith and allegiance is a vital and necessary part of Christian existence. But they differ as to the particular "moment" of the covenant-making process that is expressed in baptism and the Lord's Supper.

In the *ordinance* view, God's generosity is expressed long ago in Christ, and has also been experienced in the life of the individual Christian *prior to* baptism or partaking of the Lord's Supper. In baptism and the Lord's Supper, in this view, Christians reach out to receive this grace and promise to live their lives in grateful allegiance. So baptism and the Lord's Supper refer *primarily* to our response of grateful allegiance, and *secondarily* to God's gracious action. This distinction between primary and secondary arises because in the actual act of baptism or the Lord's Supper, God's grace has already been given in the gospel, and we are only being reminded of that grace (thus the *secondary* reference to God's grace), whereas our commitment is being expressed *in the ordinance itself* (hence this is what is *primary* in the ordinance).

In the *sacramental* view, God's gracious and generous action is the primary focus in baptism and the Lord's Supper. The sacraments are not only *signs* that point our attention back to Jesus Christ as presented in the gospel and thus remind us of his grace offered to the whole world. They are also *seals*, which assure us that God's grace and promise are given to us in particular. This word "seal," when used in the context of the Reformation, referred to the wax imprint that marked a document as official and legally binding. In this context, baptism is the seal whereby God takes the general promise of the gospel and applies it to us in particular. In the ancient world, the same word also referred to marks on the body — brands or tattoos which functioned as a mark of ownership.[1] Just so, baptism is God's mark of ownership upon us, the seal that God has entered into covenant with us. We are "marked" by Christ's death and resurrection, as witnessed both by baptism and the Lord's Supper. This action of God to place his "mark" of Christ's death and resurrection upon us is the primary focus of the sacraments (especially baptism), and the secondary focus lies upon our response of faith and allegiance. Faith and allegiance is *secondary,* not because it is unimportant, but because it is required as an ongoing response to God's action in the sacrament, rather than being primarily expressed in the sacrament itself.

So in the *ordinance* view, baptism and the Lord's Supper are primarily ways in which the church expresses its promise to God, in response to the prior gift of the gospel. In the *sacramental* view, baptism and the Lord's Supper are primarily the means by which God makes the gospel a promise to us, and requires of us a life of grateful allegiance in response.

These two views can be summarized in the following table:

Ordinance	Sacrament
Our promise to God	God's promise to us
Expression of obedience	Means of grace
Primary focus on what we do in response to God's grace, offered to all	Primary focus on what God does to extend grace to us in particular
God's *past* offer of grace in Jesus calls us to *present* obedience in the rite	God's *present* grace offered in the rite calls us to *future* obedience
Rites are *signs* which point to the gospel	Rites are *signs* of the gospel and *seals* of our participation in the body of Christ

1. Note the way in which circumcision is spoken of as a *seal* in Romans 4:11. Cf. also the use of the word in 1 Corinthians 9:2.

Which view is correct? Which view is more biblical? For the sake of brevity, we will focus especially here on baptism, and frame the question in this way: When the New Testament speaks of baptism, does the emphasis fall primarily on what Christians do (the *ordinance* view as outlined above), or on what God does (the *sacramental* view as outlined above)?

When framed in this way, I believe the clear answer is the latter: the emphasis falls on what *God* does in baptism. First, note the places where baptism is closely linked to the washing away of sin — something only God can do (Acts 22:16 "Get up, be baptized, and have your sins washed away, calling on his name." Cf. also Heb. 10:22.). Similarly, 1 Corinthians 6:11 links "washing," an obvious reference to baptism, with justification and sanctification — all pointing to God's activity, not a human response: "But you were washed, you were sanctified, you were justified in the name of the Lord Jesus Christ and in the Spirit of our God."

Baptism is also linked in Scripture to the giving of the Spirit, another pointer to divine action. 1 Corinthians 12:13 states "For in the one Spirit we were all baptized into one body — Jews or Greeks, slaves or free — and we were all made to drink of one Spirit." Note a similar linkage of water, with its baptismal associations, and the Spirit in John 3:5 and Titus 3:5. These last two texts also link the washing of baptism with new birth, clearly a reality only brought about by God's action.

Several other New Testament passages also link baptism to our union with Christ, a union not accomplished by our action, but by God's. For example, Colossians 2:12 speaks of how Christians are "buried with [Christ] in baptism" (cf. also Romans 6:3-4). Here the focus in baptism also falls on what God does in joining us to Christ's death, rather than on an action that we take in response to God's grace. Indeed, in all these texts, the overwhelming focus is on God's action in baptism, not the human response.

But what are we to make of the many New Testament passages that also link baptism with repentance and faith — human responses to God's grace? Many of these passages are speaking about John the Baptist's baptism, which is not to be identified with Christian baptism.[2] John called people to repent to prepare the way for the "coming one," who would bring in God's judgment and redemption. His baptism sprang from and was a response to his call to repentance (e.g., Luke 3:3), and it also was intended

---

2. Acts 19:1-4 recounts the story of some who were baptized into John's baptism, who were subsequently baptized "in the name of the Lord Jesus."

to lead to repentance (Matt. 3:11). Yet even here, it must be questioned whether, for those Jews baptized by John, the baptism *represented* their repentance, or whether John's baptism itself more specifically represented the receiving of divine grace, cleansing, and empowerment. The latter seems more likely, especially in light of the fact that Jesus (who, according to the gospel writers, clearly had no need to repent) submitted to John's baptism, and received the Spirit in conjunction with that baptism (Luke 3:21-22; Matt 3:13-17; Mark 1:9-11) For Jesus at least, John's baptism pointed primarily to God's action and call, and not to his own faith or repentance. So even in John's baptism, it must be questioned whether the baptism itself signified primarily the human response to God's action, or whether God's gracious action itself was its primary focus. John's was a baptism *of repentance* in the sense that it flowed from and toward repentance. But the baptism itself did not signify repentance, but rather it pointed to and looked forward to God's gracious action. This is why Jesus speaks of John's baptism as coming "from heaven" (Matt. 21:25).

It is important to remember the focus of our discussion here. We are not discussing whether faith and repentance are necessary in connection with baptism.[3] Our concern here is with the distinction between sacrament and ordinance — whether as an ordinance baptism signifies primarily our obedient action (including faith and repentance), or whether as a sacrament it signifies primarily God's action. So it is entirely to be expected that the New Testament would link a summons to repent and believe with a call to be baptized (Acts 2:38, 41; 8:12; 16:14-15; 18:8). But in light of the many texts that link divine action with baptism, it makes most sense to interpret these passages in Acts which link repentance, faith, and baptism, not so much as *equating* baptism with faith and repentance, but rather *pairing* baptism with faith and repentance as the "objective" and "subjective" side of God's covenant. Baptism does not express primarily our turning from the old life to the new, but rather presents to us the new life toward which we must continually turn. Baptism thus points to God's generous cleansing and renewing grace poured out upon us, and repentance and faith reflect our grateful response to that grace in faith and allegiance. Both are necessary, but they are not to be equated with each other.[4]

3. We discuss the relationship between baptism, faith, and repentance more fully in chapter 12.

4. One sees a similar pairing of our faith and God's action in the difficult baptismal text

As a sacrament, then (and not merely an ordinance), baptism offers Jesus Christ to us in a unique way. Baptism is a *sign* of God's grace that extends to and is promised specifically to us. It is a *seal* that marks us as God's own with Christ's death and resurrection. In baptism, God promises us that we belong to God. As a sacrament, it is primarily *God's* act, ordained by Christ and made effective by the working of the Spirit. Through the rest of our lives, God calls us to remember the promises of God that are sealed to us in our baptism, and to live out the implications of those promises in obedient faith and allegiance.

To Sum Up

▸ One important debate in the history of the church is whether baptism is to be understood as a sacrament or as an ordinance.

▸ Understanding baptism as an ordinance places the emphasis in baptism on *our* faith and repentance; understanding baptism as a sacrament places the emphasis on *God's* action and promise.

▸ The biblical texts that speak of baptism place the emphasis on God's action and promise.

▸ Baptism does not primarily express our repentance, but rather presents to us and marks us with a new life in Christ — a new life toward which we must continually turn in repentance and faith.

For Further Reflection and Discussion

▸ Sometimes, even in churches that practice infant baptism, there is an emphasis placed on the promises of the parents when children are bap-

---

found in 1 Peter 3:21: "And baptism, which this [i.e., God's saving of Noah and his family through water] prefigured, now saves you — not as a removal of dirt from the body, but as an appeal to God for a good conscience, through the resurrection of Jesus Christ." Here baptism is actually described as *saving* Christians — clearly something only God can do. Yet baptism is also described as an "appeal to God," an action that we do. Of all the New Testament baptismal texts, this is one where the distinction between primary and secondary emphases we have been exploring in this chapter is least clear. Despite the difficulties of this text, however, it clearly presents baptism as a rite in which God is decisively active. If baptism, in any sense, can be said to "save" us, then it is God's doing, and not ours. See also the discussion in chapter 14 on the relationship between baptism and salvation.

tized. Does this reflect a failure to understand fully what happens in baptism? Why or why not?

> If the focus in baptism is on God's action and promise, what further questions does this raise for you about baptism that you will want to explore as this book progresses?

> What excites you, and what worries you, when you think about baptism as a sacrament?

For Further Study

> John Calvin's discussion of the sacraments in the *Institutes* is a helpful place to dig more deeply into these questions (*Institutes of the Christian Religion,* ed. John T. McNeill, trans. Ford Lewis Battles [Philadelphia: Westminster, 1960]). See especially Book IV, Chapter XIV. If you are unable to obtain this most recent translation, an older, but still serviceable version is available online at http://www.reformed.org/books/index.html.

> You may also wish to read the *Consensus Tigurinus,* a brief document on the sacraments drafted by Calvin and Heinrich Bullinger that represented a compromise during the Reformation between the theologians of Zurich (who were more inclined to the "ordinance" theology of Ulrich Zwingli) and Calvin's more sacramental approach. This document is available online at http://www.creeds.net/reformed/Tigurinus/tigur-bvd.htm.

5 How Do the Sacraments Bring God's Grace to Us?

In the previous chapter, we explored a major debate that has occurred among the various churches of the Reformation, focusing on whether baptism and the Lord's Supper are best understood as sacraments or as ordinances. There we saw that Scripture requires that we regard baptism and the Lord's Supper as *means* or *instruments of grace,* channels through which God's grace is brought in a special way to us. In this chapter, we move to an earlier debate during the Reformation over the nature of sacraments, a debate between the reformers and late medieval Catholicism. This debate focuses on *how* the sacraments bring God's grace to us.

In order to understand this debate, we must begin at a much earlier period in Christian history, in the so-called Donatist controversy of the fourth century. During that time, some church leaders had denied their faith under persecution. Later, the church had to struggle with the question of whether the baptisms that were performed by these leaders were valid baptisms. The church decided that the efficacy of baptism did not depend on the sanctity of the officiant, but on God's faithfulness and the truth of the Word of God. Therefore these fourth-century baptisms, even if performed by sinful persons, were still valid baptisms which effectively communicated God's promise and grace. Therefore those who were baptized by these lapsed leaders should not be rebaptized.

The medieval church continued to reflect upon the efficacy of the sacraments. Building upon the decision made in the Donatist controversy, they asked the further question: What about the faith of the person *receiving* the sacraments? Is the effectiveness of baptism or the Lord's Supper in conveying God's grace diminished or enhanced by a faith which may be stronger or weaker in the recipient? Although this question was debated vigorously, and a variety of answers were brought forward, the dominant answer followed the essential lines of the Donatist controversy. The efficacy of the sacraments was based centrally in the power and faithfulness of God. Therefore, the medieval church concluded, the sacraments were effective *ex opere operato,* simply "from the work wrought," regardless of whether the faith of the recipient was strong or weak. The medieval church did not entirely remove the need for a receptive faith; if one came to the sacraments with the conscious intention to continue sinning, the sacraments would not be effective. But so long as recipients placed no "obstacle" in the way of the grace offered in the sacrament, they could be sure that they had received the grace signified in the sacrament, *ex opere operato,* ("from the work wrought"). This was true simply because they had received the sacrament, since the efficacy of the sacrament depended not on human faithfulness, but on divine faithfulness.

In the period leading up to the Reformation, however, these finer theological distinctions were lost in the practice of many churches. Instead, the assumption took hold that the sacraments were "automatically" effective, regardless of the faith of the recipient. This assumption finally led to the buying and selling of masses and indulgences as a way to obtain the grace necessary to cover one's various sins and to ensure one's salvation. From the perspective of the reformers, the result was a twofold spiritual and theological disaster: the centrality of faith in receiving salvation was obscured, and the security of salvation began practically and finally to rest not in God's faithfulness, but in the church's ecclesiastical power, as it claimed a monopoly in its capacity to administer efficacious sacraments.

Much of the energy and power of the Reformation emerged in reaction against these abuses. Central to the task of the reformers was the reformulation of a doctrine of the sacraments that would protect against these abuses. They did not want to undo or weaken the insights that came out of the Donatist controversy, for they also believed that God's grace is effective, even when brought to us through imperfect or sinful ministers. Yet the reformers also wanted to tie faith much more closely to the *reception* of the sacraments than their medieval forebears had done.

But how does one underscore the importance of faith in receiving the sacraments, without making it appear that the efficacy of the sacraments varies, depending on the depth or purity of our faith? Here is a theological puzzle of the first order. It appears that we are caught between the mythical Scylla and Charybdis, between the monster and the whirlpool. Either the efficacy of the sacrament depends finally on God, as the medieval theologians had thought *(ex opere operato)*, and the importance of faith is diminished, or else the efficacy of the sacrament depends on our faith. In the latter case, it appears that we can never be sure if the sacrament is really effective or not, because we can never be sure if our faith is great enough. Neither is a happy alternative.

Some reformers, like Ulrich Zwingli and the Anabaptists, decided to avoid the dilemma altogether. They denied that there was any special efficacy to the sacraments at all, and rejected a theology of sacraments in favor of an emphasis on baptism and the Lord's Supper as ordinances. In this view, the sacraments do not convey any special grace, beyond the call to faith which is the cornerstone of the gospel message. As we have seen in the previous chapter, however, this view requires minimizing a significant number of biblical texts that speak of God actually *doing* something in baptism and the Lord's Supper. In the Bible, the emphasis in both baptism and the Lord's Supper is not on our faith, but on God's action.

Martin Luther and others in the Reformation therefore took a different approach. Returning to Scripture, Luther sought to recover the fundamental biblical notion that both baptism and the Lord's Supper are signs of God's *promise*. He pointed to Jesus' words of institution in the Lord's Supper, which refer to the Supper as a "testament" (Luke 22:20; 1 Cor. 11:25).[1] The word here, which is also rendered "covenant" in some translations, can also refer to a will that one makes, to be executed upon one's death. For Luther, the Lord's Supper is, in essence, the promise of God's salvation to us, to be delivered upon the death of Jesus. Jesus gave us the Supper as his last will and testament. Baptism also for Luther has the same fundamental character of a promise. Luther cites Mark 16:16, "Whoever believes and is baptized will be saved," to support his argument that baptism as well has the essential character of a divine promise.[2] The sacraments are essentially divine *promises*, to be received by faith. Luther writes,

> We know that wherever there is a divine promise, there faith is required, and that these two are so necessary to each other that neither can be ef-

---

1. See especially the discussion in his tract, "The Babylonian Captivity of the Church," in *Selected Writings of Martin Luther, 1517-1520*, trans. A. T. W. Steinhaeuser and ed. Theodore G. Tappert (Philadelphia: Fortress, 1967), pp. 390ff.

2. "The Babylonian Captivity of the Church," p. 401.

fective apart from the other. For it is not possible to believe unless there is a promise, and the promise is not established unless it is believed. But where these two meet, they give a real and most certain efficacy to the sacraments.[3]

But the sacraments of baptism and the Lord's Supper do not merely present the promise of God in general; they offer God's promise of salvation in Christ to specific people. The sacraments represent God's promise of salvation engraved with our name. They are offered to us in particular. The gift of this promise does not waver depending on our faith; it stands as a promise, regardless of whether we believe it, regardless of whether we receive it. In this way, the efficacy of the sacraments depends on God, and not on our faith.

This theological move by Luther dramatically changed the theological landscape and ushered in the refreshingly new spirituality of the Reformation. In the place of a theology which had been preoccupied with increasingly subtle and technical distinctions, a theology where questions of substance and the "mechanics" by which grace comes to us had long dominated theological discussions, Luther refocused attention on the God who makes promises. Luther emphasized the distinctive character of promises. Promises *reveal* God's mind and purpose. We see God more clearly, and know God more deeply, when we hear God's promises. This focus on divine promise also underscores the *grace* of God. God freely and graciously promises to be our God, to forgive us and redeem us from all of our sins. God makes this promise in Christ, even before our repentance and faith is seen. Finally, Luther always emphasized that promises *call forth* a response of faith and fidelity from us. By building a theology of the sacraments upon promise, Luther offered a much more dynamic and relational context for thinking about the sacraments.

At the same time, this understanding of the sacraments as divine promises underscored for both Luther and Calvin the centrality and necessity of faith. The reformers insisted that God's promise is always received only by faith. We can do nothing to deserve the promise, but if we refuse to place our trust in it, we will not receive it. Thus whenever the practice of the church separates sacraments from faith (as it had done at least in the popular mind in the period leading up to the Reformation), it denies the

---

3. "The Babylonian Captivity of the Church," p. 419.

nature of the sacraments as divine promises which call forth faith from us. Yet the reformers' way of understanding the efficacy of the sacraments does not make the grace conveyed by the sacraments subject to our faith, as if we might receive more or less grace, depending on our faith. Rather, the gift of salvation is given, in its entirety, to all who receive it with the open hands of trusting faith. The promise is not measured out in tea-spoonfuls, but is given, undivided, as pure gift. If Christ is not augmented or diminished by the presence or absence of our faith, neither can our salvation be so augmented or diminished. And because the sacraments have the character of promise, we continue to carry our baptism with us, so to speak, as a permanent promise, to which we may return again and again, and receive anew the assurance of God's salvation, whenever our hearts condemn us or our weakness leads us into stumbling.

This emphasis on the sacraments as *promises* was the central answer of the Reformation to the medieval Catholic Church's emphasis on the efficacy of the sacraments *ex opere operato,* particularly as that understanding had been degraded to a kind of "automatic" effectiveness in popular practice. The reformers taught that the sacraments were indeed necessary and effective, for in the sacraments, God addresses the promises of salvation to us in particular. The efficacy of the sacraments depends on God alone, for it is only God who can make the promise of salvation, and only God can bring salvation to us. Yet the effectiveness of the sacraments must also always be linked to faith, and thus can never be subject to the manipulations or profiteering of the church. It is simply and only the open hands of faith that receive the promises of God.

This understanding of sacraments as signs of God's promise brought with it two other important emphases in the Reformation, emphases that we do well to remember. First, sacraments must always be closely linked with the Word of God. Scripture spells out for us in detail the nature of the promise that is given to us in baptism and the Lord's Supper. Without the full witness of Scripture, our understanding of the promise remains stunted, or even misguided, and as a result, our capacity to receive the promise in all its fullness will be limited. This does not mean that our salvation itself is in jeopardy if our understanding is spotty, but it does mean that we need the full witness of Scripture in order to open our hands to all that Scripture promises to us in the sacraments. Word and sacrament belong together.

The reformers were also aware that an emphasis on the centrality of faith was not without its own perils. If faith is a human accomplishment, then the sacraments, and ultimately our entire salvation, depend on the frail foundation of human weakness. Such a foundation has no security or staying power. So along with their emphasis on faith as the necessary means of receiving the promise given to us in the sacraments, the reformers also emphasized the role of the Holy Spirit in awakening and deepening faith in our lives. Calvin writes,

> But the sacraments properly fulfill their office only when the Spirit, that inward teacher, comes to them, by whose power alone hearts are penetrated and affections moved and our souls opened for the sacraments to enter in. If the Spirit be lacking, the sacraments can accomplish nothing more in our minds than the splendor of the sun shining upon blind eyes, or a voice sounding in deaf ears.[4]

We must remember that even our response of faith is ultimately not our own doing, but is mysteriously a work of God in us. Faith is regularly associated with the work of the Spirit throughout the New Testament.[5] Thus, even though the reformers insisted on the necessity of faith to receive the benefits of God's promise in the sacraments, they acknowledged that, in the final analysis, *everything* about the effectiveness of the sacraments depends upon God, and not upon us. Even the faith by which we receive God's promise in the sacraments is ultimately God's doing, and nothing for which we can claim any credit.

How, then, do the sacraments bring God's grace to us? We have seen that the sacraments do indeed bring God's grace to us, in the form of a promise that has our name written upon it. This grace does not come to us "automatically," but only when it is received in receptive and trusting faith, informed by the whole counsel of the Word of God. Yet even our faith is finally recognized, usually in hindsight, as the work of God, because the Spirit is the one who awakens within us the very capacity to hear God's promise, and to receive it with grateful trust. The power and efficacy of the sacraments thus begin and end with God alone.

---

4. *Institutes* IV.XIV.9.

5. See, for example, Luke 10:21; John 16:13; Acts 6:5; 10:44; 11:24; 15:8-9; Rom. 15:13; 1 Cor. 2:12; 12:9; 2 Cor. 4:13; Gal. 3:14; 5:5; Eph. 1:13; 1 Thess. 1:5; 2 Thess. 2:13; 2 Tim. 1:13-14.

To Sum Up

> Luther and Calvin tried to steer a middle course between the ordinance theology of Zwingli and the Anabaptists, who rejected sacraments as means of grace (making sacraments necessary only as a matter of obedience), and medieval Catholic theology which, especially in popular practice, assumed that grace was delivered "automatically" in the sacraments (making faith unnecessary).

> Luther and Calvin regarded the sacraments as signs of God's *promise,* to be received by faith. God's promise reveals God's will, expresses God's grace, and calls forth faith from us.

> Our reception of these sacramental promises must be informed by the Word of God and empowered by the Holy Spirit.

> Thus the reformers affirmed that our *confidence* about receiving God's grace in the sacraments must be based on a reliance upon God's faithfulness, rather than a reliance upon the steadfastness of our faith.

For Further Reflection and Discussion

> Every congregation tends to incline at times toward one of the extremes that Luther and Calvin tried to avoid. Is your congregation more inclined to downplay the sacraments as means of grace, or to minimize the importance of faith in receiving God's grace in the sacraments?

> Have you experienced times in your life when, in hindsight, you recognized that your capacity for faith was the work of the Holy Spirit in you?

> Have you thought of your baptism as God's promise to you? What other thoughts or questions does this idea raise for you?

For Further Study

> Martin Luther's "The Babylonian Captivity of the Church" is a marvelous introduction into Reformation debates on the sacraments. The first half, which deals with the Lord's Supper and baptism, is particularly relevant to this book. It is available online at http://www.ctsfw.edu/etext/luther/babylonian/.

6 Why Are Sacraments Necessary and Important?

In chapter 4, we explored the difference between a sacrament and an ordinance. If baptism is a sacrament, the primary focus is on what God does; if it is an ordinance, the primary focus falls on what we do. It will be important for the reader to explore that chapter before turning to this one. In this chapter, we will explore in more detail the significance of the distinction between sacrament and ordinance for wider issues in Christian faith and theology. What difference does it make whether we believe that baptism is a sacrament or an ordinance? Does this distinction really matter, or is it just something for theologians to argue about? Why is it so important to believe that God *does* something in baptism?

Baptism is a Christian *practice*. A Christian practice is an action or ritual or set of behaviors that Christians engage in to articulate, embody, and live out the gospel. Prayer, the Lord's Supper, worship, forgiveness and reconciliation, charitable giving — these are all examples of Christian practices. They give concrete expression in our daily lives to the truths on which our lives are built. We teach them to our children and encourage them to imitate us in these practices. Our practices tell a great deal about what we believe. They shape to a large extent the direction and character of our growth and maturation. Long before we learn our theology, and long after we have forgotten it, we remember the actual experience of living the Christian life — its rituals and music, its recurring behaviors — and it is that experience which shapes, at the deepest level, our Christian life. Practices are embodied wisdom; they weave the Christian faith deeply into the fabric of our lives. So the way we practice our faith matters. For this reason alone, it is important to be clear on what we mean by a sacrament, and what we believe God is doing in the sacraments.

But we can be more specific as well. The way we view the debate between "sacrament" and "ordinance" will affect the way we think about and experience our relationship with God. The basic question is something like this: How do we experience God? Is our life with God essentially a personal and private affair, or is our experience of God inextricably interwoven with our relationship to God's people, the body of Christ? Although many advocates of an ordinance theology are more carefully nuanced, in the perceptions of many, one does not need the church for any of the essentials of Christian faith and life. One can come to faith, receive the Holy Spirit, experience forgiveness of sins and the hope of eternal life entirely on one's own, or in the midst of whatever group of Christians one happens to be with at any time. Rites and rituals are simply an echo or reminder of the more basic and foundational experience of God, which is personal and intimate. For some advocates of ordinance theology, the suggestion that God might use baptism in a unique way feels as if it moves the center (the individual) to the periphery, and the periphery (the group) to the center.

A more sacramental perspective, however, holds that God assigns to human beings the task of being the conduits through which a great deal of divine grace comes to us. God has structured the redemptive plan in such a way that we cannot be drawn fully into fellowship with God without, at the same time, being drawn more closely to the body of Christ. Twice in the Gospel of Matthew, Jesus declares that what his disciples "bind on earth" will be "bound in heaven" (Matt. 16:19; 18:18). Jesus promises a divine efficacy to actions taken by his disciples. When God's people gather, Jesus is there in a special way (Matt. 18:20). What is true in these two passages is even more true of the sacraments. Particularly in baptism and the Lord's Supper, we receive something powerful and important from God, but only as we receive it from others within the Body of Christ. Sacramental theology holds that God intended it this way.

There is a tendency that all of us have to want to keep our relationship with God private and personal. This allows us to keep our own relative autonomy. There is a certain attraction we may experience to an approach to baptism or the Lord's Supper in which God's presence is not quite so directly involved with others whom we may find puzzling, frustrating, and difficult to get along with. It is far less "messy" to keep our life with God, at least in its essence, in the realm of the personal and the private, rather than in the complexities and conflicts of the Christian community. But the God of the Bible is a God who engages us directly and specifically, through each other. A sacramental theology understands and embraces this, along with its attendant questions, problems, and mysteries. A theology of ordinance is always simpler and cleaner in its understanding of God's presence in the world than a sacramental theology. But that does not make it more spiritually alive, nor more effective in building and sustaining the body of Christ. Neither does it mean that it is closer to the biblical witness.

But the distinction between sacrament and ordinance affects not only the way we think about God. It also shapes our understanding of God's salvation. There is in the theology of western Christianity in general, and in North American theology even more specifically, a tendency to focus our understanding of salvation more internally than externally, more on the mind than on the body, more on the individual than on the group. Often this tendency is expressed in a concern for religion as a "spiritual" reality (which is assumed to be "inner" rather than "outer," non-material, and private rather than public). There is a very long tradition in American Christianity of religious perspectives that focus almost entirely on one's inner mental state as the key to religious life. From extreme groups like Christian Science, which teach that right *thinking* can even cure and prevent illness, to more mainstream preachers like Norman Vincent Peale and Robert Schuller, who speak of the power of positive or possibility thinking, Americans have always been drawn to religious approaches that emphasize getting our own thinking straight as the key to religious life and happiness. We have an inherent bias toward religion as a personal, private, and "spiritual" matter, which works "from the inside out."

It is only a short step from such an approach to the assumption that our *thinking* is all that God cares about. So we see in other streams of American Christianity that are interested in apocalyptic prophecy, the tendency to see the world as slated for complete destruction.[1] The view here is that the goal of the church is to assist as many people as possible to make the "spiritual" shift to trusting in Christ for their personal salvation, so that they can be "raptured" before the world is destroyed, and enjoy eter-

---

1. A text commonly cited to support the idea that the earth is slated for destruction is 2 Peter 3:10: "But the day of the Lord will come like a thief, and then the heavens will pass away with a loud noise, and the elements will be dissolved with fire, and the earth and everything that is done on it will be disclosed." Some older versions render the end of this verse "burned up" rather than "disclosed," but "disclosed" or "laid bare" is the more accurate reading. Even judgment by fire in this passage is not for the purpose of destruction, but for the purpose of refinement and cleansing.

nal life with God. In this view, God doesn't care about this world — he intends to destroy it. God only cares about the inner state and disposition of people. God's salvation only addresses our *inner* lives.

Without diminishing or ignoring the inner and spiritual dimensions of our lives, a sacramental theology envisions salvation more holistically. It looks and hopes for the *convergence* of the material and the spiritual, the inner and the outer, the personal and the corporate. It hopes for God's action, not to destroy the world, but to knit the world back to a wholeness in which our inner and outer lives are reconciled with each other. Sacramental theology thus sees the use of material things — bread, wine, water — as enormously important, pointing toward God's reconciling and restoring purpose for the whole creation: the body as well as the soul, the material as well as the spiritual, both the individual and the group. Likewise, the location of sacraments within the worshipping *community* emphasizes the corporate and public as well as the personal dimensions of God's saving purpose.

A more technical distinction may help to illumine this integrative vision of sacramental theology: the difference between *allegory, metaphor,* and *sign.* An allegory — such as John Bunyan's well-known *Pilgrim's Progress* — tells us about something we already know, using different images. We already know what it is like to experience despair, but the image of Pilgrim being caught in the "Slough of Despond" provides a vivid image that reminds us, in an entertaining and memorable fashion, of our own experience.

For some proponents of an ordinance theology, baptism and the Lord's Supper are like an allegory. We already know by our own experience of faith what it is like to die and rise with Christ, and to be nourished and strengthened by him. Baptism and the Lord's Supper remind us of this experience in a striking and memorable way.

For others, baptism and the Lord's Supper are *metaphors* of the Christian life. With both metaphor and allegory, we speak of one thing by using another image. What distinguishes metaphor from allegory, however, is that with metaphor, we *learn* something more through the image that is used. Many of Jesus' parables, for example, are metaphorical. When Jesus compares the Kingdom of God to a set of workers who are all paid the same wage, despite working very different numbers of hours, we are jarred, and challenged to think more deeply about God's ways of working with us. Jesus' hearers did not already have this idea of God; Jesus didn't tell this story to remind them of what they already knew; he told the story to *change* the way they thought about and responded to God's graciousness in the world. That's what metaphors do: they force us to think in fresh ways.

There is a profound sense in which baptism and the Lord's Supper function as metaphors, teaching us important lessons about our life with God. No one can think in quite the same way about dying and rising with Christ, after being pushed under water and being allowed to rise again for air! Both sacramental and ordinance theology, at their best, recognize the metaphorical power of baptism and the Lord's Supper.

But sacramental theology presses further, and also understands baptism and the Lord's Supper as *signs*. I am using the word here in a more technical and specific way than I employed it in chapter 4. There I spoke of a sign as something that pointed beyond itself to a deeper reality. But sacramental theologians have refined this understanding of *sign* still further. They speak of a sacramental sign not merely as something that points beyond itself, but as something that *participates in* the deeper reality to which it points. A break in a fever is a *sign* of returning health. The giving of rings in a wedding ceremony is a *sign* of the mutual giving and bonding that will characterize the marriage as a whole. Occupying a house can be a *sign* of one's ownership of the building.

The difference between signs and metaphors is that metaphors are *dispensable,* once you have learned the lesson. You can translate the same lesson into different metaphors. Signs, by contrast, are not dispensable. When married persons permanently remove their rings, they are saying that they are no longer married. The sign and the thing signified are not entirely separable from each other, as they are with metaphors or allegories.

For sacramental theology, baptism and the Lord's Supper are signs in this more specific and technical sense. The cleansing we receive from God as Christians cannot be completely distinguished from the cleansing signified by the rite of baptism. The nourishment we receive from the Lord's Supper is a sustenance without which our faith will never be entirely whole. Sacramental theology believes that God engages the created order, our material existence and our specific relationships with others in the body of Christ, as the context of our salvation, and that these signs are not merely dispensable "visual lessons," but rather the visible and material manifestations of a much more profound spiritual transformation that encompasses the totality of our existence. Sacramental theology emphasizes this comprehensive, creational focus to God's salvation. It points not merely to the restoration of creation, but to its full consummation in Christ (Rom. 8:19-21).

Sacramental theology locates our salvation in the midst of webs of interconnectedness. The sacraments emphasize our connectedness to others, and to the creation as a whole. Our salvation is wrapped up with the salvation of all of God's people, and indeed of the whole creation.

So why are sacraments necessary and important? They emphasize the direct and personal engagement of God with our lives in the midst of the body of Christ. They call us to a vision of God's saving purpose that encompasses the whole of our lives and the whole of creation, and they bind us to one another and to the creation in a journey of faith, even as they bind us to God in ties of love and grace.

To Sum Up

➤ Sacramental theology emphasizes that God's grace comes to us in a way that also binds us to each other in the body of Christ.

➤ Sacramental theology keeps the focus of God's salvation not only on our thinking and our internal life, but also on our relationships with others and with the whole of creation.

➤ Sacraments are not simply allegories or metaphors, which are dispensable once the lesson is learned. They are signs, which cannot finally be separated from the realities which they signify.

For Further Reflection and Discussion

➤ In western culture, the prevailing assumption is that religious issues are personal and private, rather than social and public. Is this the way you tend to think about your own Christian life? How has this chapter challenged that assumption?

➤ Can you think of examples in your own Christian experience where a deepening of your relationship with God was tied together with a deepening in your relationship to the body of Christ?

➤ Some people think that if a theology places too much emphasis on rites like baptism as a means of grace, that the church will become preoccupied with its own power, and tend either toward corruption or complacency. Is this true? If not, why not? If so, what can guard against this tendency?

For Further Study

> For a helpful historical overview of the history of the church's discussion of sacraments, see James F. White, *The Sacraments in Protestant Practice and Faith* (Nashville: Abingdon Press, 1999), especially pages 13-30.

THE CORE MEANINGS OF BAPTISM

This next section (chapters 7-12) draws out the basic meanings that Scripture attaches to baptism: union with Christ in his death and resurrection, cleansing, the gift of the Holy Spirit, and new birth. The final chapters in this section discuss the *mode* of baptism (sprinkling, pouring, or immersion), especially as it relates to these four key meanings of baptism, and the "baptismal formula" which speaks of baptism "in the name of" the Triune God. These six chapters belong together, and the reader will not gain a comprehensive sense of the meaning of baptism without looking at all of them together. These meanings of baptism are essentially consistent, whether we are addressing the baptism of adult converts or the baptism of the children of believing parents.

7 What Does Romans 6:3 Mean When It Speaks of Being Baptized into Christ's Death?

In baptism, God portrays, promises, and seals to us our union with Jesus Christ. In Galatians 3:27, Paul says, "As many of you as were baptized into Christ have clothed yourself with Christ." Our clothing is the completion of our identity — the way we represent ourselves to the world around us. Paul claims that baptism gives us a new set of clothes, made up of Christ himself. This image of being united with Christ or clothed with Christ has important implications for our relationship with God and for the way we understand ourselves. It means, first of all, that God acts toward us as if we were Jesus himself. To God, the baptized look like Jesus. Another phrase commonly used to express this sense of being clothed with Christ is the expression, "in Christ." To be "in Christ" is to be united to Christ, and to have the same relationship with God that Christ has. So Romans 8:1 states, "There is therefore now no condemnation for those who are *in Christ Jesus*." Because God does not condemn Jesus, those who are united to Jesus experience no condemnation. Indeed, nothing can separate us from the love of God we have by virtue of our being "in Christ" (Rom. 8:39), since Christ is the object of God's unfailing love (Mark 1:11). 1 Corinthians 1:4 speaks of grace that is given us "in Christ Jesus." Ephesians 1:11 speaks of our inheritance "in Christ Jesus." This implies that our union with Christ makes us privileged members of God's household, along with Christ.

But this new clothing, this new identity sealed in baptism, is not merely an outer representation or façade. It represents a new self. Colossians 3:10 speaks (also in the context of baptism) of how "[you] have clothed yourselves with the new self, which is being renewed in knowledge according to the image of its creator." So great is this transformation that comes from being joined to Christ that Scripture can say, "So if anyone is in Christ, there is a new creation: everything old has passed away; see, everything has become new" (2 Cor. 5:17)!

Nowhere is this transformation spoken of more vividly than in Romans 6, which links baptism to our dying and rising with Christ. Let's explore this passage in more detail:

> Do you not know that all of us who have been baptized into Christ Jesus were baptized into his death? Therefore we have been buried with him by baptism into death, so that, just as Christ was raised from the dead by the glory of the Father, so we too might walk in newness of life. For if we have been united with him in a death like his, we will certainly be united with him in a resurrection like his. We know that our old self was crucified with him so that the body of sin might be destroyed, and we might no longer be enslaved to sin. For whoever has died is freed from sin. But if we have died with Christ, we believe that we will also live with him. We know that Christ, being raised from the dead, will never die again; death no longer has dominion over him. The death he died, he died to sin, once for all; but the life he lives, he lives to God. So you also must consider yourselves dead to sin and alive to God in Christ Jesus. (Rom. 6:3-11)

This text teaches us that baptism not only unites us to Christ's *person*, but to Christ's *history*. Not only does God look at us in the same way God looks at Christ because we are clothed with Christ in our baptism, but baptism also puts us in a new place, where what happened to Christ (*i.e.*, his death and resurrection) also, in some sense, happens to us. In baptism, we are "buried into [Christ's] death" (Rom. 6:4), "united with [Christ] in a death like his" (Rom. 6:5). We have "died with Christ" in baptism (Rom. 6:8). This gives us the further hope that we will also "be united with him in a resurrection like his" (Rom. 6:5). We see the same baptismal perspective in Colossians 3:3-4, which states, "you have died, and your life is hidden with Christ in God. When Christ who is your life is revealed, then you also will be revealed with him in glory."

In baptism, we die with Christ and we rise with Christ. But in the New Testament, the accent falls on dying with Christ. There are a few New Testament passages which also speak of our being already raised with Christ in baptism (Col. 3:1; Eph. 2:6). For the most part, however, the New Testament speaks about our resurrection with Christ as something still awaiting us in the future — it has not yet happened. Note Romans 6:8, for example, which speaks of our union with Christ's *death* as something which has already happened, and our union with Christ's *resurrection* as a future hope.

But the language of the New Testament is more emphatic on the subject of our present union with Christ in his death. Already during Jesus' own ministry, baptism and death were linked together (Mark 10:38; Luke 12:50). Our dying with Christ is always spoken of as something accomplished at baptism. The New Testament never speaks of our dying with Christ as a future event. What does it mean to say that we have died with Christ in baptism? Paul says in Romans 6:6, "We know that our old self was crucified with him so that the body of sin might be destroyed, and we might no longer be enslaved to sin." We hear a similar statement in Galatians 2:19b-20: "I have been crucified with Christ; and it is no longer I who live, but it is Christ who lives in me." What does this mean, and how does it happen in and through baptism?

There are some common misunderstandings of these passages that can be quickly cleared away. The dying with Christ signified in baptism does not refer primarily to our own act of repentance. What we have argued earlier with respect to the sacraments in general is also true of our union with Christ's death: Dying with Christ is not something we accomplish, but something God does to us by uniting us to Christ. Nor is the Bible speaking here merely of a kind of "legal fiction," by which God treats us "as if" we had died with Christ, even though we really haven't been crucified. If this were the case, it is hard to imagine why Paul would say in Romans 6:11, "So you also must consider yourselves dead to sin and alive to God in Christ Jesus."

In what sense, then, do we die with Christ when we are baptized, if this is neither a metaphor for our own repentance, nor merely an indirect way of speaking of our new legal standing before God? Before attempting to answer this question, it is worth noting that the New Testament speaks of our dying with Christ in somewhat ambiguous terms. At some points such as the Romans 6 text we are exploring, our death with Christ seems to be an event in the *past*. Scholars differ over the nuances here. Some think that Paul is claiming that we died when Christ died, back around A.D. 30, and that this prior death of ours is simply recalled in baptism. Other scholars claim (I think more plausibly) that Paul links our dying with Christ more closely to our baptism itself. In either case, however, dying with Christ is, in many New Testament passages, something that happened *in the past*. How-

49

ever, at other points in the New Testament, dying appears to be a calling that lies before us and still awaits us. Colossians 3:5, for example, urges us to "put to death whatever in you is earthly." Why do we need to put parts of our selves to death, if, as Colossians 3:3 says, we have already died with Christ? Similarly, despite the fact that Colossians 3:10 states that we have (already) been clothed with a new self in baptism, Colossians 3:12 goes on to say, "As God's chosen ones, holy and beloved, *clothe yourselves* with compassion, kindness, humility, meekness, and patience." Why do we still need to clothe ourselves with these things, if we have already been clothed with a new self in Jesus Christ? Why does Paul urge us, in Romans 13:14, to "put on the Lord Jesus Christ," if we have already "put on" Christ in our baptism?

We begin to grasp the surprising and elusive language of the New Testament on this topic when we realize that the New Testament envisages Christian identity in a way that is very different from the way we are taught to think about ourselves. We are taught to derive our identity from our past. We envision ourselves as the product of our life experiences. If we want someone to get to know us well, we tell them our life story, which carries within it our understanding of our identity.

The Bible, however, takes a different approach to identity. In the Bible, our identity is not found in our past, but in Christ's past, which is our future. Our *truest and deepest self* is defined not by what we have experienced in the past, but by what Christ experienced and accomplished for us. This past experience of Christ gives us a glimpse of who we are becoming in the future, because of what Christ has already accomplished on our behalf. This identity awaits us in the future, and we grow toward it. C. S. Lewis captures well this future-oriented aspect of Christian identity:

> It is a serious thing to live in a society of possible gods and goddesses, to remember that the dullest and most uninteresting person you talk to may one day be a creature which, if you saw it now, you would be strongly tempted to worship, or else a horror and a corruption such as you now meet, if at all, only in a nightmare. All day long we are, in some degree, helping each other to one or other of these destinations.[1]

Who we are, at the deepest level, is who we are becoming. Once this is clearly grasped, the paradoxical character of the Bible's language about our

---

1. *The Weight of Glory* (New York: Macmillan, 1949), pp. 14-15.

union with Christ makes much more sense. Our truest and deepest self is the self that has been united with Christ in his death and resurrection. This is the self given to us in Christ, sealed to us in our baptism. Of course, we don't always act in accordance with this self, so we need continually to put into practice our deepest identity. We need to *become in our daily experience* what we already *are in Christ* by virtue of our baptism into Christ. Though we have already been united to Christ's death, we still need to "put to death whatever in you is earthly." Though we have already been clothed with Christ, we still need to "put on the Lord Jesus Christ." Taking these actions is a way of claiming and expressing our truest and deepest self. It is a way of becoming who we most truly are and who we are meant to be.

Although this way of thinking about ourselves may seem odd at first, further reflection suggests that this is the real path to freedom. If we are defined by our past, we can never escape the failures of our past. We are forever haunted by the sins of our past. Even if we have accepted forgiveness for our past failings, when we fail again, a little voice goes off in our head: "There I go again." If the past gives me my identity, I can never escape completely the failures of the past. Because I have failed, I *am*, in some inescapable way, a failure. But it is a different story entirely if my identity comes from the destiny given to me by my union with Christ in baptism. Then, when I fail, the little voice in the back of my head says, "I have not been myself lately." Sin and failure are then not part of who I am in my deepest self, and I can more readily leave these behind and step into this new identity that has been given to me in Christ. This does not mean that all our past problems are magically eliminated when we are baptized and joined to Christ. The Bible makes it clear that Christians often continue to struggle with destructive patterns in their lives, along with their experiences of victory and transformation. But this perspective does transform the way I think about these struggles, and the way I relate my sense of identity to them.

It is only through this perspective that we can bring together the notion that we have died with Christ in baptism with the call of Jesus to take up the cross daily in Luke 9:23: "If any want to become my followers, let them deny themselves and take up their cross daily and follow me." If we have already died with Christ, why must we still take up our cross daily? In an important sense, baptism is answering this call of Jesus. Baptism entails a call to renounce our old life — to leave it behind and put it to death, so that a new kind of life can emerge in us as we follow Jesus. But this letting go of our old life and reaching out to a new life is not something *we* achieve; it is something that is given to us by God. And this gift needs constantly to be put into practice, so that the identity given to us by God becomes the identity that marks our day-to-day lives. We must become who we already are in Christ.

Although I will be discussing infant baptism in more detail a bit later, it is worth noting in passing here that this understanding of dying and rising with Christ in baptism is entirely compatible with the baptism of infants. Baptism signifies both to infants and adults the conferring of a new identity that is united to Christ — an identity that we spend the rest of our lives "living into."

Baptism clothes us with Christ, and in so doing, gives us a new identity. We who are baptized are to think of ourselves as "dead to sin and alive to God in Christ Jesus" (Rom. 6:12). Just as Christ died, we who are clothed with Christ are to think of ourselves as already having lost everything, and having received in its place a new and resurrected life. So what can we still lose? What have we left to fear? Those who have already died no longer need to worry about preserving their lives. Instead, as Jesus said, those who lose their lives will find them (Matt. 16:25). That is the mystery of the gospel given to us in baptism — our deepest identity and our life's calling.

To Sum Up

> One of the core meanings of baptism is union with Christ in his death and resurrection.

> Our union with Christ means that, in some sense, what happened to Christ happened to us, and what Christ has accomplished belongs to us. The crucial question is, in what sense?

> We understand our union with Christ best when we understand that it is a new *identity* given to us by God, an identity into which we grow throughout the rest of our lives. Christian identity flows from the future, already established by Christ's work on our behalf, not primarily from our past.

> The repeated association of union with Christ with baptism in the New Testament suggests that this identity is given to us in our baptism.

For Further Reflection and Discussion

▸ Can you recall a time in your own Christian experience when you based your identity on what Christ accomplished for you, rather than on your own past experience? What difference did it make?

▸ Sometimes our past experience is a powerful determinant on our future. In the case of addictions, for example, past patterns of behavior exert a powerful hold on us. How does the image of Christian identity explored in this chapter speak to such problems?

▸ Does this approach to Christian identity — as a future toward which we grow, rather than a past from which we emerge — mean that our past lives are irrelevant to our Christian identity? If we have died with Christ, is everything about our prior life worthless? (Hint: Meditate upon the use of "I" in Gal. 2:19-20.)

For Further Study

▸ For a careful and thorough discussion of the New Testament theme of union with Christ, see Lewis B. Smedes, *Union with Christ: A Biblical View of the New Life in Jesus Christ* (Grand Rapids: Eerdmans, 1983).

▸ Do a computer-based search for the phrase "in Christ" in the New Testament. You may be surprised by how frequently it is used, and the contexts where it pops up. You can do such a search online at http://www .biblestudytools.net/. (Put the phrase "in Christ" in quotation marks.)

8 If Baptism Unites Us to Christ's Death and Resurrection, in What Sense Does It Also Signify Cleansing?

Baptism is a rich and multi-faceted practice that carries within it multiple levels of meaning. In the last chapter, we explored how baptism signifies our union with the death and resurrection of Christ. In this chapter, we turn to another dimension of baptism: the way in which it points to our cleansing from sin. Recounting his conversion in Acts 22:16, Paul recalls the words of Ananias to him, just after he had recovered his sight: "And now why do you delay? Get up, be baptized, and have your sins washed away, calling on his name." Here baptism is interpreted essentially as a cleansing rite. We see a similar perspective in Ephesians 5:25-26, where the text speaks of how Christ "loved the church and gave himself up for her, in order to make her holy by cleansing her with the washing of water by the word." Here preaching (the word) and baptism are closely connected to each other, but baptism is again viewed as a "washing." Hebrews 10:22 reflects the same understanding of baptism as cleansing, exhorting its listeners to "approach with a true heart in full assurance of faith, with our hearts sprinkled clean from an evil conscience and our bodies washed with pure water." Here an explicit connection is made between the outward washing of the body (i.e., baptism) and the inner cleansing of the heart from an "evil conscience."

At first glance, it might appear as if the notion of baptism as cleansing is completely unrelated to baptism as union with Christ's death and resurrection. What does dying and rising have to do with taking a bath and getting clean? Yet as we shall see, these two images are, in fact, closely related to each other, and must be interpreted in light of their relationship to each other.

The linkage in Scripture between death and cleansing is found in the way *blood* is used in the Bible. In numerous passages, the sprinkling of blood has a cleansing function. In the cleansing ritual for lepers in Leviticus 14:14, blood is sprinkled on the leprous person in order to achieve ritual purity. In the ritual associated with the Day of Atonement, blood is sprinkled on the altar in order to cleanse it (Lev. 16:19). The same linkage between blood and cleansing is found in 1 John 1:7: "But if we walk in the light as he himself is in the light, we have fellowship with one another, and the blood of Jesus his Son cleanses us from all sin." Similarly, 1 Peter 1:2 speaks of how Christians "have been chosen and destined by God the Father and sanctified by the Spirit to be obedient to Jesus Christ and to be sprinkled with his blood."

In the logic of the Bible, to be baptized into Christ's death is also to be sprinkled with Christ's blood. This is both why and how baptism signifies cleansing. Baptism does not cleanse us because the water, in itself, has some spiritual power. Neither does baptism cleanse because the church's rites, in themselves, can cleanse. Rather, baptism cleanses because it points to our union with Jesus Christ, whose life-giving death cleanses us from sin.

Baptism thus presupposes that human beings are in need of cleansing, that sin has left us in a defiled condition that must be remedied if we are to live in God's presence as members of Christ's body. But this only raises a host of further questions: What does it mean to say that human beings are "defiled," and how does the blood of Jesus correct this problem and cleanse us of this defilement?

We get a start on answering that question when we recognize that in the symbolism of Scripture, dirt is essentially *matter that is out of place.* Soil in the garden is fine, but when it gets on my hands, my hands are "dirty." To say that human beings are "defiled" is thus to say that human life is disordered or out of its proper place, and that human beings carry within themselves the results of that disorder. God intends for us to live peaceably with each other, but we are filled with violence and hostility. God intends for us to respect the lives of others, but we use others for our own purposes. God intends human life to be lived in loving care of the creation, but we abuse the earth to our own short-term advantage. And we carry within ourselves, both individually and corporately, the consequences of that disorder, the "dirt on our hands," in the form of guilt, defensiveness, anger, fear, animosity, anxiety, and so forth. To say that human life needs to be cleansed is to say that it must be set right again — restored to the original order and intention of God for human life.

In the sign-world of baptism, it is Christ's blood, symbolized in the cleansing water of baptism, that restores God's order and intention for human life in general, and for us in particular. How does the blood of Christ do this? Christ's blood cleanses us in that the death of Jesus *atones for sin,* by removing from us the guilt we bear from our disordered lives, and by removing from us the fear of punishment, since we know that whatever punishment we deserved was borne by Jesus in his death. Christ's blood cleanses us in that our union with his death *purifies* our lives, setting them back in order, restoring them to the original harmony of God's intentions for human life. When with Christ we die and rise again, we leave behind the disorder of the past, and enter into life as God intends it, and as Christ lived it out. Finally, Christ's blood cleanses and restores order to our lives by *establishing us in covenant with God.* Note, for example how the sprinkling with blood symbolizes the establishing of covenant in Exodus 24:8. Jesus picks up this theme when he speaks of the cup, offered at the Last Supper, as the "blood of the covenant" (Matt. 26:28; Mark 14:24; cf. Luke 22:20; 1 Cor. 11:25). Although scholars differ on the exact significance of the linkage between blood and covenant, one prominent view is that blood, as the vehicle of life, symbolizes the vitality and blessing that is to come from a restored covenantal relationship with God. As our lives are restored to their rightful relationship with God and with each other, life flourishes and we become all we were meant to be. All of these themes — atonement, purity, and covenant — are part of the meaning of the cleansing signified in baptism.

If this is what baptism signifies, *how* and *when* does this cleansing signified in baptism actually happen? Does baptism itself cleanse us, or does it merely remind us of the cleansing we have already received by faith? Before we explore how and when cleansing happens, however, we must be reminded of *why* baptism points to our cleansing. Baptism points to our cleansing because it points to our union with Jesus Christ. It is only by virtue of our union with Christ that we are accepted by God and forgiven, as God treats us in the same way God treats Jesus. It is only by being united to Jesus that our lives are restored to God's original intention for human life, as lived out perfectly by him. It is only in our relationship to Jesus that we can lay claim to a covenantal relationship to God, because Jesus declared his own blood to be the blood of the covenant. It is vitally important that we not abstract the cleansing significance of baptism from our union with Christ signified in our baptism. Ultimately, the question of how and when baptism cleanses us is a question of how and when we are united with Christ.

This makes it clear that it is not simply the rite itself that cleanses us. The sign (the baptismal rite) must never be divorced from what it signifies (union with Christ). Yet this does not mean that the baptismal rite itself is irrelevant to our union with Christ, because baptism marks the point at which we are publicly welcomed into the visible church, the body of Christ. As we have noted earlier, our union with Christ always also unites us to the body of Christ. It is in the body of Christ that our lives are cleansed, slowly and sometimes painstakingly put back into order. Here is where we learn the practices of forgiveness, generosity, hospitality, mercy, and reconciliation. Here is where we begin the difficult but good work of living as Jesus calls us to live, together.

This means further that the cleansing signified in baptism comes to us as a *gift* and as a *promise,* both of which are received *by faith.* The cleansing of baptism is offered to us first as a gift. We do not earn it; we do not deserve it. We come with dirty hands and guilty hearts, and in the waters of baptism, God says to us, "You are clean again — you have a new life, set back into the order intended by me from the beginning." And yet, of course, our life after our baptism is not perfect. We fail and fall short of the life given to us in Christ, and continually need God's forgiving and cleansing grace. Here is where baptism also comes to us as a promise. In baptism, God promises to us that the atonement, purity, and covenant offered to us in our baptism will always be there for us as our truest identity and deepest calling. Indeed nothing can take it away from us.[1]

However, we receive this gift and promise *by faith.* It is not a gift and a promise to be presumed upon. We cannot say, "now that I am baptized, I can ignore God, since my sins are permanently washed away." God's promise only functions as a promise when it is embraced by faith, when we hold on to that promise, put our trust in it, and seek, as best we can, to shape our lives around that promise. Both the gift and promise come to us

---

1. There was a period of time in the fourth century of the Christian church (about 330-365) when Christians often deferred their baptism until very late in life, out of a mistaken fear that baptism offered no assurance of forgiveness for sins committed after baptism was received. This practice may have been originated, in part at least, from the influence of the Emperor Constantine, who was baptized very late in life. For further discussion see J. Jeremias, *Infant Baptism in the First Four Centuries* (London: SCM, 1960), pp. 87-97.

wrapped up in Christ, and we can only receive the gift and trust in the promise by holding fast to Jesus.

Even if we have fallen far away, however, our baptism still speaks to us as God's gift and promise of cleansing. Just as the father of the prodigal son ran out to meet him when he returned, so God's cleansing gift and promise are there in the blink of an eye, when we return to our baptism and place our trust again in God's grace promised to us in those cleansing waters in Christ. Our baptism means we are always welcome to return, and a warm shower and fresh clothes will always be waiting for us!

One final note: It was this understanding of baptism as the promise of lifelong cleansing that led the reformers to reject the sacrament of penance (now called *reconciliation* in the Roman Catholic Church) as a separate sacrament. The medieval church had held that the grace conferred in baptism could be lost through repeated sin. The sacrament of penance provided the means to receive fresh grace to address sins committed after baptism. According to the reformers, however, this approach failed to recognize that baptism signified cleansing as *both* gift and promise. Baptism not only promises forgiveness for past sins; our baptism stands as a promise of forgiveness and cleansing whenever we fail or fall short of God's purposes for us. The reformers rejected the sacrament of penance because they believed that the cleansing offered to us in baptism is abundantly sufficient throughout our lives. All that is required of Christians who fail is a return in faith to the promise of God signified in their baptism.

To Sum Up

▸ Baptism points not only to our union with Christ, but also to our cleansing from sin.

▸ The cleansing significance of baptism flows from our union with Christ in his death. There is a close link in Scripture between the waters of baptism and the blood of Christ.

▸ Cleansing is best understood as the reordering of our lives, individually and corporately, in the image of Christ by the power of the Spirit. This includes the concepts of atonement, purification, and covenant.

▸ The cleansing significance of baptism is offered to us both as a gift in the present and as a promise that sustains us throughout our lives.

For Further Reflection and Discussion

> In the minds of many people, "dirt" is closely associated with "shame." How does the discussion of cleansing in this chapter open up some new ways to think about cleansing for you?

> When you think about seeking God's forgiveness for sins committed in your life, do you think of this act as a return to the promise of your baptism? How might such an approach change the way you think about seeking God's forgiveness and cleansing?

For Further Study

> For a fascinating anthropological study of the relationship between the symbolism of cleansing and the reordering of human life, see Mary Douglas, *Purity and Danger: An Analysis of Concepts of Pollution and Taboo* (London: Routledge and Kegan Paul, 1966).

9 What Is the Relationship of Baptism to Receiving the Holy Spirit?

A quick look at the New Testament shows how closely the Holy Spirit is linked with baptism. In all four gospels, Jesus is introduced by John the Baptist as the "one who baptizes in the Holy Spirit" (Matt. 3:11; Mark 1:8; Luke 3:16; John 1:33). Moreover, the Holy Spirit, in each of the four gospels, descends upon Jesus during his own baptism by John (Matt. 3:16; Mark 1:10; Luke 3:21-22; John 1:32). It is not at all surprising, then, that the same connection between the Holy Spirit and baptism should appear in the teaching and practice of Jesus' disciples. In Acts 1:5, Jesus promises, "John baptized with water, but you will be baptized with the Holy Spirit not many days from now." Subsequently, at the close of the first sermon recorded in the book of Acts, Peter urges his listeners, "Repent, and be baptized every one of you in the name of Jesus Christ so that your sins may be forgiven; and you will receive the gift of the Holy Spirit" (Acts 2:38). Paul makes the same connection between baptism and receiving the Spirit in 1 Corinthians 12:13: "For in the one Spirit we were all baptized into one body — Jews or Greeks, slaves or free — and we were all made to drink of one Spirit." Clearly in Scripture baptism is closely linked with receiving the Holy Spirit.

There are some Christians who hold that "baptism in the Spirit" is an experience subsequent to and different from baptism by water, accompanied by supernatural signs such as speaking in tongues. One text commonly cited to distinguish Christian baptism from baptism in the Spirit is Acts 8:14-17. Here some Samaritans are baptized "in the name of the Lord Jesus," and only later receive the Holy Spirit at the hands of Peter and John. Yet the book of Acts seems clearly to regard this as an anomaly — unusual enough to record here specifically — rather than part of the normal experience of the church.[1]

In fact, Scripture makes it quite clear that one cannot be a Christian at all without also having received the Holy Spirit. Romans 8:9 declares simply and categorically that "anyone who does not have the Spirit of Christ does not belong to him." So it is inconceivable that the early church would have envisioned baptism, which marked one's entry into the body of Christ, without also envisioning, in connection with it, the gift of the Holy Spirit.

The reason for this, on closer examination, is that it is the Holy Spirit who actually unites us to Jesus Christ. The Holy Spirit is the one who makes this bond living and effective. Note, for example, the sequence of logic in Romans 8:9-10:

> But you are not in the flesh; you are in the Spirit, since the Spirit of God dwells in you. Anyone who does not have the Spirit of Christ does not belong to him. But if Christ is in you, though the body is dead because of sin, the Spirit is life because of righteousness.

In the first sentence, Paul speaks about "the Spirit of God" dwelling in you. In the second sentence, the same Spirit is referred to as the "Spirit of Christ." In the third sentence, the Spirit dwelling in you is equated with "Christ" being in you. It is the Spirit who actually makes our union with Christ a reality. We see a similar perspective in John 14. Here Jesus says in verse 16 that he will send "another advocate," the Spirit of truth, to be with them. Just a bit later, in verse 18, he says, "I will not leave you orphaned; I am coming to you." The return of Jesus to be with his disciples and the coming of the Spirit are identified with each other. Later in John 16:14, Jesus says that the Spirit will "take what is mine, and declare it to you." The Spirit takes all of Christ's wisdom, life, righteousness, and truth, and brings it to us, uniting us to it.

---

1. One plausible explanation for this anomaly is that Philip (who originally proclaimed the word in Acts 8 in Samaria) was not an apostle, but one of the seven appointed as deacons in Acts 6. At this critical juncture in the early church, the centrality of the apostles and their role needed to be underscored. Hence, Acts 8:14-17 indicate that *the apostles* sent Peter and John as emissaries. If the newly emerging Samaritan church had not stayed closely linked to the apostolic witness at Jerusalem, the entire unity of the future church might have been at risk.

This is the theological rationale that explains why baptism and the Spirit are so closely related in Scripture. The union with Christ promised in our baptism simply cannot exist apart from the work of the Spirit. Insofar as our baptism points to our initiation into Christ, it also points to our initiation into a relationship with the Holy Spirit.[2] Our union with Christ, attested in our baptism, is a living, vital, relational bond, not merely a legal or formal one. We cannot understand this bond apart from understanding the Holy Spirit's presence and work in us.

Yet for many of us, our understanding of the Holy Spirit is somewhat vague — linked to an emotional feeling or a surge of energy or conviction. We have difficulty understanding the *Holy* Spirit, in part at least, because we have difficulty understanding *spirit* in general. In this regard, it may be helpful to note that the word "spirit" in Scripture is linked with three different images.

First, "spirit" is linked with energy and vitality. The Hebrew word translated "spirit" in the Old Testament is the word for breath or wind. In Judges 14:6, for example, the text tells us, "The spirit of the Lord rushed on [Samson], and he tore the lion apart barehanded as one might tear apart a kid." "Spirit" here is equated with great strength and power. In this same general arena of meaning, to "give up the spirit" in Scripture is to lose all vitality, and thus to die. Similarly, it is spirit — God's breath — that blows on the valley of dry bones in Ezekiel 37, and restores them to life. It is God's breath — God's Spirit — that blows across the deep at creation and brings forth life. The Holy Spirit is thus the source of God's energy and vitality.

Secondly "spirit" represents the capacity for deep personal *knowing* of another. The TNIV's translation of 1 Corinthians 2:11 brings out the meaning clearly: "For who knows a person's thoughts except that person's own spirit within? In the same way no one knows the thoughts of God except the Spirit of God." A person's spirit, in this sense, is the source of feeling, insight, and will. In this sense, to receive the Spirit of God or of Christ is to know, in some deep sense, God's feeling, insight, and will, and for God to know yours. This may well be what Paul is alluding to in Romans 8:26-27:

2. For a summary of key texts linking the work of Christ and the work of the Spirit in us, see Lewis Smedes, *Union with Christ: A Biblical View of the New Life in Jesus Christ* (Grand Rapids: Eerdmans, 1983), p. 44.

> Likewise the Spirit helps us in our weakness; for we do not know how to pray as we ought, but that very Spirit intercedes with sighs too deep for words. And God, who searches the heart, knows what is the mind of the Spirit, because the Spirit intercedes for the saints according to the will of God.

Here the Spirit creates the capacity for communion with God that involves an intimacy and directness that transcends language itself. In scriptural thinking, to receive the spirit of another is to have access to the feelings, insights, and intentions of that other person. To receive the Spirit of God is to have an intimate knowledge of God's heart and mind, and for God to know ours.

This notion of spirit as the capacity for interpersonal knowing also leads to the third aspect of "spirit": although spirit can enable an intersubjective knowing that transcends language, spirit also is the source of language. Our words are, in essence, shaped and articulated breath. And so in Scripture, there is a vital link between spirit and *communication.* The Spirit of God uniquely brings the word of God. Over and over in Scripture, the Spirit of God comes on people, and they both know and speak the word of God. This speaking of God's word arises from the encounter with God mediated by the Spirit. The Holy Spirit is always intimately connected with the word of God.

All these aspects of spirit — vitality, knowledge, intimacy, and communication, are part of the Spirit's work in us promised in baptism. Through the energy of the Spirit, we experience Christ's resurrection. Through the intimacy with God engendered by God's Spirit, we experience Christ's love for us and for the world. Through the agency of the Spirit, God's word becomes real, meaningful, and alive for us.

But what is the relationship between all this and baptism? Surely the Spirit of God is at work in people before they are baptized. Otherwise, it is impossible to imagine how someone might be converted to become a Christian and seek baptism in the first place. Interestingly, Acts 10:47 speaks specifically of some who received the Holy Spirit prior to baptism. And it is also the case that many Christians have dramatically new experiences of the Spirit *after* their baptism. Indeed, for some Christians, these later experiences are so dramatic, and in such contrast with their earlier experience, that they wonder whether they "really" received the Spirit in their baptism, particularly if they were baptized as an infant. If the Spirit is poured out in baptism, how shall we understand the work of the Spirit prior to baptism, and also afterward?

Several observations may help to answer this question. First, we must remember that the Holy Spirit is God, and is not under our control. The Spirit is free, and works wherever and however God wills. We cannot restrict the presence and work of the Spirit to the rites of the church.

But neither is it helpful to say that the gift of the Spirit has nothing specifically to do with the rite of baptism. Even though the self-giving of the Spirit is not *restricted* to baptism, Scripture, by its repeated linkage between baptism and the Spirit, suggests that the Holy Spirit *uses* baptism in a special way. The Spirit gives himself to us both before and after baptism, but that self-giving takes particular expression in baptism itself. The analogy of a marriage may be helpful here. A couple loves each other before their wedding day. They will grow to love each other much more deeply as their marriage matures and grows. Yet their wedding is a unique and powerful expression of the love that binds them to one another — an expression of love that is irreplaceable by any other expression of love. In the same way, the Spirit's self-giving to us neither begins nor ends with baptism. But baptism is a visible and tangible expression of that self-giving that stands as a unique marker, a sign and seal of our relationship with the Holy Spirit from that time forward.

But there is another important sense in which we receive the Spirit in a *unique* way *in baptism itself.* Baptism is our incorporation into the church, the body of Christ. We know from Scripture that the Spirit dwells, in a special and unique way, in the body of Christ. The gifts of the Spirit are given *to the body* (1 Cor. 12). They find their meaning, their significance, and their inter-relatedness within the body of Christ. The Spirit of Christ dwells uniquely in the body of Christ. Here we confront one of the limitations of our modern and American individualism, which tends to ignore the corporate dimension to life. We tend to think about the work of the Spirit only in relation to us as individuals. But Scripture sees the Spirit at work centrally in the body. Thus when we enter the body of Christ in baptism, we enter the realm of the Spirit, and find those places and discover those gifts that allow us to make our contribution to something much larger than ourselves. This entry into this particular aspect of the Spirit's work happens uniquely in baptism, and nowhere else. If we are not baptized into the body of Christ, and if that does not express itself in tangible relationships with other Christians, there are dimensions of the Spirit's presence and work in our lives which we will never experience. In this sense, any work of the Spirit in our lives prior to baptism has the character of a prelude to the "main event."

Finally, we must remember the character of baptism as both gift and promise. In baptism, the Spirit is given to us. But this gift is not a "one-time shot." It rather carries with it the promise of the Spirit's continual presence and abiding with us, and also the promise of occasional "fillings" of the Spirit — seasons where the Spirit's work in our lives seems especially powerful and tangible. When we experience those seasons of special blessing, we can look back to our baptism with gratitude for God's faithfulness to his promise.

To Sum Up

> In baptism, we receive the Spirit of God, who unites us to Jesus Christ.

> The Spirit takes what belongs to Christ, and makes it real to us and for us.

> In baptism, the Spirit ushers us into the vitality of new life in Christ, the deep and intimate awareness of the love of Christ, and the powerful and transforming knowledge of the word of God.

> As we enter into the realm of the Spirit in baptism, we are at the same time drawn into the body of Christ, where the Spirit empowers us and puts us to work as disciples in God's mission.

For Further Reflection and Discussion

> This chapter spoke of the Spirit's work under the general categories of *energy and vitality, knowledge of God and intimacy with God,* and *a living encounter with God's word.* Which of these has been most formative in your life?

> Have you encountered Christians who believe that all Christians should expect a "baptism in the Spirit," subsequent to baptism in water? How would you respond to this claim?

> Some church members don't act as if the Spirit of God is at work in their lives, even though they may be baptized. Is the Spirit still active in a person, even when there are not outward signs of that activity?

For Further Study

> ‣ For a helpful overview of the Spirit in the New Testament, see the article on "spirit" by James D. G. Dunn in *Dictionary of New Testament Theology,* ed. Colin Brown (Grand Rapids: Zondervan, 1975), 3:693-709.

10 What Is the Relationship between Baptism and Being "Born Again"?

In order to answer this question, we need first to explore what it means to be "born again." In the mind of the average North American Christian, being "born again" usually is connected to having some sort of "conversion experience," or making a personal decision to become a Christian. To be a "born-again Christian" means to have undergone a transforming religious experience, as a result of which one has made a personal commitment to follow Jesus Christ in faith. When we explore the New Testament, however, we will discover that "rebirth" has a somewhat different range of meanings, sometimes more particular and focused, sometimes broader and more general. Once we have explored more precisely what rebirth means in the New Testament, we will return to its relationship to baptism in particular.

Perhaps the most familiar text about being "born again" is found in John 3:1-8:

Now there was a Pharisee named Nicodemus, a leader of the Jews. He came to Jesus by night and said to him, "Rabbi, we know that you are a teacher who has come from God; for no one can do these signs that you do apart from the presence of God." Jesus answered him, "Very truly, I tell you, no one can see the kingdom of God without being born from above." Nicodemus said to him, "How can anyone be born after having grown old? Can one enter a second time into the mother's womb and be born?" Jesus answered, "Very truly, I tell you, no one can enter the kingdom of God without being born of water and Spirit. What is born of the flesh is flesh, and what is born of the Spirit is spirit. Do not be astonished that I said to you, 'You must be born from above.' The wind blows where it chooses, and you hear the sound of it, but you do not know where it comes from or where it goes. So it is with everyone who is born of the Spirit."

We will return to this text several times in our discussion, but we begin by noting Jesus' words that no one can *see* the Kingdom of God without being born "from above."[1] Later, Jesus also says that no one can *enter* the Kingdom of God without being born "of water and Spirit." In other words, being born again/from above is a *prerequisite* to seeing or entering the Kingdom of God. This new birth comes from "water and Spirit," linking this new birth with baptism and the work of the Holy Spirit.[2]

As this text speaks of it, being born again is something that happens *even before* the conscious experience of conversion. One must be born again before one can even *see* the Kingdom of God, much less choose to embrace that Kingdom. In this sense, being born again is equivalent to having God's life in you — a life that enables you to see the significance of Jesus and his life, and to choose to follow him.

Although baptism may *point* to this transforming work of the Spirit, we cannot say that baptism *brings about* rebirth in the sense that is spoken of in John 3. The reason is plain: people come to baptism *because* they have seen something of the Kingdom of God, and want to be part of it. In this sense, the regenerating work of the Spirit has already begun in them. Baptism points to this rebirth or insight, but it does not bring that rebirth or that insight into existence. So even though this passage links baptism with being born again, we must recognize that baptism does not *cause* someone to be born again in the sense spoken of in John 3.

What, then, is the relationship between baptism and being born again? Another key text linking these two experiences is found in Titus 3:4-5: "But when the goodness and loving kindness of God our Savior appeared, he saved us, not because of any works of righteousness that we had done, but

---

1. It may be helpful to note that the same Greek word that is translated in this passage as "from above" can also be translated "again." Jesus intends both meanings — he is speaking of a second birth which comes "from above," that is, from God. Nicodemus understands the word only to mean "again," missing the divine origin of this life, and thus remains confused.

2. While some commentators see in the reference to "water" an allusion to the amniotic water of physical birth, separate and distinct from spiritual birth, this is unlikely. Throughout this passage, Jesus is speaking only of new birth by the Spirit. The reference to "water" here is thus an allusion to baptism.

according to his mercy, *through the water of rebirth and renewal by the Holy Spirit.*" The phrase "water of rebirth" is more literally translated "washing of rebirth," an allusion to baptism as a symbol of both cleansing and new life.[3]

Here we come to a somewhat different sense of being "born again." In the text from John with which we began, being "born again" was viewed as a *prerequisite* to seeing or entering into God's life. In numerous other New Testament passages, rebirth is viewed more broadly to encompass the totality of the transformation and renewal that we experience as Christians. Galatians 6:15 and 2 Corinthians 5:17 speak of a "new creation" as the totality of Christian life. This broader sense of rebirth and renewal is seen with particular clarity in Colossians 3:9-10:

> Do not lie to one another, seeing that you have stripped off the old self with its practices and have clothed yourselves with the new self, which is being renewed in knowledge according to the image of its creator.

Note in this passage that renewal is an *ongoing* experience of the Christian life. We already have been given a "new self," but that new self is also in the process of "being renewed in knowledge according to the image of its creator."

Here we confront the same paradox we saw in the chapter on dying and rising with Christ. If we already have been given a new self, why are we still being renewed? It is only when we recognize that Scripture speaks of our identity as our *promised destiny,* as what we are in the process of becoming, that this paradox is resolved. Christians have already been reborn in Christ, and that accomplished reality is in the ongoing process of manifesting itself in their everyday lives, more and more.

So rebirth means two things. It is the secret work of God in our lives, before we are even aware of God, by which we are able to see the Kingdom of God. In this sense, it is the work of the Spirit in us that enables us to hear the gospel at all, and to respond in faith. But rebirth also refers to the whole process of transformation in our lives, by which we gradually become more and more conformed to the image of Jesus Christ. So Paul, for

---

3. Some scholars argue that the phrase "washing of rebirth" is not an allusion to baptism, but rather to the cleansing that is brought about by our rebirth and renewal by the Holy Spirit. This is unlikely, since "rebirth" is nowhere else envisioned in Scripture as something that, in itself, brings about cleansing. (Indeed, birth, considered by itself, is not a clean, but a rather messy affair!)

example, can say, in a particularly frustrated mood, to the Galatians, "My little children, for whom I am again in the pain of childbirth until Christ is formed in you" (4:19). They are already Christians, but something still needs to be born in them, too. Just so, we are in the continual process of renewal, by which Jesus Christ is born in our lives.

Baptism points to rebirth in both of these senses. It holds before us an image of the mysterious renewing work of the Spirit, affirming what God has done in us, and promising to us what God will still do to give us new life. When we consider more particularly the baptism of infants or adults, the emphasis will shift somewhat. With infants, the emphasis falls on the *promise* of rebirth in Christ, and baptism invites the child and his or her parents to place their trust in that promise. With the baptism of confessing Christians, the emphasis falls both on the affirmation of the new life which has already begun, and the promise of God's continued renewing work, whereby the fullness of Christ's life comes to birth in us.

It is only within this larger framework that we can properly understand the subjective experience commonly spoken of as being "born again." It is characteristic of many Christians to have a dramatic experience of spiritual transformation and renewal, which they may speak of as a "born-again experience." In light of our exploration, however, we must understand such experiences neither as the beginning nor as the end of the Christian life. They are not the beginning, since the mysterious and secret work of the Holy Spirit preceded them. Indeed, it is only the prior work of the Holy Spirit giving us the capacity to see the Kingdom of God that enables such transformation to begin. "Born-again" experiences are also not the end of the Christian life. Instead, the gospel calls us to a life of discipleship, where there may be periodic times of profound spiritual growth and transformation, as we become more and more the person God has destined us to be.

This framework suggests, finally, that the absence of a dramatic "born-again" experience may not be anything for Christians to worry about. For some Christians, the process of renewal and transformation is slower and more regular — a matter of steady growth and maturation. This too is one of the ways our new life in Christ manifests itself in us. What matters is not the pace of change, but the reality of new life in Christ.

Many believer baptists insist that a subjective "born-again" experience is a necessary *prerequisite* to baptism. In their view, baptism does not *cause* new birth, but it *witnesses* to the existing reality of new birth in the life of the believer. Yet this approach is inadequate for three reasons. First, it collapses the biblical tension we have been exploring in this chapter, suggesting that new birth refers only to the beginning of Christian life, whereas Scripture speaks of new birth in two distinct senses — both the mysterious beginning of Christian life, and the totality of Christian transformation into the image of Christ. Secondly, this approach mistakenly assumes that we can confidently discern when and where the Spirit is at work to do the initial, secret work of regeneration spoken of in John 3. But it is by no means clear that Scripture teaches that we always can know when and where the Spirit is at work so clearly. Finally, and perhaps most importantly, by envisioning new birth only as an accomplished reality prior to baptism, this approach obscures the character of baptism as the *promise* of God's continual work in our lives to bring the life of Christ to birth in us. Baptism thus becomes merely an attempt to recognize what God has already done, rather than a forward-looking initiation into the journey of trust and discipleship.

But there is one further sense of rebirth in John 3, which we also must address, if we are to understand all the linkages between baptism and being "born again." John 3 is the story of Jesus and Nicodemus. It's a story of a breakdown in communication, as Nicodemus becomes increasingly confused by what Jesus is saying to him. It is worth noting that this story begins with the note that Nicodemus comes to Jesus "at night" (John 3:2). This suggests that Nicodemus doesn't want others to know that he is talking to Jesus. He wants this to be his own personal spiritual exploration, done as a private quest for enlightenment. This is a big part of his problem.

Nicodemus is like others in the Gospel of John who refuse to confess Jesus publicly because they are afraid of persecution (e.g., John 12:42). So when Jesus tells Nicodemus that he must be born of water and Spirit in order to enter the Kingdom of God, one of the implications we may draw is that baptism as a *public act* is important. Our relationship with Jesus is not merely a private affair. Nowhere is this more powerfully demonstrated than in baptism, which takes place in a public worship service. Baptism publicly marks us as a follower of Jesus. And part of what Jesus is saying to Nicodemus, I suspect, is that he won't experience the fullness of the new life Jesus is talking about until he is willing to become a public follower of Jesus. We can become so "spiritual" in our thinking about the Christian life that we lose sight of the concrete, tangible relationships in the body of Christ, through which our new life in Christ expresses itself. Baptism calls us back to these relationships as the context in which our rebirth takes place.

Baptism points to our rebirth as new creatures in the image of Jesus Christ. Baptism is neither the source of our rebirth, nor the end of the process of our renewal. But it captures and holds before us, as both identity and calling, our union with the risen Christ, whose renewing life and power flows into us through the Spirit, as we are united with the body of Christ, the church. When baptism is practiced at its best, it is a public declaration of our identity, and a kind of touchstone to which we continually return, to remember the new birth which ushered us into God's Kingdom, and the promise of the new creation in Christ we are still becoming.

To Sum Up

> In the New Testament, new birth (or to use the more technical term, "regeneration") refers both to the hidden work of God that enables us even to *see* God's Kingdom, and also to the whole process of transformation that continues throughout Christian life.

> Baptism does not cause regeneration, but points to the gift of new life and holds before us the promise of God's continuing regenerative work in our lives.

> The subjective experience of being "born again" must be understood as part of the larger process of transformation that makes up Christian life in its entirety.

> Baptism does not *presuppose* regeneration, but directs our faith both toward the mysterious work of the Spirit in ushering us into life in Christ and toward the Spirit's ongoing work of bringing new life into our lives.

> As a public event, baptism also underscores the connection between new life and our public identification with Christ and his people.

For Further Reflection and Discussion

> Think about John 3:3, and its claim that no one can see the Kingdom of God without being born again. This grates rather harshly against our normal self-understanding. Most folks believe that they can see things for

themselves and make their own decisions. How should that self-understanding be revised, if at all, in light of this verse?

> Some Christian traditions identify baptism more explicitly as the *cause* of new birth. The technical term for this is "baptismal regeneration." Are you familiar with the notion that baptism *causes* new birth? What do you make of this idea?

> What is your reaction when someone asks you if you are a "born-again Christian"?

For Further Study

> For a quick exposure to a variety of perspectives on the relationship between baptism and rebirth, do an Internet search (e.g., at www.google.com) on the words "regeneration," "rebirth," and "baptism." Just enter all three words into the search box. Here you will probably also encounter the Roman Catholic view of baptism and regeneration, which tends to link the two more closely than we have done in this chapter.

11 Which Is Better, Sprinkling or Immersion?

Although the primary debate in recent Christian history has been whether baptism should be done by immersion or by sprinkling, there are in reality three different ways in which baptism has been performed at various points in the history of the church: immersion, sprinkling, and pouring. With immersion, the entire body is submerged below the water; with sprinkling, water is applied with the hand to the head of the person being baptized; with pouring, water is poured over the head, either using some utensil or the hand to hold and pour the water.

Scholars have spent a great deal of energy trying to resolve the debate about the mode of baptism by seeking to nail down the precise definition of the Greek word *baptizo*. The results seem to indicate, however, that the issue will not be settled this way. The Greek word has a wide range of meanings, from "dip" or "plunge" to "soak" to "wash."[1] In the New Testament, the word is always used of ritualized actions that are intended to have religious significance. But the word itself has a sufficiently wide range of possible meanings that it cannot tell us by itself what the proper mode of baptism is.

If the study of an individual word cannot settle the question of the mode of baptism, neither can church history. One of the earliest Christian sources beyond the New Testament, the *Didache* (dating from approximately A.D. 90-150), calls for the use of running ("living") water, but if that is unavailable, it suggests pouring water on the head three times. It does

---

1. Luke 11:38 clearly indicates "washing" as opposed to immersion, for example: "The Pharisee was amazed to see that [Jesus] did not first wash (literally, *was not first baptized*) before dinner."

not say, however, whether immersion or pouring was recommended when using running water.[2] A similar diversity of practice is evident elsewhere as well.

We are left, then, with the New Testament materials, and the broader question, whether the biblical language surrounding baptism seems to lean toward any particular mode of baptism. Those who prefer immersion often move immediately to Romans 6, with its connections between that method and burial with Christ. Clearly, Romans 6 is most compatible with baptism as immersion. Baptism as immersion also coheres with the most common (but not the only) meaning of the Greek word outside the New Testament — "to dip" or "to plunge."[3]

At the same time, it must be noted that if the focus in immersion is on disappearing completely under the water, then immersion does not so readily lend itself to baptism as a cleansing rite. Indeed, there is no biblical evidence that any of the various ritual washings prescribed in the Old Testament law ever required the total immersion of the person or object to be cleansed. In fact, sprinkling served as the more common mode for various cleansing rites (e.g., Ezek. 36:25: "I will sprinkle clean water upon you, and you shall be clean from all your uncleannesses. . . ."). If John's baptism, which is a clear predecessor of Christian baptism, drew at all on Old Testament precedents, it seems unlikely that immersion was regarded as necessary. Overall, to the extent that baptism symbolizes cleansing, it is more fully symbolized by pouring or sprinkling than by immersion, since these are the dominant means of ritual cleansing in the Old Testament.

Similarly, immersion does not reflect the way in which the symbolism of baptism by pouring resonates with the "pouring out" of the Holy Spirit (Acts 2:17-18; 2:33; 10:45; Rom. 5:5; Titus 3:6). The Bible never speaks unambiguously of anyone being *immersed* in the Holy Spirit, and never speaks of someone entering "into" the Holy Spirit — an image that might be sug-

---

2. "Now concerning baptism, baptize as follows: after you have reviewed all these things, baptize 'in the name of the Father and of the Son and of the Holy Spirit' in running water. But if you have no running water, then baptize in some other water; and if you are not able to baptize in cold water, then do so in warm. But if you have neither, then pour water on the head three times 'in the name of Father and Son and Holy Spirit.'" *Didache* 7:1-3, trans. Michael W. Holmes, in *Apostolic Fathers* (Grand Rapids: Baker, 1999), p. 259.

3. Curiously, there is only one New Testament reference to being baptized "into" water: Mark 1:9, which refers not to water directly, but to the Jordan River. One might expect more such usages, if "dip" or "plunge" was *always* the assumed meaning of the Greek word *baptizō*.

gested by baptism as immersion, in light of the parallel phrases, "baptized with water" and "baptized with the Holy Spirit."[4] Throughout the Bible, persons do not enter into the Holy Spirit; the Holy Spirit enters into persons.[5] The Bible does, however, speak frequently of the "pouring out" of the Spirit. This suggests that an important dimension of baptismal symbolism is lost when immersion is regarded as the essence of baptism. It further suggests that the pouring of water in baptism may more effectively evoke both the symbolism of cleansing and of the pouring out of the Spirit.

These complexities suggest that no single mode of baptism can fully express all the rich symbolism of the New Testament. Immersion can convey our union with Christ in his death and resurrection, and, to a lesser degree, our cleansing by the blood of Christ, but says little about the gift of the Spirit. Pouring conveys a sense of cleansing and directly evokes the gift of the Spirit, but links less clearly with our union with Christ in his death and resurrection. Sprinkling draws on rich Old Testament images of cleansing, and also links with Christ's death, since blood is always sprinkled in the Old Testament when it is used ritually. Yet sprinkling has less resonance with the gift of the Spirit.

I believe that there is insufficient evidence in Scripture and in church history to be decisive about these matters, and that congregations should exercise freedom in their approach to the question of the mode of baptism. Indeed, congregations may be well served by employing a variety of different modes of baptism as circumstances may warrant, so that over time the congregation is exposed visually to the full range of baptismal symbolism.

To Sum Up

> There are three "modes" commonly used for baptism: sprinkling, pouring, and immersion.

> The meaning of the word "baptize" in the New Testament does not give

---

4. Despite periodic references to people going "into" water (Matt. 17:15; Mark 9:22; John 5:7; Acts 8:38), there is never in the entire New Testament a reference to persons entering "into" the Holy Spirit.

5. There are a few New Testament references to visionary states, in which people are said to be "in the spirit" (e.g., Rev. 4:2; 17:3; 21:10). But "spirit" in these texts does not refer to the Holy Spirit, but rather to a mode of existence which transcends physical limitations.

us enough information to be decisive about the mode of baptism. Neither does church history.

➤ Each mode has strengths and limitations when viewed against the full array of baptismal images in the Bible.

➤ Churches do best to use a variety of modes of baptism, so that the full range of scriptural symbolism is held before the congregation.

For Further Reflection and Discussion

➤ What mode(s) of baptism have you witnessed or experienced? How would you assess the strengths and limitations of each in terms of the actual practice?

➤ In your experience, does the tendency to use only one mode of baptism have the practical effect of narrowing down the implicit theology of baptism in your church?

➤ Usually, our practice of baptism is dictated by the architecture of our places of worship. What different kinds of baptisteries or baptismal fonts have you seen, and how might their location and design enrich or shape our understanding of baptism?

For Further Study

➤ For an interesting discussion of Christian baptisteries dating from the fourth to the ninth centuries, along with some photographs, see http://en.wikipedia.org/wiki/Baptistery.

12 What Does It Mean to Be Baptized "*in the Name of* the Father and of the Son and of the Holy Spirit," or "*in the Name of* Jesus" (and Which of These Names Should Be Used in Baptism)?

The phrase "in the name of" is one of those expressions we hear frequently (especially in Christian circles), but when we pause to think about exactly what it means, we may find ourselves a bit unsure. We are instructed to offer our prayers in the name of Jesus (e.g., John 14:13; 15:16; etc.). Scripture speaks of Christians gathering in Jesus' name (Matt. 18:20). The book of Acts tells of the apostles speaking in Jesus' name (Acts 4:18). Miracles are done in Jesus' name (Acts 3:6). Paul says that we were justified "in the name of the Lord Jesus Christ" (1 Cor. 6:11). We are instructed to give thanks to God in the name of Jesus (Eph. 5:20). Indeed, we are told to "do everything in the name of the Lord Jesus" (Col. 3:17). We need to discern what this phrase means in general, and what it means in particular to be baptized in the name of Jesus, or, as the Great Commission phrases it, "in the name of the Father and of the Son and of the Holy Spirit" (Matt. 28:19).

We get some help in understanding this phrase by looking at the Old Testament. Several patterns of meaning occur when parallels are examined. First, to do something "in the name of" someone else is to *represent* that other person and act on his or her behalf. Prophets, for example, frequently speak *in God's name* (e.g., 2 Chron. 33:18; Ezra 5:1; Jer. 11:21). By this phrase, they claim to represent God and speak on God's behalf. A similar, more mundane usage occurs in Esther 2:22, where the text reads, "But the matter came to the knowledge of Mordecai, and he told it to Queen Esther, and Esther told the king in the name of Mordecai." Clearly, what is intended here is that Esther spoke *on behalf of Mordecai* to the king.

To the extent that this pattern of meaning is relevant to baptism, what might it mean to baptize "in the name of" Jesus or the triune God? Here the accent would fall on the person who is doing the baptizing. To say "I baptize you in the name of the Father and of the Son and of the Holy Spirit" is thus to say "I baptize you representing and acting on behalf of the triune God."[1] I believe that this is an important dimension of what it means to be baptized "in the name of" the Father, the Son, and the Holy Spirit, but it is not the only meaning of this phrase.

In other usages, to do something "in the name of" someone means to *invoke the presence, vindication, or judgment* of that person. Here the "name" represents the person's presence and anticipated action. When David comes out to meet Goliath in 1 Samuel 17:45, he declares, "You come to me with sword and spear and javelin; but I come to you *in the name of* the Lord of hosts, the God of the armies of Israel, whom you have defied." The parallelism here clearly indicates that the name of God is the presence and power of God on which David will rely, instead of "sword and spear and javelin." David is not claiming to represent God here, but to rely upon God, and he invokes God's presence and help to that end. A similar sense is found in Psalm 124:8, "Our help is in the name of the LORD, who made heaven and earth." Similarly, Psalm 118:26 pronounces a blessing on pilgrims who approach the Temple: "Blessed is the one who comes in the name of the LORD. We bless you from the house of the LORD." Here as well, the thought is probably not that the pilgrims represent God, but that they make their approach to the Temple invoking God's presence and grace.[2]

In this sense, to be baptized "in the name of" Jesus is to be baptized while invoking the presence, power, and activity of Jesus. The book of Acts tells us that from the very earliest point, it was the practice of the church to baptize in the name of *Jesus*. The presence and power of Jesus occupies the place normally given to God. Here we have a very early indication of the

---

1. Martin Luther writes, "Hence we ought to receive baptism at human hands just as if Christ himself, indeed God himself, were baptizing us with his own hands. For it is not man's baptism, but Christ's and God's baptism, which we receive by the hand of a man, just as everything else that we have through the hand of somebody else is God's alone" ("The Babylonian Captivity of the Church," in *Selected Writings of Martin Luther, 1517-1520*, trans. A. T. W. Steinhaeuser and ed. Theodore G. Tappert [Philadephia: Fortress, 1967], p. 414).

2. When the same words are called out to Jesus in his "triumphal entry" (Mark 11:9), the Gospel of Mark may perhaps intend a subtle double meaning, suggesting not only the traditional meaning from the Psalms (that Jesus' approach to the city is done in reliance upon God), but also that Jesus represents the divine presence in his approach to the city. The other gospels make this double meaning even more explicit.

way in which Jesus was accorded a uniquely divine status by the early church. The formula of the Great Commission only expands on what is implicit in the formula "in the name of Jesus" by invoking the presence and action of the Father, the Son, and the Holy Spirit. So when the church baptizes someone "in the name of" the triune God, the church voices its belief and trust that in its actions, God is and will be active. We invoke God's presence in the rite of baptism to actually do what baptism signifies.

There is one further dimension to the phrase "in the name of" that should also be mentioned. This meaning comes not so much from the Old Testament as from Greek usage. Explorations of the phrase "in the name of" in Greek outside of biblical usage suggest that Greek speakers would attach to the phrase implications of *ownership,* particularly when used within the context of banking and money. In Greek usage, to place something or someone "in the name of" someone else is to assign the person or thing to the account of the "name." Objects purchased "in the name of" a god are assumed to be the property of the god. The dowry of a wife, upon marriage, is placed "in the name of" the husband, indicating that the husband takes ownership.

Baptism "in the name of" Jesus, in this sense, means that baptism indicates a transfer of ownership. The baptized person now "belongs" to Jesus. This dimension of meaning is beautifully captured in the opening of the first question and answer of the Heidelberg Catechism: "What is your only comfort in life and death? That I am not my own, but belong — body and soul, in life and in death — to my faithful Savior Jesus Christ." It is interesting to recall, in this light, how one of the early Christians' favorite ways of speaking of themselves was as "servants/slaves of Christ" (Rom. 1:1; James 1:1; 2 Peter 1:1; Jude 1:1). It may well be that this sense of being "owned" by Jesus originated with this baptismal formula.

All these dimensions of meaning to the phrase "in the name of" — representation, invocation and reliance, and ownership — are important and relevant to our understanding of baptism. When a minister baptizes someone, by faith we claim that it is not merely the action of a human being, but that, in this action, the minister not only represents the church but also *represents* and acts on behalf of God. We claim by faith that God is active in and through the action of the minister baptizing a person. In baptism, we also *invoke God's presence,* and claim by faith that God is present in the baptism itself, doing for us what the baptism signifies and promises: uniting us to Christ, cleansing us of our sins, pouring out on us the Spirit, and giving us new life. Finally, in baptism we claim by faith that we now *belong* to Jesus Christ, and that we therefore belong in the company of his followers, the church.

To say that we claim these things "by faith" is to acknowledge that baptism is not a magical rite that springs from some special power given to the church or to ministers of the church (even though God uses the church and its ministers, to be sure). Nor is there some magical power in "the name." Rather, the phrase "in the name of" the triune God reflects the church's basic posture of trust and reliance upon God, rather than upon itself. We baptize "in the name of the Father, and of the Son, and of the Holy Spirit," because we recognize that it is only in reliance upon God's gracious action, in fulfillment of God's promise, that all the blessings of baptism will flow to us and through us to the world.

One last biblical text is instructive on this question as well. When Paul speaks of baptism in Galatians 3:27, he speaks not of being baptized *in the name of Christ*, but simply as being baptized *into Christ*: "As many of you as were baptized into Christ have clothed yourself with Christ." This verse underscores the central theme of union with Christ that underlies baptism as a whole. When we say that in baptism the minister represents Christ, that the community invokes Christ's presence and power, and that Christ takes ownership of a person, these are all aspects of the more basic affirmation that in baptism God promises and seals to us our union with Christ, together with all the blessings and benefits that flow from that union.

Finally, a word should be said about the difference between "in the name of Jesus" and "in the name of the Father, and of the Son, and of the Holy Spirit." Baptism "in the name of Jesus" is the formula we see in the Book of Acts.[3] This may well have been the earliest Christian practice. The wording of the Great Commission, however, with its full trinitarian reference, quickly became the standard wording for baptism in the early church. I believe that this happened for several reasons. First, the full trinitarian reference to "Father, Son, and Holy Spirit" made explicit what baptism "in the name of Jesus" already implied: that is, that Jesus was being invoked as a manifestation of God. Secondly, the fuller reference makes clear that the whole Godhead is at work in baptism: The Father draws us to Christ (John 6:44); the Son makes us his own and gives us his life through the Spirit, who bonds us to Christ and pours out gifts and power upon us.

3. Acts 2:38; 8:16; 10:48; 19:5.

There are a few churches today that insist that baptism should be in the name of "Jesus only." However, it is difficult to see how this is not a rejection of the clear and more complete trinitarian formula of Matthew 28:19. Any real or implied rejection of that trinitarian formula represents a serious departure from the biblical witness and the entire Christian tradition. Though it may have taken a while for the early church to standardize its practice, it appears clear now that baptism should be done in the name of the triune God, Father, Son, and Holy Spirit.

To Sum Up

> To baptize "in the name of" the triune God conveys three meanings:
  – the minister *represents* the triune God when baptizing in God's name;
  – baptism in God's name *invokes* the presence and power of the triune God to do what baptism signifies and promises;
  – baptism in God's name conveys a transfer of *ownership* of the baptized person to God.

> The early Christian practice of baptizing "into the name of Christ," or "into Christ," shows the close link between baptism and union with Christ.

> The full trinitarian formula should be used in baptism.

For Further Reflection and Discussion

> Refer back to the first paragraph of this chapter, which discusses a variety of ways in which the phrase "in the name of" is used in the New Testament. How might your understanding of these texts be deepened as a result of the discussion in this chapter?

> Which of these meanings of "in the name of" was most familiar to you? Which, if any, was a new discovery for you?

For Further Study

> The definitive study on this phrase is by Lars Hartman, *Into the Name of the Lord Jesus: Baptism in the Early Church* (London: T&T Clark, 1997).

BAPTISM, FAITH, AND SALVATION

The next section (chapters 13-16) covers some general questions that arise about baptism. Here we are not addressing the core meanings of baptism in Scripture, but rather are working out the *implications* of those core meanings for our overall understanding of Christian faith and life. The issues in this section revolve primarily around how we relate baptism, faith, and salvation to each other in a coherent whole. The order and sequence of these chapters is of no deep significance, and the reader is welcome to dip in wherever interest may lie.

13 Does Baptism Presuppose Faith, or Does It Call Us to Faith?

The relationship between baptism and faith is complex, but it is vital that we understand the role that faith plays in the sacrament of baptism. In later chapters, I will discuss more specifically the role of faith in infant baptism,[1] but in this chapter, we shall explore more broadly the relationship between baptism and faith.

To do this, however, we must first understand what faith itself is. Let us begin by briefly returning to the discussion in the chapter entitled "What Is the Church?" (chapter 2). There we explored how God's relationship with human beings is shaped by the making of covenants. In these covenants, God comes to humans with generosity, kindness, and grace. In return, God expects our trust and allegiance. It is this response of trust and allegiance that the Bible is speaking of when it speaks of faith. Faith is our response to God's goodness: acknowledging that goodness, accepting it, trusting in it, and committing ourselves to the relationship and the calling that God's kindness establishes with us.

Each of these elements can be expanded upon. Faith begins with *acknowledging* God's generosity to us. Faith thus has a component of knowledge — it involves an awareness of who God is and what God has done, above all, in the life, death, and resurrection of Jesus. That is why the Bible insists that "faith comes from what is heard, and what is heard comes through the word of Christ" (Rom. 10:17). This link between faith and God's word explains why the theologians of the Reformation linked the sacraments so closely with the preaching of the word of God. In order for us to embrace our baptism with faith, we need to hear and understand the

---

1. See chapters 19 & 25.

Word of God, and acknowledge its truth. We need to hear that God loves us, that he sent his Son to be our Savior, that the Holy Spirit is at work in our lives, and that God invites us to be part of a new community in Christ. Faith begins by acknowledging that these things are so.

But the knowledge of faith is not an abstract knowledge — it is not the kind of knowledge that is merely recognized in some remote sense to be true. Faith recognizes that the goodness of God is intended not just for others, or for the world in the abstract, but also for us in particular. And faith not only acknowledges this, but it *accepts* God's goodness to us in particular. Thus Paul, for example, speaks of how we "*receive* the promise of the Spirit through faith" (Gal. 3:14). Faith and receptivity are closely linked. So faith begins by acknowledging that God loves the world and sent Jesus to be its Savior. But faith takes another step when people accept that this is true for themselves in particular, when they recognize and accept the implications of what they know for their own lives. When we undergo baptism, we are summoned not only to acknowledge that Christ died and rose for us and that we are cleansed of our sins and given new life by the Spirit. By undergoing baptism, we are publicly called to accept these gifts and promises, and to gratefully recognize that they are given to us in particular.

But faith is more than merely knowing and accepting God's goodness. It is also a matter of *trusting* God's generosity and kindness. I may see a briefcase full of cash on the ground and *acknowledge* that it is there. I may even stoop down and pick it up, *accepting* the random gift. But it is another matter entirely if someone has given that briefcase to me, and has invited me to follow him and to use the cash wisely as his disciple. Now I face a new set of questions: Do I trust this person enough to enter into this relationship? Is this person really treating me well, or simply trying to manipulate me? Will I be asked to do something crazy? If I don't trust the person who is handing me the briefcase, I had better not accept it in the first place. This is a vital element of faith. It is not only a matter of acknowledging and receiving God's goodness; it is also a matter of trusting God with our lives. Faith involves trusting in the relationship established by God's acts of kindness and generosity toward us. Consider, for example, the story of the "rich young man" in Mark 10:17-22 (cf. Matt. 19:16-22; Luke 18:18-25). He acknowledged Jesus as a "good teacher" and came to receive his wisdom. But when Jesus told him to "sell what you own, and give the money to the poor, and you will have treasure in heaven; then come, follow me," the man went away sadly because, the text tells us, "he had many possessions." What was lacking in this relationship was trust — the man lacked sufficient confidence; he wasn't sure whether Jesus would lead him astray. Faith always involves *trust.*

This leads to the last component of faith: our trust in God expresses itself in *allegiance* to God. Faith leads to faithfulness. This allegiance is not something other than or in addition to our trust in God; it is rather the natural expression of our trust in God. We noted earlier that being a Christian means, at its core, being a disciple of Jesus. Faith is what establishes this relationship of discipleship. If we place our trust in Jesus Christ, the natural consequence is to follow him as disciples. If we do not trust him, we will, just like the rich young man, also decline to follow him. Allegiance is the natural extension of trust and the clearest indicator of its presence. And so baptism involves the making of promises on our part. We respond to God's call and promise in baptism by declaring our commitment to be disciples of Jesus. We renounce evil and promise to be faithful to God's call to us in Christ. Faith expresses itself as allegiance.

Scripture links faith and baptism in a very close way. Several times Scripture speaks of how people "believed and were baptized" (Acts 8:12f.; 18:8; cf. Mark 16:16). Indeed, this close link between baptism and faith is the central argument of advocates of believer baptism over against infant baptism. Only those who have faith, they argue, should be baptized. Since infants are incapable of the response of acknowledgment, acceptance, trust, and allegiance outlined here, advocates of believer baptism insist that they should not be baptized until they are capable of and have expressed this response.

It is one thing, however, to note that baptism and faith are closely related; it is quite another to insist that baptism exists in order to express the faith which we subjectively have experienced. We have already noted in chapter 4 in the discussion of sacrament and ordinance, that the primary emphasis in baptism is not on what we do (our faith), but on what God does. The primary purpose of baptism is not to give expression to our faith, but rather to give expression to the grace and promise of God directed toward us.

But this is not to say that our faith is irrelevant to baptism. Quite to the contrary, baptism both requires and summons from us a response of faith. Baptism points to God's generosity, grace, and kindness in making us his own, in joining us to Christ, cleansing us from sin, and renewing us by the power of the Holy Spirit. Baptism calls us to acknowledge this gift, to accept it as our own, to trust the giver of this gift, and to be loyal to him our whole life long. But we don't do this only once; we do it throughout our lives. So baptism does not so much *express* our faith as *call* us to a life of faith.

Throughout much of the history of the church's wrestling with baptism, especially since the Reformation, Christians have found it hard to hold baptism and faith together. As we explored in chapter 5, the churches of the Reformation reacted against a view of the sacraments that regarded them as working automatically, even apart from the faith of the recipient. Baptism, in this view, seemed to make faith superfluous or unnecessary. In response, the Reformers rightly insisted that the grace offered in the sacraments is effective only in hearts that are receptive in faith. However, some churches after the Reformation tilted the balance in the opposite direction, emphasizing faith so strongly that baptism was either irrelevant or merely a peripheral or secondary expression of faith, or support to faith. Faith, in this view, seemed to make baptism superfluous or unnecessary.

But this position also distorts the biblical witness. Scripture repeatedly links baptism and faith, minimizing neither faith nor the importance of baptism. Indeed, almost all the blessings that Scripture speaks of as flowing from faith are also spoken of as flowing from baptism, including cleansing,[2] justification,[3] union with Christ,[4] adoption,[5] membership in the body of Christ,[6] giving of the Holy Spirit,[7] and the inheritance of the Kingdom of God.[8] The reason for this is simple enough. Baptism offers what faith reaches out to receive. Without baptism, the gift is not fully given; without faith, the gift is not fully received. Neither is dispensable, unnecessary, or superfluous.[9]

2. Linked to baptism: Acts 2:38; 22:16. Linked to faith: 1 John 1:9.

3. Linked to baptism: 1 Cor. 6:11. Linked to faith: Rom. 3–4.

4. Linked to baptism: Gal. 3:27. Linked to faith: Eph. 3:17.

5. Linked to baptism: Gal. 3:26-27. Linked to faith: Gal. 3:26; John 1:12; Gal. 6:10.

6. Linked to baptism: 1 Cor. 12:13; Gal. 3:27. Linked to faith: Gal. 6:10.

7. Linked to baptism: John 3:5; Titus 3:5. Linked to faith: John 1:12f.

8. Linked to baptism: John 3:5. Linked to faith: John 3:14-17. All these citations are drawn from George R. Beasley-Murray's study *Baptism in the New Testament* (London: Macmillan, 1962), pp. 272f. Beasley-Murray, of course, draws quite different conclusions from the juxtaposition of baptism and faith. He concludes that baptism is an *expression* of faith, thereby underscoring the necessity of believer's baptism. In contrast, I argue in this chapter that baptism is a *summons* to faith.

9. I discuss elsewhere, in chapters 14 and 19, the unusual circumstances of those who die without being able to be baptized. God's grace is more than adequate to accommodate these extraordinary circumstances. But we must recognize them as extraordinary and atypical in God's purpose and design.

Moreover, the elements of faith — acknowledgement of God's grace, acceptance of that grace, trust and allegiance — are not singular events expressed only at one moment in time. They are instead expressive of a lifelong disposition that deepens and grows over time. There is a very profound sense in which the whole of Christian life is simply the deeper embrace of the grace offered to us in our baptism. Throughout our lives, we learn to recognize, at deeper and deeper levels, the goodness of God to us in Christ. We are continually surprised to discover the levels at which God gives gifts specifically to us. We are continually summoned to trust this God more deeply, and continually challenged to lay aside everything that stands in the way of total allegiance to God. The life of faith is not so much like an "on-off" switch as it is like a small creek that flows into a larger stream, eventually entering into a wide river, and into the depths of the sea.

The Gospel of Matthew expresses this notion of small and growing faith with the expression "little faith." "Little faith" in Matthew is not the same as faith the size of a mustard seed, which is sufficient to move mountains (Matt. 17:20). Rather, "little faith" is faith that is immature, subject to doubt, uncertainty, and lack of trust. The disciples show "little faith" when they worry about what they will wear (Matt. 6:30), when they panic in the midst of storm (Matt. 8:26), when Peter loses his nerve after stepping out to walk on the water (Matt. 14:31), or when they are anxious because they don't know where their next meal will come from (Matt. 16:8). Even when Jesus appears to the disciples after his resurrection in Matthew 28:17, the text tells us that "some doubted." "Little faith" describes most of us, most of the time! But those with little faith are never condemned for their weakness by Jesus. Instead, he gently but insistently invites them to greater trust and firmer allegiance. This is the life of faith into which baptism ushers us, and to which baptism calls us.

So the basic question to be asked about faith and baptism is not whether any particular individual has enough faith to be worthy of being baptized. We humans are incapable of seeing into the heart as God does, and cannot entirely determine whether the seeds of true faith are present or not anyway. The basic question is rather whether there is reason to believe that God is extending God's gift and call to this particular individual, and summoning this person to a lifetime of grateful faith. Where the outward signs of God's grace summoning us to a life of faith are evident, as in the case of the adult converts recorded in the book of Acts, there is good reason to baptize. There is also good reason to baptize others for whom the church has scriptural warrant for believing that God's gift and call is offered specifically to them, especially the children of believers, as we shall explore in coming chapters.

In either case, however, baptism does not so much *express* our faith as it *calls us to faith*. Yet without a life of growing faith, we will experience none of the blessings that are promised to us in baptism. Faith is our opening of our hands to receive the gifts God gives to us in baptism. If our hands are not open, the gifts may still be offered, but we will not receive them.[10]

There are some who say that faith itself is given to us in our baptism. At the deepest level, Scripture does acknowledge that faith is a gift of God. Ephesians 2:8 declares, "For by grace you have been saved through faith, and this is not your own doing; it is the gift of God." As we noted in the chapter on new birth (chapter 10), John 3:5 declares that one cannot even *see* the Kingdom of God without receiving God's new life by being born again/from above. But even though Scripture regards faith itself as a gift, it never speaks of faith as something given *in baptism*. As we also noted in that earlier chapter, baptism does not *cause* new birth to happen, but rather presents new life to us as gift and promise, to be received by faith.

But in another sense, baptism surely deepens our capacity for faith. In baptism, the promise of the gospel is vividly portrayed and sealed to us. Whatever doubt or uncertainty we may encounter in our lives, we can, with Martin Luther, remember, "I am baptized." To reassure ourselves in this way is not to rely on a magic rite, but rather to focus our trust again upon the promise sealed to us in our baptism. Our baptism is always with us as a window into the heart of God toward us, through which again we can always look to find our bearings and the meaning of our lives. The promise of our baptism is as close as a memory, as real as the touch of water upon skin. And Scripture is clear that no one who trusts in God's promise will be put to shame (Rom. 10:11).

Moreover, in baptism, we enter the community of faith, and are joined to those who walk beside us as we take our faltering steps as disciples of Jesus, and who pick us up when we fall or are tempted to give up. In baptism, we enter the body of Christ, the dwelling place of the Spirit, where all of God's gifts are at work to take the word of Christ and make it alive and real

---

10. Of course, even the opening of our hands to receive God's grace is possible only with the working of the Holy Spirit in us. The totality of our salvation is God's gift. Yet this fact does not remove the need for us to respond to God in faith.

to us. Here are brothers and sisters in Christ who will challenge us by their words, by their example, and by their love to recognize God's goodness more clearly, to accept God's gifts more openhandedly, to trust God more unreservedly, and to follow Jesus Christ more fearlessly. This is the life of faith — not just our own but the life of the body of Christ — to which our baptism summons us.

To Sum Up

➤ Faith involves *acknowledging* God's goodness toward us, *accepting* God's gifts, *trusting* God, and living a life of *allegiance* to God.

➤ In Scripture, all the blessings attributed to baptism are also attributed to faith. This is true not because baptism is an expression of our faith, but because baptism promises what faith receives.

➤ Faith is a response that grows in us over time.

➤ Baptism does not so much express our faith as call us to faith.

➤ Faith is not given in baptism itself, but baptism strengthens our faith.

For Further Reflection and Discussion

➤ When you think of the four aspects of faith discussed in this chapter (acknowledgement, acceptance, trust, and allegiance), where is your congregation strongest in faith? Where does it most need to grow? How about you personally?

➤ Look through your church's liturgy for baptism. How does baptism *call us* to faith as baptism is practiced in your church?

For Further Study

➤ Explore the biblical passages in footnotes 2 through 8 of this chapter in more detail, as an exercise in understanding the many connections and linkages between baptism and faith.

➤ For John Calvin's discussion of faith and baptism, see the *Institutes,* IV.15, 14-18, available online at http://www.reformed.org/books/institutes.

14 Can Someone Be "Saved" without Being Baptized? Can Someone Be Baptized without Being Saved?

The short answer to both of these questions is *yes*. But it will take a bit more discussion before we can clarify and qualify both the questions and their answers. In order to do so, we must first come to grips with the whole notion of salvation as it is found in the Bible. Salvation means much more than the popular understanding of "going to heaven when you die." The word in Greek *(soteria)* has a wide range of meanings, from "deliverance" to "security" to "healing." To experience salvation is to be rescued out of a tight spot, to escape from what threatens your life, to experience life without fear, or to be healed.

The connection between healing and salvation is particularly important to note, since it does not come through in most English translations of the Bible. In the New International Version of the New Testament, for example, the verb meaning "save" in Greek is translated 13 times as "heal."[1] In the New Testament, salvation and healing are not seen as two distinct things, but as different expressions of the same basic reality — deliverance and protection from what threatens life, health, and well-being.

In the Graeco-Roman world in which the New Testament was written, salvation, in this broad sense, was understood to be the responsibility of the government, especially the emperor. The Roman emperor claimed for himself the title of "savior." This was understood to mean that Rome provided the peace and security that enabled life to carry on without fear or threat. Indeed, the Christian designation of Jesus as "Savior," and the claim that Christianity offered "salvation" would have been understood, when the New Tes-

---

1. Matt. 9:21f.; Mark 5:23, 28, 34; 6:56; 10:52; Luke 8:48, 50; 18:42; Acts 4:9; 14:9. Cf. also these texts in which the word "save" in Greek refers to healing: Luke 17:19; James 5:15.

tament was written, as a kind of counterclaim and critique of Roman claims to be the final source of peace and security. Early Christians were, in effect, saying that it was *Jesus,* and not the emperor, who was the source of ultimate safety, security, wholeness, healing, and freedom from fear.

This echo of Roman usage also underscores the *corporate* dimensions of salvation. Although the New Testament does speak clearly and frequently about the salvation of individuals, the interest in individual salvation needs to be set in this larger context. Ultimately, God's concern in providing salvation is not merely to rescue individuals from danger, but to establish a people in safety and wholeness.[2] This concern with a people recalls again the language of covenant. Salvation is what God intends for us when God comes to us and makes covenant with us, extending to us kindness and generosity, and calling for faith in return. God seeks to restore the bond with us that enables life to flourish as God originally intended it, free from brokenness and fear as a community.

This connection between salvation and God's covenant-making with us also underscores the centrality of faith — our reception of God's generosity and kindness — as necessary for salvation. Indeed, throughout the Bible, salvation in the broad sense we have been speaking of is received *by faith.* When Jesus healed people, he frequently said to them, "your faith has saved (or healed) you."[3] By this he clearly did not intend to say that the healing originated with human faith, rather than with God's gracious action. Instead, he was calling attention to the critical role of faith in receiving God's generosity and kindness.[4]

We see the same connection between faith and salvation echoed frequently in the rest of the New Testament. Among many possible texts, the following are illustrative: Acts 16:31 declares, "Believe on the Lord Jesus, and you will be saved." Romans 10:9 promises, "if you confess with your lips that Jesus is Lord and believe in your heart that God raised him from the dead, you will be saved." Ephesians 2:8 tells us, "For by grace you have been saved through faith." Clearly Scripture teaches us that we are saved by faith. Faith is the necessary opening of our hands to receive the gifts God gives. It is the bond of trust that unites us to Jesus Christ through the Holy Spirit.

---

2. See, for example, Matt. 1:21; John 3:17; 12:47; Rom. 11:26.

3. Matt. 9:22; Mark 5:34; 10:52; Luke 7:50; 8:48; 17:19; 18:42.

4. For further exploration of the nature of faith, see the previous chapter on the relationship between baptism and faith.

There is one further dimension of salvation that we must address, if we are to address adequately the questions with which this chapter begins. We must also explore *when* salvation — in all of its many dimensions — happens. Here we must recognize that the old evangelical question, "Are you saved?" only gets at part of the biblical witness regarding salvation. The Bible talks about salvation as something already accomplished when it is speaking of healing, such as when Jesus says, "Your faith has saved you." Here the restoration and deliverance has already happened. But these references, for the most part, are not speaking of salvation in the comprehensive sense of deliverance from sin and death.

When we examine the biblical passages which speak of salvation in this more comprehensive sense, it becomes clear that the majority of these passages envision salvation as something that happens *in the future*, when all of God's gracious purposes for the world come to their culmination.[5] This is the primary point of reference for most of Scripture when it speaks about our salvation in the broadest sense as deliverance from sin and death. Our salvation is not complete until death itself is finally and completely defeated (1 Cor. 15:26).

So from the full perspective of Scripture, the answer Christians must give to the question "Are you saved?" is "Not yet," or better still, "Not entirely." We still await the completion of God's saving work in us and in our world. Yet the New Testament also wants to proclaim that this future salvation is not in doubt. Rather, we can be completely confident of it, because it is based on God's promise, which we know to be absolutely reliable. The essential New Testament proclamation is the sure promise of Acts 16:31: "Believe on the Lord Jesus, and you will be saved." Indeed, the New Testament is so confident of this future salvation that the biblical writers can, at times, speak of this future salvation as if it is already accomplished, using the past or perfect tenses. So, for example, Ephesians 2:5-8 can speak of how we "have been saved" by grace through faith. Or Titus 3:5 can speak of how God "saved us" because of his mercy.

It is vital to recognize, however, that these affirmations that we "have been saved" are confessions of faith, not observations of fact. When we say, "We have been saved," we are saying that the future deliverance from sin and death God offers to the world is ours, not because we deserve it or have

---

5. For example, Matt. 10:22; 24:13; Mark 8:35; 13:13; Luke 9:24; Acts 2:21; Rom. 5:9-10; 10:13; 11:26; 1 Cor. 3:15.

already achieved it, but because we are trusting in God's unshakeable promise to us. We are in effect declaring our reliance on the promise of Scripture that "everyone who calls on the name of the Lord will be saved" (Rom. 10:13).

Like so many themes in Scripture, salvation thus has both a present and future reference. We experience God's salvation in the present, as prayers are answered, healing is given, and as we are delivered in various ways from the power of sin in our lives and in our world. We also claim in faith the sure hope of our future salvation, when God "will wipe away every tear from their eyes; death will be no more; mourning and crying and pain will be no more" (Rev. 21:4). Then, and only then, will our salvation be complete.

All this, of course, has direct implications for the way we think about baptism and salvation. Baptism itself does not save us; baptism gives to us God's promise of salvation, and summons us to a life that is formed by trusting in that promise. So any baptized person can say with confidence: "God has promised to save me in my baptism. I am trusting in that promise. Therefore my salvation is certain." Yet God is not miserly with the promise of salvation. Again, Scripture tells us that "everyone who calls on the name of the Lord shall be saved" (Rom. 10:13). So we must recognize that it is possible for someone who has not yet been baptized to place their hope and trust in God's promise. (In chapter 19, we will explore some more specific questions about the salvation of baptized and unbaptized infants who are not yet capable of conscious faith.) Baptism is thus not *necessary* for salvation in the strict sense of the word, but it is a significant aid to our faith, a wonderful and powerful reminder to us that God's promise is there for us, beckoning us to hold fast to that promise in faith.

But what of those who have been baptized but are not living in faith? Will they be saved? Here we must recognize the consistent witness of Scripture that there is no hope of salvation apart from faith in Christ. Even 1 Peter 3:21, which speaks of how baptism "saves you," speaks also of baptism as an "appeal to God for a good conscience, through the resurrection of Jesus Christ." Baptism saves us only as it becomes the means through which we place our faith in God's promise in Christ. Scripture also clearly says that "the one who endures to the end will be saved."[6] The promise of God given to us in our baptism is not to be presumed upon, but is given to

---

6. Matt. 10:22; 24:13; Mark 13:13.

be grasped in faith our whole life long. Baptism is not a ticket to heaven, but a summons to a life of faith in Christ. Yet even when we have fallen far away, and our lives show the brokenness of that departure, still our baptism calls to us and invites us to trust again in God's promise, which is still offered to us in particular. And only God knows the depths of the heart of those who have been baptized and appear to have "fallen away." I am convinced that even the smallest and most hidden effort truly to trust in God's promise will not be disregarded by the merciful God revealed to us in Jesus Christ. Scripture encourages us that "a bruised reed he will not break, and a dimly burning wick he will not quench" (Isa. 42:3).

But if it is possible to be saved without being baptized, and it is possible to be baptized without being saved, what good then is baptism? Why not simply make it an optional rite to assist in faith those who feel the need for it? The first answer, of course, is that Jesus did not declare baptism to be optional, but commanded his disciples to do it in the Great Commission (Matt. 28:19f.), presumably for good reason! But this is only the beginning of an answer. Sometimes, this impulse to minimize the significance of baptism is related to the assumption that Christianity is solely concerned with what happens to us after we die; nothing else really matters. In this view then, baptism only matters if it provides some additional security regarding life after death. Scripture is clear, however, that we are called to a life of discipleship here and now, and it is this life of discipleship in the here and now that begins with baptism.

In baptism, we are publicly marked as Christ's own and called to a life of discipleship. We are given brothers and sisters in Christ, and we enter into explicit relationships of mutual accountability to help us to be faithful to the call of God in Christ. We enter the visible church, where the Holy Spirit is active, pouring out gifts for the strengthening of the body of Christ in its mission to the world. And God gives a shared calling to be this visible church, to be the salt of the earth and the light of the world. We are not only held, encouraged, and sustained in our own pilgrimage as we await God's full salvation, but as participants in God's mission to the world, we also become the agents through which God's salvation begins, more and more, to break into the lives of those around us right here, and right now. Without baptism none of this would have its focus and center, for baptism ushers us into the visible church, where these realities are lived out in specific relationships in real day-to-day life.

God never intended for individuals merely to experience a private salvation; God intends the renewal of human community, and the renewal of creation. This is what "salvation" finally means. God has called us to be disciples, partners in Christ's mission to the world. Baptism is the central "entry point" through which we enter and begin to participate in this larger and greater purpose of God, a purpose lived out in the specific and tangible relationships we enter when we are baptized. In this deeper sense, there can be no final salvation of the world without the body of Christ, a real body of real disciples of Jesus that takes shape in space and time only through our shared baptism.

To Sum Up

> In the broadest sense, "salvation" in the Bible is deliverance and protection from whatever threatens life, health, and well-being, both individually and corporately.

> We experience God's salvation in the present, but its fullness is usually spoken of in Scripture as a future reality.

> We receive salvation only by faith.

> It is possible to be saved without being baptized in exceptional cases, and baptism offers no guarantee of salvation for those who are not living in faith.

> Yet by ushering us into the visible church, baptism brings us into the place where God's salvation is being experienced and offered to the world.

For Further Reflection and Discussion

> When we say today that Jesus is the Savior, who or what are the competing "saviors" who claim to offer peace, security, health, and wholeness to people?

> How has your congregation experienced glimpses of God's salvation in its present experience?

> Do you naturally associate baptism with salvation, or do you see baptism only in terms of church membership?

For Further Study

➤ You may want to read the article on "salvation" in the *Anchor Bible Dictionary* (New York: Doubleday, 1992), or another Bible dictionary available to you.

15 Does Baptism Actually Bring About Any Change in Us and in Our Relationship to God?

This question is often one of the sharp points of contention between those who take the "ordinance" view of baptism and those who see baptism as a sacrament (see chapter 4 for further discussion of this distinction). If baptism is a sacrament and a means of grace, as we have argued, then we should be able to point to some significant changes in a baptized person's life that are a direct result of baptism itself. If we cannot point to such changes, then perhaps the ordinance view is correct, that baptism is essentially done in obedience to Christ, and that it is no more of a *special* means of grace than any other Christian practice commanded by Christ, such as prayer, giving, hospitality, Christian fellowship, discipline, worship, and so forth. Is there some decisive change in a person and his or her relationship to God brought about only (or at least *centrally*) by baptism?

I believe the answer is *yes*. However, before answering in more detail, we must first explore some assumptions that are often hidden behind this question. In North America, we live in a highly individualistic culture. We also live in a culture that is deeply shaped by our economic system, the capitalist economy. As a result both of our individualism and of the shaping influence of our economic system, we tend to think of ourselves primarily as people with needs, and as people who make choices to meet those needs. We believe that our core identity, and the drama of our lives, is found in the struggle to identify and meet our deepest needs.

We think this way about ourselves in part at least because there are thousands of businesses that spend billions of dollars to teach us to think this way about ourselves. We are constantly bombarded with advertising designed to awaken a sense of need or desire in us, and to offer us goods and services that will meet those needs and desires. This culture of advertising and consumption tells us that we are most truly human, and that we most fulfill our destiny, when we are making choices to meet our needs.

When these assumptions are brought into the Christian faith, the result is an inevitable diminishment of the significance of baptism. The reason is that our awareness of our *need* for God's grace in Christ, and our *choice* to respond to the gospel of Christ, both happen outside of the baptismal rite itself. For adult converts to Christianity, both the awareness of need and the choice to become a Christian *precede* baptism. For baptized infants, the realization of need and the choice personally to embrace the gospel *follow* after baptism. Given the way we naturally construct our sense of identity, it is not surprising that many people ask the question, "Does anything important really happen in baptism itself?" It seems to us that all the really important things happen *outside* baptism.

We must recognize, however, that there is a distinct downside to this way of constructing our identity, including our Christian identity. The result of this type of identity formation in North America has been a proliferation of passively oriented churches where members see themselves as "shopping" for religious goods and services from professional clergy, rather than as participants in a fellowship of disciples of Jesus, following him in mission. When we see ourselves primarily as people with (religious) needs, we can easily lose sight of the biblical image of the body of Christ, where the central motif is not the needs people bring, but the gifts they have to offer for the upbuilding of others. Indeed, from a biblical perspective, the central question in our identity is not so much the drama of how we will get our needs met, but rather how we can be drawn into something much larger and more beautiful than ourselves, into God's redeeming mission to the world.

So we must be prepared, in exploring the differences baptism really makes, to reconsider what we think is significant or important. In so doing, we may just discover that more happens in baptism than we had realized:

In baptism, I am publicly identified as a Christian, as belonging to Jesus Christ. In many missionary contexts, this change is particularly clear. Indeed in many parts of the world, when a person is baptized, he or she may be disowned by family, shunned by neighbors and former friends, and even threatened with death. Baptism is the public divide between those who follow Jesus and those who do not. Of course, one may follow Jesus without being baptized, but sooner or later, that person must confront the words of Jesus, "Everyone therefore who acknowledges me before others, I also will acknowledge before my Father in heaven; but whoever denies me before others, I also will deny before my Father in heaven" (Matt. 10:32-33). This public identification with Jesus is not an optional "extra" for disciples of Jesus; Jesus requires it of us, hard as it may be. This is true even of baptized children. Though they have had no choice in the matter, still they are publicly identified as Christians, and subject to treatment by others as Christians, unless they renounce their connection to Christ and his church.

Moreover, as we have noted in the chapter on baptism "in the name of" Jesus (chap. 12), baptism is a mark of divine ownership. For both believers and baptized children, baptism is the public mark upon them, signifying that they belong to God in Jesus Christ. Both those baptized in infancy and adulthood may subsequently renounce this mark of ownership, but that mark stands, nonetheless, even as a witness against them. The baptized belong to God in a unique way. Of course, there are also some who are not baptized who belong to God as well. But they have, so to speak, no ownership papers to prove it, to themselves or to anyone else. In baptism, and nowhere else so clearly, we are publicly assigned to God's household.

This theme of belonging leads to the next major change brought about by baptism: *In baptism, I become a member of the covenant community — the church — and am subject to its discipline, a participant in its struggles and sufferings, and heir to its blessings.* Insofar as baptism points to our union with Christ, it also enacts our entry into the body of Christ, the church. This means, for example, that the baptized are subject to the discipline and nurture of the church in a way that those who are not baptized are not. The entire church (and not merely the parents) has a spiritual responsibility for the oversight and nurture of baptized children, just as it has that responsibility for those baptized in adulthood. When I become part of the church, I become part of the network of mutual accountability, responsibility, and discipline that makes up the church as a whole. The baptized are those who assist each other "on the way" as disciples of Jesus, trusting in God's grace to assist them at each step of the journey. As the baptized journey together as the visible body of Christ, they share both in the sufferings and the power of Christ. When one member suffers, all the baptized suffer. When one triumphs, all share the joy (1 Cor. 12:26).

Our incorporation into the visible body of Christ leads naturally to the third major change effected in baptism: *In baptism, I am given a new identity, into which I am called to grow.* When we are baptized into the name of Jesus, we are given a new name, the name of Christian. Names are curious things. We rarely choose them for ourselves; they are given to us by others. Yet names carry within themselves powerful markers of our identity. My son recently started attending college, and during the first few days, decided to use his Rollerblades to get around campus. Quite quickly, he picked up the nickname "Blade." If the nickname sticks, it will doubtless shape part of his identity, and the way others perceive him around campus. It will shape who he actually becomes.

As we noted in chapter 7 (on dying and rising with Christ), this is the central way in which the Bible understands the formation of our identity. We become our name; our name becomes us. Our identity arises not from our past (and not from the choices of our past, be they good or bad), but rather from who we are becoming in Christ. This is the new identity, the new name given to us in our baptism. Of course, that gift was ours even before we were baptized, and can be given to those unable to be baptized, but these are all merely exceptions to the norm. We are not isolated individuals; our identity is formed in relationships with others. Our names are spoken primarily not by us, but by those around us. And baptism is the public rite whereby we are given a new name, a new identity, and thus a new destiny.

Finally, *in baptism, I am promised enormous grace and power, to be received by faith.* As we have noted in earlier chapters, baptism takes the general promises of the gospel, and assigns them to us in particular. And it takes the general summons to faith found in the gospel, and assigns it to us in particular. In baptism, Jesus offers all his goodness to us: union with himself, cleansing from sin, new birth and the gift of the Spirit. "Take it," he says, "and follow me." Of course, this promise was available before I was baptized, but in baptism, it comes in a package with my name engraved on it, a gift given not just once, but ready to be given again and again.

Rick Warren began his chart-topping bestseller, *The Purpose-Driven Life,* with a striking sentence: "It's not about you." He calls Christians to a form of identity that places God, rather than themselves, at the center. We do well to apply this exhortation to our thinking about baptism. Of course I must confront my own deep need for God's grace. Of course, I must choose to lay hold of the promise of the gospel in faith. Of course, I must live that life of faith out in countless day-to-day choices. All that happens outside of baptism. But it is supremely in baptism that I am compelled to recognize that I am not alone, that Jesus Christ goes ahead of me, the Spirit is at work within me, and that there are many fellow disciples beside me. Nowhere in the Christian life, more centrally and pivotally than in baptism, is this reality acknowledged, enacted, and celebrated.

Does anything actually *happen* in baptism? Yes, a lot happens! But we will not see it if we are so preoccupied with our own choices, our own needs, or even our own faith. Baptism sums up the whole of our Christian life — past, present, and future — and offers it to us in a single, powerful sign and seal. Baptism makes us members of a new body, a group of Christians who gather for worship in a specific place, and who share a common calling to follow Jesus. It gives to us, with our name written on it, the promise of a new life, a new identity that originates in the future, and over time breaks more and more into our present. It is an identity that begins with the whole body of Christ, in which we more and more will find our place. It is an identity that begins with Christ, into whose image we are slowly but surely being transformed, not by our own efforts, but by the gracious promise of God and the power of the Holy Spirit.

To Sum Up

> We miss much of the significance of baptism because we tend to focus exclusively on our own needs and choices.

> What happens uniquely in baptism? In baptism,
>   – I am publicly identified as a Christian, as belonging to Jesus Christ;
>   – I become a member of the covenant community — the church — and am subject to its discipline, a participant in its struggles and sufferings, and heir to its blessings;
>   – I am given a new identity, into which I am called to grow; and
>   – I am promised enormous grace and power, to be received by faith.

For Further Reflection and Discussion

> Do you agree with the argument of this chapter that our culture inclines us to focus only on our own needs and choices? How have you seen this to be true?

> What sort of difference has it made in your life, if any, to be publicly identified as a Christian?

➤ Do you agree with the central thesis of this chapter, that there are important changes brought about in us centrally at our baptism? Why or why not?

For Further Study

➤ For a provocative overview of the ways in which our economic system shapes and distorts our approach to spiritual things, read David Matzko McCarthy, *The Good Life: Genuine Christianity for the Middle Class* (Grand Rapids: Brazos Press, 2004).

16 Does Baptism Assure Us of Our Salvation?

For some Christians who view baptism as a sacrament, the simple response to the question, "Are you saved?" is to say, "Yes, I am baptized." Generally speaking, this kind of answer is nourished in churches that have a "high" view of the sacrament of baptism, and emphasize baptism as a means of grace — sometimes even a means of grace that is effective regardless of our response, so long as we do not resist the grace given us in baptism.[1] Other Christians (and this may include both adherents of sacramental and ordinance theology) are wary about appealing to baptism as a ground for assurance about our salvation. They fear that doing so will divert attention away from faith in Christ who is the source of our salvation.[2] The perspective of this book has something in common with both these responses, affirming that baptism is a means of grace, but also affirming the necessity of faith, in order to receive God's grace promised in the sacrament. So the crucial issue, as we address this question here, will be this: *In what sense,* if at all, does baptism assure us of salvation?

Before we speak of baptism and the assurance of salvation, we first must explore what "assurance of salvation" is in the first place. In the period leading up to the Reformation, when the church had not clearly articulated the gospel truth that we are saved by God's grace in Christ, rather than our own efforts, there was tremendous anxiety over one's future salvation. The sale of indulgences in the late medieval church was one of the corrupt ways in which the church preyed on this anxiety for its own benefit. The reformers, by contrast, rightly insisted that one's assurance of sal-

---

1. See chapter 5 for further discussion of this view.
2. See chapter 4 for further discussion of this view.

vation came not through pronouncements of the church, nor through our good works, nor through the church's sacramental system, but solely through faith in Christ. It is only in total reliance upon Christ that our salvation is secure, and those who rely completely upon Christ for their salvation can be assured of their salvation.

As time went on during and after the Reformation, however, the question of the assurance of salvation began to emerge again, in somewhat different dress. Now the anxious question was not "What must *I do* in order to be sure I am going to heaven?" but rather, "How can I know if I really have true faith that relies on Christ alone?" This anxiety springs from the realization that even our faith is fragile and weak, motivated often by self-interest, and driven often by fear rather than by trust and allegiance. We find ourselves to be such jumbled masses of contradictions that we wonder if we are even capable of a deep faith and trust in God. How can we, so fearful and timid, ever trust Christ enough to cast our lot entirely upon him and rely on him alone for our salvation?

The reformers, especially Martin Luther, correctly recognized that there is only one way out of this kind of anxiety. As long as you are examining your own consciousness, probing whether your faith is strong enough, you will never come to true faith. You will be endlessly absorbed in introspection, and all you will discover on that road are deeper levels of self-contradiction and ambivalence. It is only when you take your gaze off yourself, and place it instead upon Jesus Christ — on his love for you, and his ability to save you — that the fog of anxiety will lift and you will see clearly. Paradoxically, the only way to be sure of your salvation when you become aware of all your internal contradictions is to trust *in Christ,* rather than *in your capacity to trust Christ* purely. This is what pure faith is. You can't have faith in faith; you can only have faith in something or someone outside of yourself. Only when our gaze turns from ourselves and our own capacities — even our own capacities for faith — to trust instead in the living God, will we find any peace, and any assurance of salvation.

We see this perspective in 2 Timothy 1:12: "But I am not ashamed, for I know the one in whom I have put my trust, and I am sure that he is able to guard until that day what I have entrusted to him." The writer's confidence emerges, not from his own strength or endurance, or even the vigor of his own faith, but from the ability of God to guard and keep his life. A similar insight appears in 1 John 3:19-20: "And by this we will know that we are from the truth and will reassure our hearts before him whenever our hearts condemn us; for God is greater than our hearts, and he knows everything." Even if our own hearts condemn us, aware as we are of all our shortcomings, ambivalences, and failures, God is still greater than our hearts, and God's love for us encompasses even all our contradictions and ambivalences. Like Peter, confronted with his own failures and ambivalences and internal contradictions, when asked for the third time if he loved Jesus in John 21:17, we too must finally say, "Lord, you know everything; you know my heart better than I know it myself. I'll let you make the call." Such acquiescence to Jesus *is in itself* the expression of faith. Scripture is clear that no one who casts himself or herself on the mercy of Christ in such a way will be disappointed. Indeed, "everyone who calls on the name of the Lord will be saved" (Acts 2:21).

Reliance upon God's grace in Christ is the central and final source of our assurance of our salvation. Assurance of salvation does not come through introspection. It does not come because we have satisfied some checklist of duties and responsibilities. It does not come because we have fulfilled a set of religious requirements (even including baptism). We experience assurance of salvation only in the existential act of reliance upon God's grace in Christ, rather than upon ourselves. Assurance of salvation comes, therefore, only through *the gospel,* the good news of God's grace shown to us in Christ's life, death, and resurrection.

But there is another aspect of this question of assurance that we must address. The question can be framed in this way: How can I be sure that God intends the gracious promises of the gospel *for me in particular?* I may believe that God loves the world, and that God graciously promises salvation to all who trust in Christ. But how do I know that all this goodness is intended for me in particular, and therefore that the Holy Spirit is at work in me to bring me to understand and trust in the gospel? I may *wish* this to be true, but this wishing of mine may be my own selfish tendency to want to make my own future secure, and thus the very opposite of trust in God. Indeed, my own desire for salvation may well lead me to construct a God in my own image and after my likeness — a God who conveniently panders to my wishes and desires. How then can I be sure that the gospel is truly good news *for me,* and not simply the result of my own wishful thinking?

For the theologians of the Reformation, the answer to this is simple and clear: In the proclamation of the gospel and in the sacraments, God's promise comes to us *from outside of ourselves,* mediated through God's emissary, the church. We didn't invent God's promise; it is not the projection of our own wishes and desires. It has been given to us by faithful witnesses, handed down through the ages in the preaching of the Word and in the sacraments. We thus come to assurance of salvation by humbling ourselves, and by hearing the word of promise mediated to us by brothers and sisters in Christ. In receiving the proclaimed and enacted word, in both sermon and sacrament, we receive God himself, not a figment of our imagination nor a creation of our own desire. Left to ourselves as isolated individuals, our spiritual quest always finally will turn in upon itself, leaving us no grounds for assurance. But when we hear the gospel from another, and when we are baptized by another, we are delivered from the prison of our subjectivity to hear and trust the promise which alone can make us new.

This is what Luther meant when he said that the assertion "I am baptized" was his final assurance of salvation. He did not mean that the church had the power to perform sacraments that were automatically effective. Rather, he was saying that the promise of God, signified in baptism, had come to him from beyond himself, delivering him from his own anxious subjectivity. It was his trust in this promise, delivered to him by the church, that was the final ground of his assurance.

The church is no alternative to faith, as if we might trust in the church rather than in God. But the church is the necessary context where faith can emerge and grow secure, freed from our idolatrous tendencies, so that we may receive the promise and trust in it. Salvation is by faith alone. But the fullness of faith is finally only possible in the church, where we receive and trust in a word that comes from beyond ourselves, which alone has the capacity to deliver us from our weakness and idolatry.

There are also some "helps" that God provides to us to strengthen and confirm our faith, to sharpen and clarify the focus of our faith on God alone. One of these is the presence of good works, evidence in our lives that the Holy Spirit is at work in us, and that transformation is happening in our lives, even if it is slow, fitful, and partial. For example, 1 John 3:14 states, "We know that we have passed from death to life because we love one another." The presence of such fruit of the Spirit's work is not a substitute for one's reliance upon God's grace in Christ. If a focus on our good works becomes a substitute, it is merely "works righteousness" that will lead us away from trust in Christ. However, it can be an enormous encouragement to us when we see the fruit of God's work in our lives. It can strengthen a faith that is already there, even if it cannot substitute for faith.

Even the absence of such good works, however, ought not to lead us to despair, for it is not our good works that make us pleasing to God, but rather the death of Christ on our behalf. The gospel calls even those who have *no* good works of their own still to trust in God's mercy revealed in Christ. Scripture promises that no one who trusts in him will be put to shame (Rom. 10:11). The only antidote to weak and failing faith is deeper faith, a return to trust.

Baptism can be another such aid to our faith. We see this, for example, in Question and Answer #67 from the *Heidelberg Catechism:*

Q: Are both the word and the sacraments then intended to focus our faith on the sacrifice of Jesus Christ on the cross as the only ground of our salvation?

A: Right! In the gospel the Holy Spirit teaches us and through the holy sacraments he assures us that our entire salvation rests on Christ's one sacrifice for us on the cross.

Note that the sacraments do not assure us *of salvation;* they assure us *that our salvation rests in Christ and his sacrifice for us.* The difference is significant. The sacraments help us to get our gaze off from ourselves and on to Christ. This is particularly true in baptism, with its central focus on God's initiative and God's promise to us. Baptism reminds us that our salvation, from the very beginning, was God's idea, rather than ours. It is the coming of the Spirit, signified in baptism, that regenerates us and creates in us the capacity for faith itself. Baptism testifies to our union with Christ, which creates in us the tension between the "old" person we are by nature and the "new" person we are becoming in Christ, between the "flesh" and the "Spirit." Indeed, much of the ambivalence we experience in the Christian life originates not because the Spirit is absent from our lives, but because the Spirit is at work, and we feel the tension between those aspects of our lives that are already transformed, and those that are still awaiting renewal.

Ultimately, however, the Spirit brings assurance of salvation to us, not by reminding us of concepts or ideas, but by making the presence of Jesus Christ real to us. Paul speaks of the Spirit "bearing witness with our spirit that we are children of God" (Rom. 8:16). Assurance of salvation is, in the final analysis, not a matter of mental conviction, but of interpersonal trust.

Assurance of salvation is grounded in the God who promises, who seeks us out before we even think to seek for God. The promises of God conveyed to us in our baptism are words of personal address — God speaking to us, and calling forth a response of trust from us. It is the Spirit of God who awakens us to this personal form of address, opening our eyes to the fact that when we were baptized, God himself was there, loving us, making promises to us, and calling us. This same God continues to address us, day by day, throughout our lives. It is the Spirit who gives us the ears to hear God's voice.

Just as in the case of good works, however, we must take care not to let baptism serve as a substitute for faith. We can start to rely on the fact that we are baptized, rather than on the God who makes promises to us in our baptism. To do so will always and inevitably result in self-righteousness and a displacement of our faith from its proper object, which is God's grace revealed to us in Christ. Revisiting and remembering our baptism is meant to be a helpful way of taking our eyes off ourselves and placing our focus and trust back upon the God who comes to us in baptism as the only sure source of our assurance and hope. We need continually to remember whose we are, and where our life comes from. Baptism helps us to do that.

So *does* baptism assure us of our salvation? Not in the ultimate sense. Ultimately, our assurance of salvation comes only in a radical and complete trust in God's free pardon, mercy, and love revealed to us in the life, death, and resurrection of Jesus. But in a secondary way, baptism can steer our minds and hearts in the right direction, and in so doing, can assist our faith, weak and wandering as it may be, to find its resting place in the gospel.

To Sum Up

> Assurance of salvation does not come from reliance upon our good works or upon the church. Nor does it come from reliance upon our own capacity for faith. It comes only through reliance upon God's mercy shown to us in Christ.

> When we receive the promise of God in the preached word and in the sacraments, we are summoned out of the prison of our own subjectivity and our own tendency toward idolatry to receive God's promise from outside of ourselves, as pure gift.

➤ The presence of good works or other signs of the Spirit's work in our lives can assist our faith, though it can never serve as the *basis* for our assurance of salvation.

➤ Baptism can assist our faith by directing our attention to God's promise, rather than to our capacity for faith. Yet faith in baptism must never be substituted for faith in God.

➤ Assurance of salvation is a work of the Holy Spirit, who makes the presence and power of the promising God real to us.

For Further Reflection and Discussion

➤ Is the question of assurance of salvation a live one in your congregation? If so, is the primary threat to assurance of salvation the fear that we haven't *done* enough to be pleasing to God, or that our faith is not strong enough?

➤ Some people are naturally inclined to see baptism as an *aid* to their trust in God; others see it as a *threat* to their trust in God — a diversion into trust in rituals rather than God. Why do you think this difference exists? What different understandings of ritual might lie beneath this difference in approach?

For Further Study

➤ The first part of Martin Luther's treatise "Concerning Christian Liberty" is a classic exposition on the theme of assurance of salvation. It can be found at http://www.iclnet.org/pub/resources/text/wittenberg/luther/web/cclib-2.html.

➤ To read more about Luther's claim that the statement "I am baptized" expresses one's assurance of salvation, see part four of Luther's Large Catechism, available online at http://www.ccel.org/luther/large_cat/large_catechism25.htm.

THE CASE FOR INFANT BAPTISM

The next four chapters lay out a basic Reformed argument for baptizing infant children of Christian parents. The argument move from general and broad issues to increasingly specific questions. Chapter 17 lays out the case for reading the entire Bible as expressive of a single covenant purpose of God. Chapter 18 then explores the place of *families* in this great covenant purpose. Chapter 19 explores whether infants can be saved, and the theological basis of infant salvation. Finally, chapter 20 examines the relationship between baptism and circumcision. These four chapters should all be read and considered as a unit by those who are particularly interested in the biblical basis for baptizing the infant children of Christian parents.

17 If the Church Is a *Covenant Community,* What Distinguishes the *New Covenant* from the *Old Covenant?*

One of the most basic and important Reformed assumptions underlying infant baptism is that baptism is the sign of God's covenant with us. Just as circumcision marked one's participation in God's covenant with Abraham (Gen. 17:10-14), so baptism now marks those who are members of God's covenant, fellow-heirs with Christ of all of God's covenant blessings and promises (Col. 2:11-12). The next several chapters will be exploring these themes of covenant and covenant membership in more detail, especially as they apply to the question of infant baptism. To begin with, however, we must explore how God's covenant with human beings changes over time, and how it remains consistent over time. In particular, we might rephrase the opening question of this chapter something like this: What has *changed* in God's covenant with humans after the coming of Christ, and what has *remained the same?* What's the difference between the "Old Covenant" (2 Cor. 3:14; Heb. 8:13), and the "New Covenant"?

This question becomes particularly important when the question of infant baptism arises. Advocates of infant baptism tend to emphasize the *continuity* between the Old Covenant and the New Covenant, and they typically argue that the sign of circumcision in the Old Covenant is replaced by baptism in the New Covenant. Just as infants were circumcised in the Old Covenant, so they should be baptized in the New Covenant.

Advocates of believer baptism, on the other hand, question this linkage between circumcision and baptism, and tend to emphasize the *discontinuity* between the Old Covenant and the New, at least as far as it applies to the relationship between circumcision and baptism. They typically charge that infant baptism fails to recognize the "newness" of the New Covenant, particularly the centrality in the New Covenant of personal faith in Christ. Because faith is so central to the New Covenant, they argue, the sign of membership in the New Covenant can only be given to those who exhibit personal faith in Christ. Other advocates of believer baptism argue that the discontinuity between the Old Covenant and the New centers on the distinction between the promise of earthly and temporal blessings like physical descendants and land in the Old Covenant, and the promise of heavenly and spiritual blessings in the New Covenant.[1] The circumcision of infants is appropriate to the Old Covenant, with its focus upon physical descent, but this does not translate into baptism in the New Covenant, since it is no longer physical descent and the attendant promise of land that defines membership in the covenant, but rather faith in Christ and the attendant promise of heaven (e.g., John 1:12-13).

We will be exploring aspects of this argument in more detail in coming chapters, but to begin with, it will be helpful to acquire a more general overview of the relationship between the New Covenant and the Old Covenant. Clearly there are aspects of the covenant narrated in the Old Testament that are unique to Israel, and not carried over into God's New Covenant with the church. The Letter to the Hebrews tells us that, because of Jesus' once-for-all sacrifice of himself, the sacrificial system that structured the Old Covenant is no longer in force. God's covenant in the Old Testament included the promise of a land (Gen. 15:18-21), but in the New Covenant, God's people are sent "into all the world" (Mark 16:15) to be the agents of God's mission. Moreover, God's promise of a covenant faithfulness "to the thousandth generation" was understood by Israel to mean that God's covenant established Israel as a nation, defined by physical descent, and marked by circumcision.[2] The New Covenant is no longer restricted to those who are physically descended from Abraham, but gentiles are now included, without being required to be circumcised (Gal. 3:26-29).[3] Paul's letter to the Galatians also describes how the role of the law in the life of

---

1. Paul K. Jewett writes that in the New Covenant, "the temporal, earthly, typical elements of the old dispensation were dropped from the great house of salvation as scaffolding from the finished edifice. It is our contention that the Paedobaptists, in framing their argument from circumcision, have failed to keep this significant historical development in clear focus." *Infant Baptism and the Covenant of Grace* (Grand Rapids: Eerdmans, 1978), p. 91.

2. See, e.g., Exod. 20:6; 34:7; Deut. 5:10; Jer. 32:18.

3. Even the Old Covenant was not entirely restricted to those who were physically descended from Abraham. Matthew's genealogy of the Messiah notes, for example, the presence of two women from outside the covenant people: Rahab and Ruth (Matt. 1:5).

God's people has shifted since the coming of Christ and the pouring out of the Spirit. In the New Covenant, the Spirit transforms us into the image of Christ, whereas in the Old Covenant, the law could only be imposed as an external constraint. Unlike Israel during much of the Old Testament period, the church is not a theocratic nation under direct divine rule, but "salt" and "light" in the midst of the world, recognizing a distinction between its allegiance to God and its allegiance to various governments (Rom. 13; Acts 5:29). Much has changed since the coming of Christ, in the movement from the Old Covenant to the New Covenant.

But though much has changed, much also remains in the movement from the Old Covenant to the New. The New Covenant is not a *substitute* for a failed Old Covenant (contrary to what is taught by many Dispensationalists[4]), but rather is its extension and completion. Israel is not rejected and replaced by the church; rather, in the church God is at work purifying and restoring the people of God, a people that includes both Jew and gentile (Acts 15:16-21; Rom. 11:17-24). Though Scripture speaks at times of an "Old Covenant" and a "New Covenant," there is still in essence only one covenant that unfolds throughout Scripture.

In fact, what was most central to the Old Covenant is precisely what is deepened and expanded in the New. Already in the Old Covenant, God's central summons was to faith and allegiance, in response to God's gracious kindness (e.g., Exod. 19:4-6). In the New Covenant, this response of faith is deepened and made even more central. In the Old Covenant, God's Spirit worked through judges and prophets to empower Israel to be faithful to the covenant. In the New Covenant, God's Spirit is poured out on all of God's people (Acts 2:17), empowering them for a life of faithful mission. Already in the Old Covenant, the ultimate purpose of God's covenant blessing was understood to extend beyond Israel, to "all the families of the earth" (Gen. 12:3). In the New Covenant, this promise moves toward fulfillment, as the church is sent out in mission to the world. In both the Old and the New Covenant, salvation is ultimately given only through the grace and mercy of God. It is received and actualized only by faith. The Old Covenant looked forward to the coming of the Messiah as its goal and consummation; the New Covenant is built precisely on this coming as its foundation, and looks forward to Christ's return as its consummation. Ultimately there is only one

4. For a good example of dispensationalism, see the teaching found in the notes of the *Scofield Reference Bible.*

covenant in Scripture because all of God's covenant-making activity finds its center and goal in Christ, whose death provides the "blood of the covenant" (Mark 14:24) that sums up *all* of God's gracious activity toward the world, and calls the world to faith and allegiance.

So there is both continuity and discontinuity between the Old Covenant and the New Covenant. One of the most important and challenging tasks of the church is to sort out this continuity and discontinuity in the interpretation of Scripture. Jesus himself noted that "every scribe who has been trained for the kingdom of heaven is like the master of a household who brings out of his treasure what is new and what is old" (Matt. 13:52). Sorting out the new and the old, and relating them properly to each other, is important.

So it will not do to contrast the Old Covenant and the New by saying that the Old Covenant had to do with "works," and the New Covenant is concerned with faith. Paul makes it clear that God's covenant with Abraham (the covenant marked by the sign of circumcision) is based not on works, but on faith (Gal. 3:7-9; Rom. 4). Nor is it accurate to say that the Old Covenant is concerned with "physical" or "temporal" or "earthly" blessings, as opposed to the New Covenant, which is concerned with "spiritual" and "heavenly" blessings. The poets and prophets in the Old Testament are constantly seeking to focus Israel's attention on the spiritual dimensions of God's covenant with them, calling for a transformation that focuses not only on exterior appearances or behaviors, but on the heart (Deut. 10:16; Ps. 51:10, 17; Jer. 4:4; Ezek. 11:19). Moreover, the New Testament is not solely concerned with "spiritual" matters. In the Lord's Prayer, Jesus instructs his disciples to ask not only for forgiveness of sins, but also for daily bread (Matt. 6:11). Indeed, Jesus makes our reception of the spiritual blessing of divine forgiveness contingent on our willingness to forgive others the debts they owe us (Matt. 6:12). Jesus was just as concerned to heal physical diseases as he was to cast out demons and confront spiritual illness. Throughout all of Scripture, the temporal and the spiritual, the earthly and the heavenly are envisioned as integrated in a holistic reality that encompasses all of life.

Nor will it even suffice to say that the Old Covenant focused upon the *promise* of salvation, while the New Covenant focuses upon the *fulfillment* of salvation. There is much fulfillment of salvation in the Old Testament, as Israel is delivered from Egypt, given the promised land, and restored from exile. Yet the Old Testament also concludes with a profound sense of expectation, in hopes of the coming of God's promised Messiah and both the physical and spiritual renewal of God's people. The New Covenant, by contrast, begins with the profound and joyful affirmation that God's Messiah has come. God's central promise has been fulfilled. But the New Testament also ends with a future hope in the book of Revelation, and the realization that *all* God's promises are not yet fulfilled in this world. The whole of Scripture, from beginning to end, including both the Old and New Covenants, situates our lives in the tension between promise and fulfillment, between hope for future redemption and thanksgiving for present blessing.

Unless this central *unity* of the Old Covenant with the New is clearly perceived, we will be unable to grasp the coherent and consistent witness of the Bible. Of course there are differences, as we have described above. The differences arise centrally from the fact that the central thrust of God's saving purposes has been revealed in Christ. Now everything centers on him. But these differences are not a matter of replacing one thing with another, but of clarifying, widening, and deepening the vision of God's redemptive purposes, and anchoring them to Jesus Christ, in whom all God's promises find their "yes" (2 Cor. 1:20). In the coming chapters, we will explore further what all this means for our understanding of baptism in general, and infant baptism in particular.

To Sum Up

‣ One of the central areas of dispute between believer baptists and paedobaptists concerns the relationship of continuity and discontinuity between the Old Covenant and the New Covenant.

‣ Reformed theology emphasizes the continuity of God's covenant purpose throughout Scripture. This continuity derives ultimately from the fact that the whole of Scripture finds its center in Christ.

‣ Therefore it will not do to contrast the Old and New Covenants along polarities such as physical/spiritual, promise/fulfillment, external/internal, earthly/heavenly, or works/faith. Rather, we must read the Bible holistically, as moving toward an integration of these various dimensions of life.

For Further Reflection and Discussion

> Frequently one hears Christians speak about the God of the Old Testament as a "God of wrath," in comparison with the New Testament "God of love." Is this a valid distinction? Why or why not? What passages are commonly used to support this distinction? How should they be interpreted?

> Do you think that John 1:12-13 means that physical descent has no significance in God's eyes? Why or why not?

> How might the perspective of this chapter shape the way Christians look at Jews?

For Further Study

> There are many excellent resources that expound the message of Scripture in terms of a single covenant purpose of God. For a brief but powerful scriptural exposition of the single covenant purpose of God, which especially highlights its missional character, see Richard Bauckham, *Bible and Mission: Christian Witness in a Postmodern World* (Grand Rapids: Baker Academic, 2003).

> You might also wish to read John Calvin's treatment of the relationship between the Old and New Covenants in the *Institutes*, II.9-11, available online at http://www.reformed.org/books/institutes/books/book2/bk2ch09 .html.

18 Does God Have a New Covenant Saving Purpose Not Just for Individuals, but *for Families*?

In our earlier chapter on the question, "What is the church?" (chapter 2), we explored how the church is a *covenant community*, established by God's covenant-making activity, and structured around God's generosity and promise, to which God's people respond in faith and allegiance. In the previous chapter, we explored the similarities and differences between the Old Covenant and the New Covenant. But as we enter into a discussion of infant baptism, we must address a more focused question about the New Covenant on which the church is built. The question can be focused in this way: Does God make this New Covenant in Christ only with individuals, or also with families?

It is clear that God's covenant with Israel in the Old Testament was not only with individuals, but with families. Circumcision was the mark of this covenant, and was given to infant males at the age of eight days, marking them as members of the covenant (Gen. 17:12-14). We see a similar pattern including families in God's covenant-making activity throughout the Old Testament. God's covenant with Noah includes his descendants as well (Gen. 9:9). God's covenant with David includes a promise that David's descendants will reign over Israel forever (2 Sam. 7:8-16). Throughout the Old Testament, God's covenants promise blessings not just to individuals, but to their families and descendants, even to the "thousandth generation" (Exod. 20:6; Deut. 7:9; Ps. 105:8).

If the Old Covenant included families, what about the New Covenant? Does God have a New Covenant saving purpose not just for individuals, but *for families?* Those who hold to believer baptism say No. They say that the link between God's covenant and physical descent was an aspect of the Old Covenant that passed away, and that now God's covenant addresses only individuals by faith. Believer baptists argue that physical descent is of no significance in the New Covenant. Paul K. Jewett, in his defense of believer baptism, writes, "But now that the age of fulfillment is come, the literal seed, like the literal land — so those who advocate believer baptism would hold — is no longer covenantally significant."[1]

We would agree with Jewett that the literal land is not covenantally significant any longer, since now God's people are sent in mission "to the ends of the earth" (Acts 1:8). We would also agree that physical descent in the sense of racial lineage — particularly the ability to trace one's genealogy back to Abraham — no longer *limits* the scope of God's covenant (though Rom. 11:28-32 suggests that physical descent from Abraham still has significance in God's eyes). It is not physical descent, but faith, that marks the children of Abraham and heirs of the covenant (Rom. 4:16).

But does the New Covenant's move to transcend physical descent as a limiting factor on the people of God also mean that physical descent has no significance at all in God's New Covenant? The answer to this question is clearly No. There is a New Covenant purpose that God has for families and households.

We see this beginning in the Old Testament itself, and carried forward into the New Testament. The Old Testament promises that when God's redemptive work comes to its culmination and God renews the covenant with Israel, this saving work of God will include the restoration of *families,* and not merely the salvation of individuals. These same promises are recalled and affirmed in the New Testament. For example, the very last words of the Old Testament in Malachi 4:5-6 speak of the coming of Elijah, when all God's covenant promises will come to their fulfillment and renewal. Elijah, it is promised, will "turn the hearts of parents to their children, and the hearts of the children to their parents." This text is cited in Luke 1:17, which understands it to be fulfilled first in the coming of John the Baptist, and ultimately in Christ. This turning of the hearts of the children to the parents and the parents to the children is not to be understood merely as familial reconciliation, but also as the shared devotion of *families* to their covenant responsibilities before God.

We see a similar promise of God's renewal of the covenant in Jeremiah 32:38-40:

---

1. *Infant Baptism and the Covenant of Grace* (Grand Rapids: Eerdmans, 1978), p. 115.

They shall be my people, and I will be their God. I will give them one heart and one way, that they may fear me for all time, for their own good *and the good of their children after them* [italics mine]. I will make an everlasting covenant with them, never to draw back from doing good to them; and I will put the fear of me in their hearts, so that they may not turn from me.

Here again, the renewal of the entire family is envisioned as part of God's New Covenant activity, an activity that is not merely external, but encompassing the whole of life, including its inner and spiritual dimensions.

This promise of God for families, linked to the renewal of the covenant, was always envisioned by God's original covenant with Israel itself. Note the connection between circumcision and this transformation of the hearts of families promised in Deuteronomy 30:6: "Moreover, the LORD your God will circumcise your heart and the heart of your descendants, so that you will love the LORD your God with all your heart and with all your soul, in order that you may live." Paul incorporates this same language in a New Covenant perspective in Romans 2:29: "Rather, a person is a Jew who is one inwardly, and real circumcision is a matter of the heart — it is spiritual and not literal. Such a person receives praise not from others but from God." What is important to note here is that Deuteronomy explicitly promises this "circumcision of the heart" for whole families, and not merely for individuals. This is not an Old Covenant "externalism," but a deeply integrated perspective encompassing all of life.

This awareness that God has a covenant purpose for families is also reflected in 1 Corinthians 7:14. Here Paul is addressing the question of whether a wife who has become a Christian should remain married to her husband who is not a Christian. In responding, Paul reasons from what is known to what is unknown. He states, "For the unbelieving husband is made holy through his wife, and the unbelieving wife is made holy through her husband. Otherwise, your children would be unclean, but as it is, they are holy." Biblical interpreters puzzle over the exact sense in which the unbelieving husband or wife is "made holy," but what is most clear in the text is that Paul takes it for granted that the *children* are "holy." This is what is known. It is on this basis that he addresses what is not so clearly known, and argues that the unbelieving partner is also, in some sense, "made holy." If that were not so, then the children would not be holy (which they obviously are, in Paul's mind). However we might seek to define this "holiness" more precisely, for our purposes it is sufficient to note that this holiness must, in some sense, indicate that God's sanctifying activity continues to extend, not only to individuals in the New Covenant, but to their families as well.

God's saving purpose for families in the New Covenant is also reflected in the extensive instruction given to members of households in the New Testament.[2] The writer of Ephesians assumes, for example, that all the members of the household, including children, should be subject to one another "out of reverence for Christ" (Eph. 5:21). Here a fundamental response characteristic of faith is expected of all children, without making any distinction between baptized and unbaptized children. It is unimaginable to suppose that those children who lack reverence for Christ would be excluded from this exhortation. It is simply assumed that the entire household is subject to instruction based upon a shared participation in Christ. The same assumption underlies the household instruction found in Colossians 3:18–4:1. Note in particular the way children are instructed (Col. 3:20): "Children, obey your parents in everything, for this is your acceptable duty in the Lord." The phrase "in the Lord" suggests that Paul is speaking to children assuming they are "in the Lord," that is, united to Christ.[3] The practical exhortation to families given in the New Testament presupposes that God's New Covenant salvation addresses families *as families*.[4]

We see the same pattern of a New Covenant purpose for households reflected in the actual practice of the early church in the book of Acts, where on several occasions, Acts reports the baptism, not of individuals, but of households (Acts 16:15, 31-33; 18:8; cf. 1 Cor. 1:16). A similar pattern of thought, emphasizing households as the recipients of salvation, though

2. See, for example, Eph. 5:21-33; Col. 3:18–4:1; 1 Tim. 6:1-2; Titus 2:1-10; 1 Peter 2:18–3:7. The same pattern of instruction to households continues in early Christian literature. See, for example, *Didache* 4:9-11, *Barnabas* 19:5-7, *1 Clement* 21:6-9, Ignatius *Pol.* 4:1–6:1, Polycarp, *Phil.* 4:2–6:3.

3. The same phrase "in the Lord" is applied to children's obedience to parents in Eph. 6:1. Here the phrase functions not to limit which parents should be obeyed, but to describe the basis for the behavior that should be directed toward parents.

4. It is a painful stretch of the imagination to suppose that Paul knew that all the children in all the families addressed by these letters had made public profession of their faith! They are addressed "in the Lord" solely because of their membership in a household of believers.

without the reference to baptism, is found in Acts 11:13-14, where the gentile Cornelius is told by an angel, "Send to Joppa and bring Simon, who is called Peter; he will give you a message by which you and your entire household will be saved." The word "you" in this verse is singular, as is the verb "will be saved." Thus we might paraphrase verse 14, "He will give you [singular] a message by which you [singular] will be saved, along with your entire household." Here the embrace of the message of salvation by the head of the household is understood to implicate salvation for the entire household.[5]

This same New Covenant perspective encompassing families appears in Peter's Pentecost sermon in Acts 2. In verses 17-18, Peter cites the great prophecy from Joel 2:28-32, and speaks these words:

> In the last days it will be, God declares, that I will pour out my Spirit upon all flesh, and your sons and your daughters shall prophesy, and your young men shall see visions, and your old men shall dream dreams. Even upon my slaves, both men and women, in those days I will pour out my Spirit; and they shall prophesy.

What is easy for us to miss, but what ancient readers would have caught immediately, is that the Joel prophecy cited here is speaking about *households*. Sons and daughters, old men and young men, and slaves were all the various members of individual households. The members of the entire household, Joel promises, will be the recipients of the Spirit. It is only in this context that we can understand why Peter says in Acts 2:39, "For the promise is for you, for your children, and for all who are far away, everyone whom the Lord our God calls to him."

Proponents of believer baptism are quick to move to the end of this verse, emphasizing that the promise is only for "everyone whom the Lord our God calls." They believe that there is no scriptural basis for believing that God calls the children of believers simply because they are members of the same household. This is the consistent application of the claim that physical descent has no covenantal significance in the New Covenant. But

---

5. The same assumption apparently did not hold when the Christian convert was not the head of the household. Note the various New Testament instructions given to slaves or to wives whose masters or husbands are not believers, and are not necessarily regarded as recipients of salvation: 1 Tim. 6:1-2; 1 Cor. 7:14-16; 1 Pet. 3:1.

why, then, does Peter mention children at all, if God's call does not extend in some particular way to them? Why doesn't Peter simply say, "The promise is for you and for all whom the Lord our God calls to him"? Clearly, Peter says "the promise is for you *and for your children*" because the Joel prophecy he cites mentions children; it promises that the Spirit will be poured out *on your sons and daughters.* This is the "promise" spoken of in Acts 2:39, and it specifically references children.

In Acts 2:21, the end of the Joel prophecy also promises that "everyone who calls on the name of the Lord will be saved." We thus see a correspondence between the Joel prophecy and the "promise" cited in Acts 2:39:

- Joel's words, "Your sons and daughters will prophesy" (cited in Acts 2:17), are summed up in Peter's words (Acts 2:39), "The promise is for you and for your children."
- Joel's words, "Everyone who calls on the name of the Lord will be saved" (cited in Acts 2:21), are summed up in Peter's words (Acts 2:39), "[the promise is] for all who are far away, everyone whom the Lord our God calls to him."

So we see at the very beginning of the church, on the day of Pentecost, this great theme of God's covenant purpose for families is brought to its climax and culmination. The promise is not just for believers, but for their children as well. God's Spirit will be poured out on them and on their children. This is not just an aspect of this text alone, but part of the great covenantal purpose of God attested throughout Scripture. God continues to promise to be not only our God, but the God of our children (Gen. 17:7).

But there is also a countervailing movement in the New Testament that we must keep in mind. There are texts in the New Testament that indicate that Jesus expects to create *division* in families (Matt. 10:34-37; Luke 12:51-53). There are also texts where Jesus calls his disciples to be willing to *leave* families (Matt. 19:29; Mark 10:29-30; Luke 14:26). How do these passages fit with this theme of the *renewal* of families?

We begin to find the answer to this question when we note that it is explicitly in this context of divisions within families and leaving families that Jesus also speaks about *taking up one's cross* to follow Jesus (Matt. 10:38-39; Luke 14:27). Despite the goodness of the created world (including families), and God's intention to restore the original integrity and blessing of the created world (including families), it is seductively possible for our attachment to any aspect of this life to supplant our radical commitment to follow Jesus. No other allegiance can compete with one's allegiance to follow Jesus — even those most near and dear, like our allegiance to our families.

Like every other aspect of our lives, it is only when we relinquish our families and take up our cross that we can receive them back again, not as a natural right, but as a gift from God (Matt. 19:29; Mark 10:29). It is interesting that the same Jesus who calls his disciples to be willing to *leave* father and mother also criticized the religious authorities for failing to observe adequately the commandment to *honor* father and mother (Matt. 15:4-6; Mark 7:10-13; cf. Matt. 19:19). What is at stake here is not the dissolution of families, but the re-ordering of families in response to the coming of God's Kingdom.

This means, of course, this New Covenant promise is no more to be presumed upon than the Old Covenant promise was. It is still possible for children to spurn the promise and to fail to respond in faith. Households may struggle with divisions within them, as they groan in awaiting the fullness of God's redemption. Yet the promise remains, and is not eclipsed in the movement from the Old Covenant to the New. No longer is physical descent a *limiting* factor on God's promise. And physical descent is not a substitute for faith (nor was it such in the Old Covenant) — indeed, God can raise up children of Abraham from stones (Matt. 3:9). But the New Covenant does not leave families behind. The ancient promise of Deuteronomy 30:6 still holds:

> Moreover, the LORD your God will circumcise your heart and the heart of your descendants, so that you will love the LORD your God with all your heart and with all your soul, in order that you may live.

Of course, some proponents of believer baptism accept this inclusion of families within the New Covenant, but still object that infants should not be baptized. It remains to be seen whether it is possible to hold such a position with consistency. In the coming chapters, we will explore how and why this inclusion of families in God's New Covenant purpose expresses itself in infant baptism.

To Sum Up

> One of the central issues in the debate between believer baptists and paedobaptists is whether God has a New Covenant purpose not only for individuals, but for families.

> Old Testament passages that look forward to the New Covenant mention the renewal of families as part of the New Covenant. These passages are picked up and affirmed in the New Testament.

> The New Testament discussion of families presupposes that families are included *as families* in the New Covenant.

> The baptism of households in the New Testament confirms this same pattern.

> Yet this focus on families can never be a substitute for discipleship, and members of families must place loyalty to Christ before loyalty to families.

For Further Reflection and Discussion

> In the ancient world, individuals were understood to be deeply embedded in their families. For example, in the Roman world, only the head of the family (the *paterfamilias*) could legally own property. In our culture, this familial identity is not so central. How does this fact shape the way we hear and respond to the gospel as families?

> One sub-debate in the controversy over infant baptism is whether there were infants as members of the household baptisms recorded in the Bible (Acts 16:15, 31-33; 18:8; cf. 1 Cor. 1:16). How significant is this debate, in light of the broad themes of this chapter?

For Further Study

> A recent conservative Reformed study advocating infant baptism has a number of chapters related to the role of families in the New Covenant. See Gregg Strawbridge, ed., *The Case for Infant Baptism* (Phillipsburg, N.J.: P&R Publishing, 2003), especially chapter 3, "Unto You and to Your Children" by Joel R. Beeke and Ray B. Lanning, and chapter 4, "The *Oikos* Formula," by Jonathan M. Watt.

19 Can Infants Be Saved, Despite Their Inability to Express Their Faith? If So, How Does This Clarify the Relationship between Salvation and Faith?

Infants know nothing about salvation through Jesus Christ. They do not know that Jesus lived, died, and rose for them. They do not know that they are sinners. They do not know that they are forgiven in Christ. They do not know what it means to follow Jesus. Since they do not know these things, they cannot consciously accept these things as gifts for themselves, and respond in gratitude to God. They do not understand what it might mean to trust the God who gives these gifts to them, nor can they comprehend what it might mean to live their lives in faithful allegiance to this God, in response to these gifts. In short, infants are incapable of expressing the faith which the gospel calls forth from us.

Nor will it suffice to interpret romantically the infant's trust in his or her parents as trust in God, and to speak of the infant's faith in this sense, as if the mere posture of reliance upon another is all that is required for our salvation. Human beings are constantly placing their faith in persons, ideas, institutions, and objects other than God, and this tendency lies at the heart of the human problem. The Bible calls it *idolatry*. As lovely and touching as the parent-child bond is, it is not to be equated with our relationship to God. The fact that infants may trust and love their parents does not, in itself, mean that they trust and love God.

The decision to baptize or not to baptize infants therefore poses in the sharpest possible way a fundamental question: can the salvation signified in baptism (including our union with Christ, cleansing, new birth, and the gift of the Holy Spirit) be said, in any meaningful way, to belong to an infant who is baptized? Advocates of believer baptism believe that infants may be saved, but they do not believe they should be baptized. They insist that to baptize infants who are incapable of expressing faith is, quite simply, to say by our actions that faith is not necessary for receiving salvation. To give to infants the mark of salvation, without any expression of faith on their part, is to proclaim that the salvation signified in baptism does not require faith. To do so, they argue, is to betray the gospel which calls us to faith. It is to relinquish one of the fundamental tenets of the Reformation, that salvation is *sola fide,* by faith alone.

We will return to this challenge. To do so, however, we need to turn the same question around in a slightly different way: Does the Bible itself acknowledge and affirm the salvation of infants who are incapable of expressing faith? If so, what might this teach us about salvation in general, and about the relation of faith to salvation? As we shall see, believer baptists have a very different understanding of the *basis* for the salvation of infants than do paedobaptists. It is this difference that we will explore in this chapter.

A careful reading of Scripture leads to the conclusion that at least *some* infants are members of God's kingdom, recipients of salvation. Perhaps the most important text here is Jesus' blessing of the children (Matt. 19:13-15; Mark 10:13-16; Luke 18:15-17). When the disciples try to keep some children from Jesus, he rebukes the disciples, demands that the children be allowed to come to him, and insists that "it is to such as these that the Kingdom of God belongs." It is worth noting in particular that Luke emphasizes in 18:15 that at least some of the children brought to Jesus were *infants* (the Greek word indicates a very small child). Since, according to John 3:3, one must be born again/from above in order even to see the Kingdom of God, we may reasonably infer that the children of which Jesus was speaking may be said in theological terms to be regenerated, or "born again." That's what it means, theologically, to say that the Kingdom of God belongs to them.[1]

What was it about these children that Jesus was pointing to as exemplary and significant? Why does the Kingdom of God belong "to such as these"? Earlier, in Matthew 18:3, Jesus insisted that "Unless you change and become like children, you will never enter the kingdom of heaven." There, the emphasis falls on humility and lowliness. In the ancient world, chil-

---

1. The attempt of some to argue that Jesus only meant that the Kingdom of God belonged to those who were *like* children, rather than to children themselves, is not convincing. The children were, after all, brought to Jesus so that he might touch them and pray for them. If this is not a request for the grace of God's Kingdom, I don't know what is. Jesus' response clearly suggests that the request was granted.

dren were at the bottom of the social ladder, with no power at all. But for our discussion at present, it is sufficient to note that Jesus publicly announces the salvation of children — even infants who are inherently incapable of expressing faith. Those who can do nothing for themselves — even those who cannot express any faith — can be saved by God. Indeed, the disciples have something to learn from such as these.

Jesus is not innovating when he makes this claim regarding the salvation of infants. Both Isaiah and Jeremiah wrote of how God's work in their lives originated while they were still in their mother's womb (Isa. 49:1-3; Jer. 1:5). The apostle Paul picks up the same idea in Galatians 1:15. If we are to be faithful to Scripture, we must acknowledge that God's salvation can belong to infants, who are, as infants, incapable of expressing faith.

But recognizing this fact in Scripture only raises a further question: On what basis does Scripture say that infants can be saved, if not through faith? This is not an easy question to answer, but some of the speculation involved in attempts to answer it may at least point out some "dead ends" which we would do well to avoid. Some might argue that infants are saved on the basis of their own *future* faith which God foresees and therefore grants salvation to them while they are still infants. While this argument may appear initially attractive, one needs only to think of the fate of those who die in infancy to realize the problem here, since such persons have no future faith for God to foresee. The almost inevitable result would appear to be a diminishment of the personhood of those who die in infancy. They *cannot* be saved, since they can have no future faith. This, therefore, hardly seems to be a satisfactory solution, and there is no scriptural evidence to support this notion of future faith in any case.

Still others have attempted to appeal to the *innocence of infants* as the basis on which they are saved. Just as infants are incapable of expressing faith, so (this argument claims) they are also incapable of rebellion against God and are thus in the realm of salvation until they consciously sin. Such was the position of the monk Pelagius in the fifth century, who denied the existence of original sin — that is, sin that accompanies and debilitates us from the very beginning of our existence. Unfortunately, there *is* scriptural evidence that speaks to this question, and it all runs against the notion that infants are born in innocence. Paul insists in Romans 3:9 that *all* are "under the power of sin." We carry within ourselves the guilt and the debilitating consequences of the sin of our forebears, so that Paul can say that "all die in Adam" (1 Cor. 15:22). Infants cannot escape this "all." The same verse goes on to affirm that it is only "in Christ" that we are made alive. If infants are saved, it is not because they are innocent and have no need of Christ's saving work on their behalf.

It also will not suffice to adopt the "semi-Pelagian" solution expressed in the writing of theologians such as James Arminius in the seventeenth century. Here the idea is that the work of Christ is applied to humanity in two stages. Despite the universality of original sin, *all* human beings benefit from the work of Christ in one specific way: because of the work of Christ on behalf of the whole world, and by divine decree, all persons now have sufficient free will to choose for or against the gospel.[2] If they choose to embrace the gospel, then they enter the second stage of grace, in which they are joined to Christ and partake of *all* of Christ's benefits. If they reject the gospel, of course, they fall again under the power of sin and death. So some might argue that infants are saved because they benefit from this first "stage" of the work of Christ and are, by virtue of this work of Christ (and not their own native innocence), still innocent and free from condemnation.

Unfortunately, this "semi-Pelagian" position is also lacking in any meaningful scriptural support. Nowhere does the Bible speak of such a "two-stage" application of Christ's redemptive work. Moreover, Paul's words in Romans 3:12 seem to give little room for the idea that humans are capable of any good in God's eyes whatsoever in themselves. He states, "All have turned aside, together they have become worthless; there is no one who shows kindness, there is not even one." If humans have free will at all — even if it is a result of the work of Christ — how is it that *all* continue to live in sin, apart from the gospel? Any attempt to say that infants do not need the full saving work of Christ eventually undermines the biblical announcement that the gospel is good news that must be heard by all.

If all these attempts to find another basis for the salvation of infants have failed, we must instead conclude that if infants are saved at all (and Scripture states that at least some infants *are* saved), it must be that they are saved in the same way all humans are saved, on the basis of Christ's redemptive work on their behalf, despite the fact that they cannot express

---

2. Arminius speaks of a "third divine decree," which is "that by which God decreed to administer *in a sufficient and efficacious manner* the MEANS which were necessary for repentance and faith." *The Works of James Arminius,* trans. James Nichols, vol. 1 (Auburn and Buffalo: Derby, Miller, and Orton, 1853), p. 247 (emphasis original).

personal faith in this work done for them. It must be that God unites them to Christ by the power of the Holy Spirit, cleanses them of the guilt and power of their sin, puts to death their old nature and plants a new kind of life in them, even before these infants can know or understand or express what has happened to them. This, of course, is precisely what the doctrine of infant baptism says happens to those infants whom God saves.

In the next chapter, we will explore the implications of this discussion for our understanding of the church and our understanding of baptism. In demonstrating that some infants are saved, and in exploring the basis of that salvation, we have not yet said anything about infant baptism, and whether the salvation of some infants by God justifies the practice of infant baptism. That discussion is still to come. But at present, we need to focus on several preliminary conclusions that result from our exploration of infant salvation.

This exploration underscores, first of all, that God's saving grace is given to us *prior to* our expression of faith. Scripture's affirmation, "We love because he first loved us" (1 John 4:19), applies to us not only corporately, but also individually. God always takes the initiative, and we are always responding to God. As we have already noted on several occasions, this priority of divine action is one of the basic characteristics of God's covenant-making activity in Scripture. God begins by showing generosity and kindness, and *then* we are called to respond in faith and allegiance. The salvation of infants underscores dramatically the priority of divine grace in our salvation.

The salvation of infants also underscores the role of faith as a *response* to salvation, rather than as a *means* of salvation. There is a tendency among some Christians to think of our relationship with God as something like an electrical circuit. One wire is God's grace, and one wire is our faith. Unless both wires are in place, the current will not flow, and we will not experience salvation. But if infants can be saved, this analogy breaks down. They have no capacity yet for the "second wire" of faith.

The language of *call and response* may be more helpful than the image of electrical circuits — and closer to the Bible's imagery. God calls us by showering upon us generosity and kindness — in essence, the beginnings of our salvation. This divine generosity is intended to call forth from us the response of faith. As faith responds to God's goodness, the covenant relationship is established, and begins to grow deeper through time. This is entirely in keeping with our everyday experience of the growth and development of infants. As they experience love, they respond in trust, and the relationship between infant and parent deepens. In just the same way, as an infant learns and experiences more of the love that God has shown to us in Christ, the capacity to respond in faith and allegiance to God deepens and grows as well.

Finally, our exploration of the salvation of infants has provided an important answer to the critique of believer baptists with which this chapter began. We began by noting the complaint of some believer baptists that the practice of infant baptism seemed to suggest that God's salvation does not require faith, thereby undermining the Reformation's insistence that salvation is *sola fide,* by faith alone.

We are now in a better position to respond to this complaint. We can begin by observing that the Reformation also insisted that salvation is *sola gratia,* by grace alone. As we have seen, the salvation of infants dramatically underscores this truth. We ought not to interpret *sola fide* in a way that undermines *sola gratia.* In fact, the reformers never understood these two affirmations to be in conflict, or even in tension with each other. Rather, the affirmation that salvation is "by faith alone" was always set in contrast to the medieval notion that it was faith in combination with good works that brought one to salvation. But the reformers also always envisioned faith as the response to God's *prior* grace. They rejected the "synergism" implied in the electrical circuit analogy.

It simply is not the case, therefore, that the baptism of infants "sends the wrong message" about the importance of faith, or about the relationship between faith and baptism. In fact, our exploration suggests that the baptism of infants can and should be understood as sending exactly the right message about the relationship between faith and salvation: God initiates a relationship with us, before we even know it, by showering grace upon us. This happens historically, in that Christ died for us even before we were born. It also happens personally, as the Spirit begins to work in us before we are even consciously aware of God's grace. It is only in response to this saving action of God that our faith emerges. This, of course, does not in itself prove that infants *should* be baptized, but it removes a major objection to that practice.

To Sum Up

> The question of the salvation of infants, and the basis for that salvation, provides an important and illuminating "test case" for the way we think about faith and salvation.

> Scripture clearly tells us that some infants are saved, despite their inability to express faith.

> These infants are not saved because they are innocent, nor because God's grace applies in a general way to all young children. If they are saved at all, it is through the work of Christ.

> The salvation of infants thus underscores the fact that God's grace *precedes* our faith. This is precisely what the practice of infant baptism teaches.

> Hence faith does not complete our salvation, but simply responds to God's prior call to salvation.

For Further Reflection and Discussion

> Some Christians find it hard to think that infants are implicated in human sinfulness and therefore need God's salvation. What might be some arguments for or against this idea, both from Scripture and from human experience?

> Almost all Christians believe that at least some infants can be saved. The disagreements concern the *basis* on which they are saved. Have you heard additional theories beyond those discussed in this chapter? What are they? (One theory that will be discussed in more detail in chapter 21 involves the so-called "age of accountability.")

For Further Study

> For a classic discussion of the doctrine of original sin, see Book 2, chapter 1 of Calvin's *Institutes,* available online at http://www.reformed.org/books/institutes/bk2ch01.html.

20 Does Baptism Take the Place of Circumcision as the Mark of the New Covenant?

In the previous three chapters, we have laid the foundation for an understanding of infant baptism. In chapter 17, we explored how the whole of Scripture bears witness to a single covenant purpose of God spanning the whole Bible. Although this covenant unfolds and develops over time, it is expressive of a single divine purpose that comes to its culmination in the life, death, and resurrection of Jesus as God's Messiah. In chapter 18, we explored more specifically the role of families in God's covenant purpose, and determined that God continues to hold a place and purpose for families in the New Covenant. Then, in chapter 19, we explored whether infants can be saved, and the basis upon which they are saved. This exploration underscored the priority of grace in the way we think about God's salvation. Faith is an ongoing and developing response to God's grace, which always comes to us first, before we are even aware of it. Thus the inability of infants to express faith is no reason to exclude them from God's gracious covenant, despite the fact that faith is central to the New Covenant.

However, none of these observations, in themselves, compels the baptism of infants. Together, the previous three chapters demonstrate that there is nothing in Scripture that forbids the baptism of infants, and much that is entirely compatible with the baptism of infants. In this chapter, we move to a positive case for baptizing infants by exploring how baptism is understood in Scripture to take the place of circumcision. The argument is essentially a simple one: If indeed baptism is the New Covenant fulfillment for circumcision, then the burden of proof is clearly on those who would deny infants access to baptism, since infants were clearly the recipients of circumcision, the sign of the covenant with Abraham.

We begin with some broad parallels between circumcision and baptism. Both circumcision and baptism are, first of all, *rites of entry* into the people of God. Genesis 17:10-14 indicates that every male, either born into God's people, or bought as a slave, was required to be circumcised in order to belong to God's people. Any resident aliens who wanted to eat the Passover were required to be circumcised, and no one who was uncircumcised was allowed to eat the Passover (Exod. 12:48). Anyone not circumcised was "cut off" from the people (Gen. 17:14). If males wanted to be part of God's people, they were required to be circumcised.

Similarly, baptism is the rite of entry into the New Covenant people. Repeatedly in the book of Acts, it is the first response made by those individuals and households who respond to the gospel, and marks the point at which they become part of God's people (Acts 2:41; 8:12, 36; 9:18; 10:48; 16:15, 33; 18:8; 22:16). Galatians 3:27 declares that baptism is the mark of those who have clothed themselves with Christ. We also noted in chapter 12, in the discussion on baptism "into the name of Jesus," that this phrase was associated, especially in Greek-speakers' minds, with the transfer of ownership. Baptism marks the point at which we belong to Jesus Christ.

As rites of entry, both circumcision and baptism function to *distinguish the people of God from those outside the covenant.* For circumcision, this became particularly true in the period after the Maccabean crisis in the second century B.C., when Jews were threatened with death for observing their religion.[1] Even the Roman writer Tacitus observes this phenomenon among Jews: "They adopted circumcision to distinguish themselves from other peoples by this difference" (*Historiae* 5.5.2). In the same way, the New Testament can use a kind of verbal shorthand to speak of the whole distinction between Jew and Gentile using the language of circumcision and uncircumcision (Rom. 2:25-29; 3:30; Gal. 2:7; Eph. 2:11; Col. 3:11).

John's baptism already had the same character. Luke 7:29-30 indicates that it distinguished those who were part of the divine purpose from those who were not. The same is true of Christian baptism. Mark 16:16 declares that "the one who believes and is baptized will be saved." Baptism marks the community that lives in the hope of God's salvation in Christ. In the Great Commission, baptism marks those who are made disciples (Matt. 28:19). Acts 2:38 links repentance and baptism with the giving of the Holy Spirit, the great empowering gift that marks the New Covenant. Acts 2:41

1. See 1 Macc. 1–2; 2 Macc. 6; 4 Macc. 4:15-26.

speaks of how three thousand people were "added" after being baptized. The New Testament "counts" people as Christians once they are baptized.

But this distinguishing role of baptism is not only social; it is also spiritual and ethical. Paul can appeal to the baptism of Christians in Romans 6 in order to explain why Christians must live differently from others, and abandon their sinful ways. If you are baptized into Christ, he says, you are baptized into his death, and you cannot go on living the way you did before (Rom. 6:3-14). Similarly, Galatians 3:27-28 appeals to baptism as the fundamental source of Christian identity: "As many of you as were baptized into Christ have clothed yourselves with Christ. There is no longer Jew or Greek, there is no longer slave or free, there is no longer male and female; for all of you are one in Christ Jesus." The realities signified in baptism are the fundamental markers of Christian identity that distinguish Christians from others, just as circumcision distinguished the Jewish people from all others.

So both baptism and circumcision are *rites of entry* into the people of God. In both cases, these rites of entry *distinguish* the people of God from others. But there is a third parallel between circumcision and baptism as well: *both rites pointed to a deeper spiritual transformation.* Circumcision was never intended merely as an "external" rite, but rather as a symbol of something deeper, involving the stripping off of aspects of one's life (just as a small portion of one's actual flesh is removed) in devotion to God. Circumcision of the flesh always pointed to circumcision of the heart (Deut. 10:16; 30:6; Jer. 4:4). It was thus a metaphor for the life of trust and allegiance to God, including the notion of *sacrifice*, the offering of one's entire life back to God in grateful allegiance.

The spiritual significance of circumcision is taken to a far deeper and richer level, of course, in baptism in the New Testament. In addition to the imagery of sacrifice and self-offering found in circumcision, baptism speaks powerfully of union with Christ, cleansing, new life, and the gift of the Spirit. But our broad survey has made the bond linking circumcision and baptism clear: both are *rites of entry* into the people of God, both *distinguish* the covenant people of God from all others, and both point to a *deeper spiritual transformation.* These striking parallels, in themselves, should invite us to think in fresh ways about the baptism of infants. Since infants were included in circumcision, and since there are so many parallels between circumcision and baptism, why should infants *not* be baptized? But some may wonder whether the New Testament makes this link between circumcision and baptism more explicit. In order to answer this question, we need to turn to the key text of Colossians 2:11-12.

In this text, Paul makes the link between circumcision and baptism explicit, and notes the inner spiritual connection between the two. In order to see this more clearly, let's first begin with a very literal translation of Colossians 2:11-12:

> In him also you were circumcised with a circumcision made without hands, in the stripping off of the body of flesh in the circumcision of Christ, having been buried together with him in baptism. In him you also were co-raised through faith in the working of God who raised him [*i.e.* Christ] from the dead.

Note that the text begins by saying, "you were circumcised." Given the likelihood that the readers are gentiles (Col. 1:21, 27, etc.), Paul is not referring to their literal circumcision. The next clause indicates that a different sort of circumcision is in view — one made "without hands." These gentile Christians have also been circumcised, but not in a way that any human being can do. What sort of circumcision is this?

The next clause goes on to tell us more about what this new and different circumcision made without hands actually is. This is a circumcision that is accomplished "in the stripping off of the body of flesh in the circumcision of Christ." This reference to the "stripping off of the body of flesh" is speaking of our dying with Christ in baptism. Both Colossians in particular and the New Testament in general speak of the "body of flesh" as the sinful nature which God has put to death for us in Christ, and which we must continually put to death. Colossians 3:9 speaks of how we have "stripped off" the "old self," another probable reference to our union with Christ signified in baptism. Romans 6:6 speaks, in conjunction with baptism, about the destruction of the "body of sin" as God's purpose for us. Romans 8:13 promises that "if by the Spirit you put to death the deeds of the body you will live." So there are extensive parallels in the New Testament for understanding "stripping off the body of flesh" to refer to what God does to and in us in baptism.

The next clause, "in the circumcision of Christ" speaks of our union with Christ in his death as a "Christian circumcision," which consists not in physical circumcision, but in baptism. This is confirmed by the next clause, which refers explicitly to baptism. The link between circumcision and baptism in these verses is also confirmed by the use of the unusual word for circumcision used here: "stripping." Just as in English, the normal meaning of this word in Greek has to do with removing clothing. We know from early sources that the ancient church practiced baptism in the nude.[2] Old clothes were ceremonially removed, and after baptism, a new robe was put on, symbolizing the "putting off" of the old self, and the assumption of a new nature and identity in Christ. Given the reference to baptism in this text, the natural meaning is to interpret this "stripping off of the body of flesh" as a reference to what happens to us in the sign-world of baptism, as we are united with Christ in his death and resurrection by faith.

Hence the text as a whole should be paraphrased in this way:

> In him also you were circumcised with a circumcision made without hands, when God stripped you of your sinful nature in the circumcision of Christ, when you were buried together with him in baptism. In him you also were co-raised through faith in the working of God who raised Christ from the dead.

Here the broader parallels we have noted between circumcision and baptism all come into clear focus and expression. Baptism is the "circumcision of Christ," the New Covenant equivalent of the Old Covenant sign.[3]

This same linkage between circumcision and baptism appears indirectly in the New Testament through the use of the word "seal": In Romans 4:11, circumcision is the "seal" of Abraham's righteousness by faith, and in 2 Corinthians 1:22, the marking of Christians with a "seal" is linked to the gift of the Holy Spirit, an indirect allusion to the gift given in baptism (cf. Eph. 1:13; 4:30). Baptism and the gift of the Spirit fulfill what circumcision already pointed to. Both baptism and circumcision are "seals" of God's covenant. But if baptism really is the fulfillment of circumcision, infant baptism suddenly appears in a different light. We have already noted in previous chapters

---

2. Hippolytus, *Apostolic Tradition*, 21:3, 20.

3. Believer baptist exegesis of this verse tends to read "the circumcision of Christ" not as a reference to baptism but as a reference to the death of Jesus. Thus, in this view, it is *Jesus'* "body of flesh" that is stripped away in "the circumcision of Christ." See, for example, G. R. Beasley-Murray, *Baptism in the New Testament* (London: Macmillan, 1962), pp. 152ff. Yet the notion that Christ's "body of flesh" was stripped away in his death has no parallels anywhere in the New Testament or early Christian literature. Such an interpretation runs the risk of suggesting that Christ's resurrection was only spiritual and not bodily. In contrast, the image of the "body of flesh" as representing *our* sinful humanity that is put away in baptism is echoed in Col. 3:9, and at several other points in the New Testament, as was noted above.

the unity of God's covenant purpose throughout the Bible, the inclusion of families throughout the Bible in God's covenant purpose, and the inclusion even of infants in God's saving grace, despite their inability to express faith. Given all these things, and given the clear connection between baptism and circumcision, the natural inference is that infants should be baptized in the New Covenant, just as they were circumcised in the Old Covenant.

Why, then, was circumcision replaced by baptism in the New Covenant? We could point to the movement away from bloody sacrifice to spiritual sacrifice. We could note the abolition of the ceremonial law in the New Covenant. We might point to Jesus' attempts to express the deeper intent of the law, rather than merely its external demands. We could point to the full inclusion of women in the church (Gal. 3:28), and the need for a covenant sign that included them (which circumcision could not do). All these factors doubtless played a part. But at bottom, a large portion of the answer must also be that circumcision was so closely identified with Jewish ethnicity that to continue to circumcise believers would have distorted the missional movement of the gospel beyond Israel to the "ends of the earth." The early church struggled in the process, but finally clearly affirmed that gentiles are included in the people of God without first being required to become Jews. This meant circumcision could no longer be mandatory. On the other hand, much of what was expressed in circumcision needed to be preserved, and reinterpreted in light of Christ's death and resurrection, and the pouring out of the Spirit. Baptism brought together these new realities with the best of what circumcision also brought: the clear delineation of the new people of God and the summons to spiritual transformation.

The corporate mindset assumed in circumcision, inclusive of children, is also indicated, as we noted earlier in chapter 18, in the repeated references to household baptisms in the New Testament (Acts 16:15, 31-33; 18:8; 1 Cor. 1:16). Believer baptists insist that there is no explicit mention that infants or young children were included among those baptized. But in light of our exploration, the burden of proof really falls the other way. Given the fact that all of Scripture witnesses to a single covenant purpose of God centering in Christ; given that this covenant purpose includes families and households, who were baptized *as households;* given that even infants are clearly part of this New Covenant saving purpose of God; given the many parallels between circumcision and baptism, and given the fact that Colossians 2:11 even speaks of baptism as "the circumcision of Christ," why should we expect that infants were *not* included, just as they were in the

Old Covenant? Perhaps believer baptists are wondering about something that the New Testament writers simply took for granted. Perhaps the lack of any explicit reference to the baptism of infants in the New Testament reflects a practice which was deemed so obvious it was assumed to need no comment. This is the cumulative biblical and theological argument on which the practice of infant baptism is based.

To Sum Up

➤ The earlier chapters suggest that infant baptism does not *contradict* key biblical themes, but it remains to be seen whether Scripture *commends* the practice.

➤ Both circumcision and baptism are *rites of entry* into the people of God; both *distinguish the people of God* from those outside the covenant; and both *point to a spiritual transformation.*

➤ Colossians 2:11-12 speaks clearly and explicitly of baptism as the New Covenant equivalent of circumcision.

➤ Thus the burden of proof falls on those who wish to say that infants should *not* be included in the New Covenant sign, since they were included in the Old Covenant.

For Further Reflection and Discussion

➤ Take a look at your church's baptismal liturgy, and explore if and how it expresses baptism as a rite of entry, a means of distinguishing the people of God, and a pointer to spiritual transformation. What comes through clearest? What is more obscure?

➤ Are you convinced that Colossians 2:11-12 identifies baptism as the New Covenant equivalent of circumcision? Why or why not? Does this persuade you that infants of Christian parents should be baptized? Why or why not?

For Further Study

➤ For a more extended argument advocating baptism as a covenant sign, see Geoffrey W. Bromiley, *Children of Promise: The Case for Baptizing Infants* (Grand Rapids: Eerdmans, 1979), especially pp. 1-26.

DISPUTES AND QUESTIONS SURROUNDING INFANT BAPTISM

The next four chapters address some common objections and questions about infant baptism. Chapter 21 addresses whether infant baptism can provide assurance to the parents of the salvation of those baptized children who die at a young age, before they are able to confess their own faith. The two chapters after it explore the theological implications of the sad fact that some people who are baptized as children reject the faith into which they were baptized. Chapter 22 addresses the question of whether this fact weakens the case for infant baptism generally, and chapter 23 addresses the more specific question of whether this fact calls into question God's faithfulness to his promise, signified in baptism. Finally, chapter 24 explores the ambiguous evidence surrounding infant baptism in the early church, in the period after the New Testament was written, and assesses how that evidence should be interpreted.

21 Can We Be Confident of the Salvation of Baptized Children Who Die at a Very Young Age?

It's one thing to believe, as we explored in chapter 19, in the salvation of infants as a general possibility. We observed in that chapter that at least some infants are indeed included in God's saving purpose. However, it's another question to consider whether any *particular* infant is saved, and whether baptism provides us with any assurance that a particular baptized person who dies in infancy will enjoy eternal life with God. Yet it is always in this more focused form that the question arises in real Christian experience. Grieving Christian parents do not ask whether baptized children in general can be saved; they desperately want to know if their small child, whom they have lost, will enjoy eternal life with God. That is a serious question, and deserves a serious answer.

One does not need to think too long about this question before encountering the obvious difficulties: Not all baptized infants grow up to behave as if they are united to Jesus Christ, despite the fact that baptism sets before us our union with Christ as both identity and calling. Some baptized infants grow to old age and never show any sign of God's regenerating work in their lives — they may even be hostile to Christian faith. We have already noted that baptism, *in itself,* provides no final assurance of salvation: It is not baptism itself, but the promise of God expressed in baptism, that saves us.[1] So if some baptized children are thus shown by the established pattern of their lives *not* to be united to Christ, and hence *not* to be saved, we confront a problem: Can we have any assurance about baptized children who die in infancy, before we can see either confirming or disconfirming evidence of their union with Christ?

1. See chapters 5, 16.

It would appear at first that we are driven to one of several unhappy conclusions by this example of some baptized infants who later turn away from their baptism: We might say that *all* baptized persons are united to Christ and saved, regardless of whether they show any evidence of God's grace in their lives. But this position would seem to contradict the strong biblical emphasis that Christians are known by the fruit they bear in their lives (e.g., Luke 6:43-45). We might say that all baptized infants are saved, but that some eventually *lose* that salvation. Yet the Reformed tradition has always emphasized that our assurance of salvation depends finally on the fact that God's hold upon us matters far more than our hold upon God. God doesn't start the work of salvation in us without finishing it (see Rom. 8:28-39). Any salvation that can be lost does not overcome the greatest threat to our salvation — our own weakness. Or we might say that baptism tells us nothing about whether infants are saved and united to Christ. The baptism of infants may express our hopes and prayers for their salvation, but little more than that. Yet this seems to evacuate God's promise, upon which baptism is based, of all its meaning. Can God's promise then be trusted?

All these conclusions are unsatisfactory. We will need to explore further, however, before we can find a better one. As we do so, however, we must also remember that this question of the salvation of infants is not only a problem for paedobaptists. Believer baptists must also wrestle with the pastoral problem of parents who have lost young children who are unable to confess their own faith. In many respects, the theological problems of believer baptists are even more difficult. If there is no saving purpose of God revealed in Scripture for the children of believers, and if profession of faith is truly necessary for salvation, then sheer logic would dictate that those who die before being able to profess their faith lack not only *assurance* of salvation, but even the *hope* of salvation. Of course, I know of no believer baptists who hold such a position. But in their desire to affirm the salvation of infants, believer baptists are often driven to positions we explored and rejected in chapter 19: assertions that children are innocent and do not need the saving work of Christ, or that a more general aspect of Christ's atoning work is all that they need. But these solutions have no grounding in Scripture, either. It is an odd contradiction to say that children of believers who die in infancy are saved, if we say at the same time that they don't really need the full saving work of Christ.

One common way to address this problem among believer baptists is to speak of an "age of accountability" before which all are saved. Appeal is sometimes made to the Bar Mitzvah or Bat Mitzvah in Judaism as a precedent for this practice. Still more often appeal is made to texts such as Deuteronomy 1:39, which speak of children who "do not yet know right from wrong." Yet even if we grant the relevance of this text to the question of infant salvation, it would only address the youngest of children. Even two-year-olds know when they have done something wrong.[2] But this entire line of reasoning has the air of desperation about it. There is nothing in Scripture that sets forth an age of accountability, either in the Old or the New Covenant. Even the Jewish practice of Bar and Bat Mitzvah has very little scriptural support in the Old Testament. Attempts to ground the salvation of infants in a doctrine of the "age of accountability" not only lack real scriptural warrant; they weaken the Bible's persistent emphasis that sin affects us from the moment we are born.

One further clarification is needed, before we attempt to answer this question of the salvation of baptized children who die in infancy: We are focusing here on *baptized* children, that is, children of believing parents. There are a variety of theories and doctrinal positions about the salvation of those who are outside of the church and who have never had the opportunity to hear the gospel. I do not address that question here, since it is not germane to the topic of baptism. Instead, I want to address the more focused question of the salvation of those within the church who are baptized and die in infancy. Can we have any assurance about their salvation?

We must begin, of course, by recognizing that we are probing into matters about which Scripture does not always speak clearly, and at some points, we may simply not know the answers to the questions we have raised. We do know that the God revealed in Jesus is supremely merciful. We do know that Jesus assures us that the Kingdom of God belongs to children, and to those who become like children (Matt. 19:14; Mark 10:14; Luke 18:16). So regardless of the complexities and turns of our theological systems, we can say with confidence that everything we know of God suggests that God's grace extends to our children, and that, in the final analysis, all we can ever do is to hope and trust in this grace. This is where all our more precise theological work must begin and end.

2. One web site I discovered in my research suggests that all who are under the age of 20 years are saved (http://www.biblebell.org/accountability.html)! Yet in such cases, Deut. 1:39 can scarcely be said to apply.

But we can be more precise as well. First, we must address the necessity of baptism itself. Reformed theology baptizes children and adults on the basis of God's promise and call (Acts 2:38-39). God's *promise* is salvation by grace, received through faith in Christ. This promise is made both to the children of believers and to those who have heard the gospel and repented of their sins. This promise is in force even before baptism is administered. God's *call* is the summons to participate in God's mission to the world as disciples of Jesus, as part of the body of Christ. This call is extended both to children of believers and to those who have heard the gospel and repented of their sins. This call also is in effect even before baptism is administered.

Baptism is thus, for both the children of believers and for adults who repent in response to the gospel, a *sign* and *seal* of the salvation and calling which Christians receive by God's sovereign grace. Therefore the absence of *baptism itself* does not nullify the promise nor abrogate the call. In this sense, Reformed theology differs from Roman Catholic theology, as well as from some streams of Lutheran and Anglican theology, which see baptism itself as necessary for salvation, at least ordinarily.[3] Reformed Christians are typically not overly anxious about baptizing newborns in the hospital who may not survive. The hope of salvation is grounded in God's promise and call, of which baptism is the sign and seal, rather than grounded in the rite of baptism itself. For this reason also, from a Reformed perspective, Christian parents who, because of conscience, have not baptized their small children, but have decided to wait until those children can profess their own faith, can also still be assured of the salvation of those children who die in infancy.

But we still must return to the more challenging question: Given that some baptized children never profess faith for themselves, but instead reject the faith into which they were baptized, and given that even some baptized in adulthood also fall away from their faith, does the baptism of children give us any grounds for confidence or hope in their salvation, or must we remain "agnostic" about the relationship between baptism and salvation generally?

---

3. Most theological systems that postulate the necessity of baptism for salvation also propose a number of exceptions for unusual circumstances, appealing to a "baptism of desire," or more generally to the mercy of God.

The classical Reformed answer to this question is found in the Canons of Dort, a Reformed confession from the seventeenth century:

> Since we must make judgments about God's will from the Word, which testifies that the children of believers are holy, not by nature but by virtue of the gracious covenant in which they together with their parents are included, godly parents ought not to doubt the election and salvation of their children whom God calls out of this life in infancy.[4]

This is the starting point of the Reformed tradition on this question. If God's promise is given to believers and to their children, then believing parents ought not to doubt that promise when their children die in infancy, regardless of the fact that some children of believers may grow up to reject the faith of their baptism. The basis for this hope is not that these children die before reaching the age of accountability. Neither is this hope grounded in the innocence of children in general. It is grounded solely and completely in the covenant promise of God, which believing parents claim by faith.

But can Christians lose this "election" of which the Canons speak? Is it the case that *all* those baptized in infancy are "elect," chosen by God for salvation, but that some of these baptized children later lose that election? Here the answer is No. The same Canons of Dort also teach the *perseverance of the saints* — that all those whom God chooses (elects) also persevere to the end, and obtain the salvation won for them by Christ. Our security in our salvation depends ultimately not on our "staying power," but on God's faithfulness. Reformed theology teaches that the elect cannot lose their salvation.

But this language of election complicates the discussion of baptism. The Canons appear to be saying that *all* baptized children who die in infancy are elect, and therefore saved (not because they are baptized, but because they are children of God's promise). However, *not all* baptized children who grow up to adulthood are elect, and therefore saved, since some obviously do not persevere to the end.

The skeptical mind will immediately ask, "How can you have it both ways?" How can baptism (and the covenant promises on which it is based) be a sure sign of election for those who die in infancy, but *not* a sure sign of

---

4. First Main Point of Doctrine, Article 17.

election for those who grow to adulthood? The answer is to be found by exploring more deeply the nature of God's *covenant promise*. God's covenant promise to unite us to Christ and to the salvation found in Christ is given to us unconditionally. We have done nothing, and can do nothing to be worthy of this gracious promise. It is entirely by God's grace that we are given this promise at all.

And yet, while the promise is *given* unconditionally, its *fulfillment* is conditional — based upon our continued and growing response of faith. Where there is no faith, the promise is void (Rom. 4:13-14; Gal. 3:14-29; Heb. 4:1-3). Yet a consideration of infants clarifies further the nature of this promise of salvation and the response of faith which it requires. For surely the capacity for faith is something that grows over time. Infants know nothing of God and the promises of the gospel. Three-year-olds know something. Eight-year-olds know even more, and 18-year-olds are capable of even deeper responses of faith. We might go on to observe that 50-year-olds and 80-year-olds also are capable of still deeper responses of faith and obedience, in response to the gospel.

The gift of God's promise of salvation remains entirely of grace. We can never, at any point in our lives, do anything to deserve it or to be worthy of it. But God expects differing responses from us as we grow and mature. God expects nothing of infants — the promise is a pure and lavish gift of grace. That is why the Canons of Dort insist that believing parents should not doubt the salvation of their children lost in infancy. But as time goes forward, God's promise calls forth from us a deepening response of faith. Those who persistently fail to embrace that call to a deepening faith over the course of a lifetime demonstrate that they are not included in God's elect, for they do not receive God's promise in faith. But to use such examples to undermine the faith of grieving parents in God's promise is to fail to recognize that God expects something different from infants than from adults. As Jesus said, "From everyone to whom much has been given, much will be required" (Luke 12:48). God does not require from infants the same response God expects of adults; nor does God hold infants responsible in the same way that God requires faith of those who have the capacity to know and to trust God.

The promises of God on which baptism is based are sure and reliable. No one who trusts in those promises will ever be disappointed. And for those recipients of the promise who, because of their young age or mental disability, are limited in their ability to respond to the promise, its graciousness appears in all the stronger form. God asks much of us in the response of faith, to be sure. But God never asks from us what we cannot give, and God's mercy accepts our feeble attempts to trust God, as if those attempts were the gestures of Christ himself. Such is the beauty and the power of God's covenant promise, the ground of hope for our salvation, and for that of our children.

So believing parents can have confidence in the salvation of their children who die at a young age — not because their children are innocent or because they died before the "age of accountability"; not because they have had a "magic rite" performed upon them; but simply because of the firm foundation on which baptism itself rests, that God promises to be our God and the God of our children. Parents therefore need not be driven by anxiety over their child's salvation so as to manipulate the child into a climactic profession of faith at an early age. What is needed is steady Christian education and nurture, encouraging the child to take the steps of faith that are appropriate to each age and level of their lives. As the child takes a more public role in the world, their profession of faith should become public as well. (We will explore this in more detail in chapter 25.) As they continue to mature in years, their faith and allegiance to God should deepen along with their deepening years. At each level of our lives, baptism points us to God's gift and call, a gift and call that addresses us right where we are with the gracious promise of God.

To Sum Up

▸ There are many *unsatisfactory* answers to the question about the salvation of baptized children who die in infancy. Unsatisfactory answers include appeals to the innocence of children, appeals to an "age of accountability" before which all are saved, and solutions that allow for the possibility that one might lose a salvation already received.

▸ The Reformed hope for the salvation of baptized children is grounded not in the rite of baptism itself, but in the covenant promise of God sealed in baptism. This is a sure basis of hope and confidence regarding the salvation of believers' children who die in infancy.

▸ This confidence does not result in a diminishment of the significance of faith. Rather, this confidence flows from the realization that God expects differing responses of faith from us at different stages of our lives. For infants, the promise is pure gift.

For Further Reflection and Discussion

> What kinds of answers have you heard to the question of the salvation of those who die in infancy? How would you evaluate those answers in light of this chapter's discussion?

> In the first decade of the twentieth century, the northern Presbyterian church adopted a statement affirming that *all* those who die in infancy are saved, regardless of whether their parents are believers. What do you make of this claim?

> How has your own response of faith deepened as you have matured in your Christian life?

For Further Study

> Richard Mouw provides a fascinating historical overview of debates within Reformed Christianity on the topic of this chapter in "Baptism and the Salvific Status of Children: An Examination of Some Intra-Reformed Debates," in the November 2006 issue of *The Calvin Theological Journal* (vol. 41, no. 2).

22 Does the Fact That Some People Baptized in Infancy Never Confess Christian Faith for Themselves Weaken the Case for Infant Baptism?

Jesus tells us that "the one who endures to the end will be saved" (Matt. 10:22; 24:13; Mark 13:13). Yet one of the sad facts of the life of the church is that not all who are baptized endure to the end. At one level, we ought not to be surprised at this, since Jesus' words anticipate that such a problem would confront the church. But at the same time, the fact that some baptized persons abandon the faith of their baptism poses painful questions to the church about the meaning of baptism.

Troubling questions arise not only for paedobaptist parents, whose baptized children may not always embrace their parents' faith. These questions also arise for believer baptists. It is not only some baptized infants who abandon the faith, but also some of those who are baptized as teenagers and adults. The failure of a baptized person to show true faith appears already in Scripture (e.g., Simon the magician in Acts 8:9-24). So at the surface level, it would appear that this problem, as troubling as it may be, does not address infant baptism in particular. It appears to be a more general problem to be addressed in an overall theology of baptism, rather than a problem unique to the baptism of infants.

Indeed, in the next chapter, we will address that more general problem. But many believer baptists think that the failure of some baptized infants to embrace their faith betrays a deeper problem with infant baptism in particular. Some voice the objection along these lines: "It's one thing for baptized adults to abandon their own confession. They clearly bear responsibility for their own failure. But it's another matter for baptized children to abandon a 'confession' that they never made for themselves in the first place. This should not be called 'falling away' at all. These children are simply showing that they were never part of the church. They never should have been baptized to begin with."

From a Reformed perspective, this objection contains two mistaken assumptions. It assumes, first of all, that baptism is primarily a confession of faith. Reformed theology, by contrast, holds that baptism is primarily a sign and seal of God's promise toward us.[1] So when baptized infants abandon their baptism, they are not abandoning a confession unwillingly imposed on them; they are abandoning a promise made by God to them.

But the next point in the objection is even more important. Believer baptists say that when those baptized as infants refuse to confess Christian faith for themselves, they are showing that "they were never part of the church" and therefore should never have been baptized. At one level, of course, the same can be said for adults who fall away — perhaps they too should never have been baptized. But at one time, those backslidden adults did confess their faith, in an apparently genuine fashion. So if the church is made up of those who confess faith, they certainly *should* have been baptized. The same cannot be said of infants, who never confessed their own faith.

The deeper assumption that lurks beneath this challenge has to do with the nature of the church itself, and what it means to be a member of the church. In chapter 3, we explored the difference between membership in the church and our culture's usual approach to voluntary organizations. But now we need to be more precise about the church. What is it, specifically, that distinguishes those who are part of the church (its members) from those who are not?

The believer baptist answer is almost always the same: the church is defined by its *public confession of Jesus Christ.* It is made up of those who have publicly declared their faith in Christ and their determination to live by that faith. Baptism, for believer baptists, *is* precisely this public declaration, and therefore the means by which we become part of the church. Of course, believer baptists also recognize that some may have faith in Christ, but for practical reasons may not yet have made public profession. They too are part of the church in the broadest sense, but these cases need to be understood as exceptions rather than the norm. In essence, the church is defined by its public *confession* of faith. The church is made up of those who have publicly declared themselves to be disciples of Jesus. This way of

1. See chapters 4 & 5.

defining church, of course, also excludes infants who have not yet publicly confessed their own faith. If public confession is the central defining characteristic of the church, then no one can confess your faith for you. You must wait to join the church until you are ready to make your own confession.

But is this really the right way to define the church at its core? From a Reformed perspective (and I believe from a biblical perspective), the answer is No. The people of God, the community of faith in whom the Spirit is at work, cannot be understood to be restricted to those who have publicly confessed their faith in Christ. Public confession is not the final delimiter of the church. Not all who publicly confess Christ are included in the true church, since some reveal by their actions the emptiness of their words (e.g., Matt. 7:21-23; Luke 6:46), and not all who do not publicly confess Christ are excluded, as we have seen in the discussion of infant salvation in chapter 19. If the Kingdom of God belongs at least to some children who cannot confess their faith, they cannot be excluded from one's core definition of the church.

How then do we know who is part of the church and who is not, if it is not on the basis of public confession? Let's begin by returning to some core principles. The church is the body of Christ, the fellowship of those whom God has joined to Jesus Christ. It is the community of the disciples of Jesus. But theologians also distinguish between the *visible church* and the *invisible church*. The invisible church is the true church as God sees it. It is made up of all those who God knows will persevere to the end in true faith. It is made up of those who have been truly and effectually joined to Christ and regenerated by the Holy Spirit. It is the community of those who have been saved, are being saved, and who will be saved in the end.

The *visible church,* on the other hand, is the community of flesh and blood Christians who gather to assist each other in their life of discipleship. Not all members of the visible church are members of the invisible church, since some may fall away. The visible church is the ordinary and somewhat messy manifestation of the invisible church in our human experience. We *believe* in the invisible church; we *see* the visible church, warts and all.

Both Reformed paedobaptists and most believer baptists recognize this distinction. The disagreement lies not in understanding the invisible church, but in grasping the essence of the *visible* church. How do we define the boundaries of this fellowship, when we recognize that our perceptions are limited? We cannot see people as God sees them. How, then, are we to decide who belongs to the visible church, the flesh and blood (as well as spiritual) fellowship into which baptism ushers a person?

We begin to find an answer by accepting our human limitations. We cannot see the heart as God sees it, and thus *we do not know for sure* who finally will be saved — who belongs to the "invisible church." Only God knows that. Jesus was emphatic in his prohibition against "judging" others (Matt. 7:1; Luke 6:37). By this he did not mean that we should never form judgments about whether someone's words or behavior are appropriate. Scripture is full of instances where the people of God are to hold each other accountable — a task which involves the forming of judgments about such things. What Jesus was talking about, I believe, was attempting to form a final judgment about the salvation of another; that task, and the ability to form that judgment, resides with God alone. So the decision whether or not to admit someone to church membership, or even the decision whether or not to baptize a person, is not a decision about that person's final salvation. It can never be so, since it is only at the final judgment that this decision is rendered, and only "the one who endures to the end will be saved" (Matt. 10:22).

This does not mean we are totally in the dark about the salvation of others. Scripture gives us many ways to discern the evidences of the Spirit's work — more than enough to live out our lives of discipleship and fellowship. And Reformed theology holds that one can gain an even deeper assurance about one's own salvation, through the inner witness of the Holy Spirit (see chapter 16). But recognizing the limitations of our understanding does mean that decisions about church membership, from the perspective of the church's practice, are *not* matters of discerning who is *saved* — that is God's decision. Nor can those decisions be based only on confession, as we have seen. They are instead matters of discerning who is *called* by God in Jesus Christ.[2] The Bible regularly refers to Christians as those who are *called,* both to salvation and to discipleship (e.g., Acts 2:39; Rom. 1:7; 1 Cor. 1:2, 9, 24; 1 Peter 5:10; Jude 1:1). This focus on *call* centers the for-

---

2. The Second Helvetic Confession, an early Swiss Reformed confession, defines the church in this way: "The Church is an assembly of the faithful *called or gathered out of the world;* a communion, I say, of all saints, namely, of those who truly know and rightly worship and serve the true God in Christ the Savior, by the Word and Holy Spirit, and who by faith are partakers of all benefits which are freely offered through Christ" (chap. 17, emphasis mine).

mation of the church not on our commitment, but on God's promise and initiative. But those who are called are called as *disciples* of Jesus, and thus must enter into relationships of mutual accountability and discipline as they seek to follow Jesus Christ. Paul refers to Christians not as *confessors*, but as those *called to be saints*, or *called to be holy ones* (Rom. 1:7; 1 Cor. 1:2). So we are called not just to salvation, but more specifically to be holy (the same word as "saints"); we are asked by Jesus to hold each other accountable to this calling, to warn each other and discipline each other if it appears that we are falling away from this calling, and to encourage each other to be faithful to the end.

The visible church, then (i.e., the flesh and blood fellowship into which we are baptized), is not defined in its essence by *confession*, but by *God's calling*. Nowhere in the New Testament is the *church* as a body addressed or defined as those who *confess* their faith. The church is addressed, however, as those who are *called* (Rom. 1:6-7; 1 Cor. 1:2; Jude 1:1). This is not to minimize the importance of confession of faith, but simply to note that confession is not the biblical basis for membership in the church. Thus the basic question with respect both to baptism and to church membership is not whether or not a person is saved (that decision belongs to God), or even whether they have confessed their faith (even though public confession of faith is vital in Christian discipleship). Rather, the basic question is whether there is reason to believe that God is extending God's promise and call to this particular individual. Of course, if God is calling someone, there is every reason to believe that God will save that person. God always finishes the saving work he begins (Phil. 1:6). But the church's focus is more modest in making its decisions about whom to baptize. It is sufficient to have a reasonable basis for believing that God's call — the beginning of the process of salvation (and not its end) — is given to a person.

With adult converts, we discern this call in their response to the gospel in repentance and faith. That tells us that, as best we can discern, God is working in their hearts, calling them to himself. But the essential question, with respect to infants, is this: Is there a reasonable basis for believing that God has called these infants, despite the fact that we do not yet see faith in them? The essential answer has already been explored in previous chapters: When God calls believers, he also calls their children. This is, at its heart, the essential rationale for infant baptism, and for infant membership in the visible church.

But this understanding of the basis for membership in the church puts the believer baptist's objection in a very different light. If the church is defined by public confession, then the baptized infant who rejects Christianity should never have been included in the church to begin with. However, if the church is defined as those whom God is calling, then both the baptized infant and the baptized adult who later fell away were called by God — the one by virtue of being born into a believing family, and the other by virtue of his own prior confession. In each case, there was good reason to believe that God was calling that person.

So if the church is defined at its core by God's call, rather than by our confession, there is no reason to exclude infants from membership. Moreover, the fact that some baptized infants do not profess their faith poses no greater difficulty than the case of baptized adults who later fall away. Both have turned away from the calling that the church had good reason to believe God had placed on their lives. This God-centered way of thinking about the church stands closer to the biblical witness, which understands the church at its core (both visible and invisible), not in the light of its limited human response to the gospel, but always in light of God's purposes and plans for the people of God.

But defining the church in terms of God's calling raises some further questions of its own, especially with respect to those who have fallen away (both baptized infants and adult converts). In both cases, if baptism points to God's promise, and the baptized person does not endure to the end in faith, does that mean that God's promise failed? It is to this question that we turn in the next chapter.

To Sum Up

> When the baptized fail to live out the faith of their baptism, they are not abandoning their former confession; they are abandoning the promise God made to them.

> When we inquire into the implications of baptized children who do not confess their faith, we are inquiring into the basis for membership in the church.

> Although believer baptists base church membership on public confession, the Bible more consistently bases church membership on God's calling.

➤ Therefore church membership is not based upon salvation. Rather, church members are those who appear to be, by a charitable judgment, called by God *to* salvation and discipleship.

➤ With this understanding, there is no substantial theological difference between the falling away of those baptized in infancy and those baptized as adults.

For Further Reflection and Discussion

➤ Some Christians fear that if church membership is not based on public confession, then people will become slack about public confession of their faith. Do you agree? Why or why not? Is church membership a "reward" for faithfulness?

➤ Beneath many believer baptists' objection to infant baptism is the deep-seated feeling, long established in America, that religion should never be "imposed" on someone else. Is this assumption warranted in the case of parents, children, and baptism?

For Further Study

➤ A classic conservative Reformed exposition of infant baptism that addresses carefully the question of the basis for church membership is B. B. Warfield's "The Polemics of Infant Baptism," available online at http://www.the-highway.com/InfantBaptism_Warfield.html.

23 Does the Fact That Some Baptized Persons Abandon the Faith of Their Baptism Call into Question the Reliability of God's Promise?

With this question, I believe we come to the heart, or at least close to the heart, of the dispute between Reformed theology and advocates of believer baptism. The core issue is not about baptizing infants; it concerns the *basis* on which baptism is done. Reformed theology says we baptize on the basis of God's promise and call, and since the children of believers are included in God's promise and call (Acts 2:39), they too should be baptized. Believer baptists hold that we baptize on the basis of repentance and professed faith in Christ, *not* on the basis of God's promise, and therefore only those should be baptized who confess their faith in Christ.

But this disagreement can be posed more sharply and precisely. Believer baptists do not baptize based on the promise of God, but based on the person's repentance and profession of faith. There are deep reasons for this approach, which focus particularly on the understanding of a divine promise. Believer baptists reject any divine promise as the basis for baptism not only because they do not believe that Scripture teaches such, but also, at least in part, because if someone's profession of faith proves false, it can be seen as a human failing, which says nothing about God or God's faithfulness. Reformed theology, however, baptizes on the basis of God's promise. Therefore when some of the baptized fall away (so believer baptists argue), it appears to be due to the failure of *God's* promise, and not merely to the weakness of human profession.[1] God appears to be the one

---

1. Paul K. Jewett writes, "Hence baptism is lawfully administered to all who make a credible profession, even though some may prove foolish virgins at last. In the latter case we have an instance of the frailty of human judgment but not the failure of a divine promise." *Infant Baptism and the Covenant of Grace* (Grand Rapids: Eerdmans, 1978), p. 150.

who is unreliable, rather than the person making the profession of faith. This, according to many believer baptists, is the core problem with infant baptism. It assumes that God makes promises that are not always kept, and in so doing, attributes unfaithfulness to God. Believer baptists conclude that it is better to leave talk of God's promise out of our understanding of baptism, and focus instead on baptism as an expression of our repentance and faith, a human response to God's grace.

It is evident, when we touch on these core issues, that this is not merely an abstract theological debate; it is a question that touches on deep pain in the lives of some parents, and brings us to the limits of what we can know and understand about the ways of God. Parents who deeply love their child experience acute anguish when that child refuses the gift that is most profoundly precious to them — the gift of a vital and transforming relationship with Jesus Christ. Few sorrows run deeper than this one, re-gardless of one's theology of baptism. But as is so often true in the life of faith, it is only when we name our pain and face it squarely that we begin to see the light of God's truth dawn, a light which may not always answer all our questions, but which eventually shows us a path forward, in the midst of our confusion and sorrow.

The first thing to note, however, is that there is no easy way out of this pain, regardless of our theology of baptism. Paedobaptists and believer baptists alike pray for their children, and Scripture gives strong assurances about answered prayer: Matthew 18:19 baldly declares, "If two of you agree on earth about anything you ask, it will be done for you by my Father in heaven." Mark 11:24 makes even stronger promises about prayer: "So I tell you, whatever you ask for in prayer, believe that you have received it, and it will be yours." Yet the earnest and believing prayers of parents for the sal-vation of their children sometimes go without any clear answer. Even if we were to remove the notion of promise from our understanding of baptism, we still cannot remove the promises of God from Scripture, and we cannot always explain how some of these promises of Scripture remain unfulfilled in our experience. We do not invite people to cease claiming God's prom-ises in prayer, or to cease making decisions based on those promises, sim-ply because sometimes those promises do not appear to be kept. So why should we remove the basis of God's promise from baptism, simply be-cause there are times when that promise does not appear to be kept? What believer baptists charge is a special problem stirred up by the doctrine of infant baptism turns out to be a general problem in Christian faith and life, stirred up by the language of Scripture more broadly: Does the fact that we do not always see God's promises kept mean that God doesn't keep the promises made in Scripture, and therefore that God cannot be trusted? As painful as this question is, however, it is not a question that implicates only infant baptism. If we cannot answer this question satisfactorily, it may suggest that Christian faith as a whole is an illusion, and God cannot be trusted at all. Baptism on the basis of the divine promise is not the only issue at stake here.

We can get a start at addressing this question by noting some considerations that, while not answering the question itself, put it in a different light. We must recognize, for example, that the hyper-individualism of our culture poses this question to us in a way that few in the New Testament period would have imagined. The New Testament understands the promises of God as addressed first and foremost to the church as a whole, and only secondarily to individuals. Because we lack the corporate mindset of the Bible, we think first (sometimes only) of individuals, and only secondarily of the group. We feel the force of the failure of individuals more powerfully, I suspect, than did the New Testament church. It may be that some of our questions, therefore, were never envisioned by the New Testament writers. This does not make our questions any less valid or pressing, but it does help us to understand why there appears at times to be a disconnect between Scripture's promises and our questions.

So Paul, for example, asserts God's faithfulness to his promises to Israel in Romans 11:29, insisting that "the gifts and call of God are irrevocable." At the same time, he can say, in Romans 9:6-7, that "not all Israelites truly belong to Israel, and not all of Abraham's children are his true descendants." Paul's thinking is corporate and general rather than individualistic here, and leaves us with some puzzling questions, because we think differently. But if the promises of God are to be interpreted in this more corporate manner, rather than individualistically, it may help us to understand how these promises might still be true, even if they don't appear to be met in specific and individual cases. This analysis does not, of course, immediately help the grieving parents whose child is one of those who has rejected the faith of his baptism. Their pain is no less real. But it does invite them to look beyond their own pain to the larger purposes of God in the church as a whole. Pain closes us in on ourselves, and one of the ways to move beyond our pain is to realize that the sun does not rise and set on us alone. God has purposes at work in the world that extend beyond us as individual families.

But that can never be the whole answer. Another perspective on this problem provides no comfort to grieving parents, but does help to inform the theological question of whether God's faithfulness is impugned by the failure of some baptized children to profess their faith: not all parents who bring their children for baptism are real believers. For some, baptism is a mere formality, a "rite of passage" or a "backup plan," just in case all this talk about final judgment turns out to be true. It is not surprising in such cases that these children do not grow up to confess their faith, because the faith is not embraced by the parents. This is not a failure of God's promise, but a failure of discipline on the part of the leaders of the congregation where such a baptism takes place. Congregational leaders have the responsibility of determining whether parents who bring their children for baptism are themselves believers. We have no promise in Scripture that warrants baptizing children of unbelievers. This is a partial line of insight into the problem we are addressing, but certainly not the central answer. Indeed, the church must be careful to encourage those grieving parents whose faith is genuine, and whose children nonetheless do not embrace that faith for themselves. We must resist the temptation quickly to blame the failure of the children on a lack of faith in the parents, even if, in some obvious cases, this may be true. Lack of faith *may* be the reason why we do not see God's promises fulfilled, but if we take the entire witness of Scripture seriously, it is scarcely the only reason. Indeed, the Psalms are full of the laments of the righteous, who cry out to God in anguish, and insist that their suffering is unjust and unwarranted. The book of Job carries the same lesson. We must stand with grieving parents, without accusing them. Indeed, their grief itself reflects the genuineness of their faith. Those who do not love and trust God also do not grieve when their children fail to believe the gospel.

We get at least a step closer to the answer when we recognize that public profession of faith, while vitally important, is also not *always* the final determinant of our salvation. In Matthew 10:32, Jesus says, "Everyone therefore who acknowledges me before others, I also will acknowledge before my Father in heaven." Yet the context of Matthew 10 is one of public conflict and controversy, in which the refusal to publicly confess one's discipleship is the same as a denial of one's faith. Such circumstances may and often do apply to life today, but this context of conflict suggests that public confession is a matter of obedience in one's call to mission, rather than a generic requirement of salvation. In the history of the church, whenever

163

the church's witness has encountered conflict and persecution, public confession has risen to the forefront of the church's call to obedience. In many of these contexts, it *is* the final determinant of faithfulness to Christ.

However, there are also many very human factors, even sinful factors, which may keep those baptized in infancy from confessing their faith in some situations — factors which have nothing to do with our obedience in mission. Churches, and even parents, sometimes do a poor job of Christian education and nurture. We do not always live out the faith we profess, and we may need to confess our failures and to receive divine forgiveness. Yet the consequences of those failures often live on in the lives and hearts of our children. Tragically, at times baptized children even experience the church not as a loving and welcoming place but as a place of hypocrisy, or even a place of abuse. There are very many human failures that can impede the freedom and joy with which baptized children embrace the faith into which they are baptized.

Shall we simply write off the promise of God because of these human failures? Absolutely not! These are the points at which we most desperately need to be reminded of God's promises. The Spirit of God has many ways of working in human hearts. Baptized children grow up in the context of the church. They hear the good news of Jesus Christ. They know that he died and rose for them. Who are we to deny that this good news may be the seed of a new life that is growing, but never breaks the surface of the soil to be seen? I am convinced that with baptized children, the bias should be in favor of our belief that the Spirit is at work within them, based on the promise of God, rather than on the assumption that they are unregenerate until they confess their faith. God does not break the bruised reed (Isa. 42:3). Everything in the gospel leads us to believe that God's grace abounds, particularly where human beings have failed (Rom. 5:20). How much more should we base our hope on this, when God has also promised, not only to be our God, but the God of our children? We have reason to believe that God welcomes, in the baptized, even the slightest turn of the heart towards trust in the gospel, even the most faltering intention of the will toward allegiance to Jesus Christ, even the most conflicted opening of the heart in repentance.

This does not mean that there are no consequences to the unbelief and disobedience of our baptized children. Damage may be done that lasts for generations. Scripture itself speaks of some who are saved "as if through fire" (1 Cor. 3:15). There is still a tragic loss of potential fruit for God's

Kingdom in those baptized children who fail to publicly profess their faith, or who wander in the far-off country and, so far as we can see, waste their lives. But let none of these losses stand against the promise of the same God who promises to save up all our tears in a bottle, and who promises to wipe away every tear from our eyes. This is the God portrayed to us by Jesus, who likened him to a father who ran out at the very first sight of his prodigal son returning home, even before probing the integrity of his heart and the purity of his motives. We dare not believe less of God, particularly God's demeanor toward those to whom God has promised, "I will be your God."

Does this mean that all the baptized are saved? Scripture gives us no grounds for such presumption. Instead, it persistently directs our attention back to Jesus Christ, and urges us to trust in him, warning of the utter peril that awaits those who hear and then spurn his call. There is a mystery of unbelief in some of the baptized that we cannot understand, sorrows that will only be consoled at the end of time, when all of God's purposes become clear. But God does not leave us in the dark when it comes to our children. God promises to be God to us and to our children. And despite the fact that we do not always see how this promise is fulfilled, it is the only sure basis on which to build our families' lives. And still deeper trust in the promise is our only rescue from despair, when we do not see the promise fulfilled as we have hoped in our children's lives.

Hebrews 11 is one of the New Testament's great chapters on faith. It chronicles a long list of saints who trusted in God's promise, even though they did not receive that promise in their lives. Faith, it says, is "the assurance of things *hoped for,* the conviction of things *not seen*" (Heb. 11:1, italics mine). When we speak of holding fast to the promise of God, even when our experience seems to contradict that promise, we are not speaking of some peripheral topic in Christian faith and experience; we are talking about the very essence and heart of faith itself. To evacuate the promise of God from baptism may make for a smoother and less problematic theology, but the reluctance clearly to proclaim and trust in God's promise to the children of believers will finally result in the loss of something vital in faith itself. The promise of God is the only final, full, and true basis for baptism. Even when some aspects of their experience shout that they are fools to do so, still Christians are called to trust in God's promise, rather than in their own strength, even the strength of their own faith.

To Sum Up

‣ Some object to infant baptism because the falling away of some baptized children appears to indicate that God's promise, on which infant baptism is based, cannot be trusted.

‣ On closer examination, however, this is not a problem peculiar to infant baptism, but a challenge that runs throughout Christian faith.

‣ The problem is complicated by the hyper-individualism of our culture, and by the absence of appropriate pastoral oversight of baptism in some cases.

‣ Public confession of faith is an important part of obedience in discipleship, but is not a generic requirement for salvation.

‣ Sometimes the weakness or sinfulness of the church places obstacles in the way of those who might otherwise publicly confess their faith.

‣ The only final response to the seeming failure of God's promise is a deeper reliance on God's promise.

For Further Reflection and Discussion

‣ Have you experienced a time in your life when it appeared that God's promise had failed you? How did you respond? What did you learn?

‣ Do you agree with the statement that "the bias should be in favor of our belief that the Spirit is at work within [our baptized children], based on the promise of God, rather than on the assumption that they are unregenerate until they confess their faith"? Why or why not? What difference will your answer make in the way you think about topics such as Christian education in the life of the church?

For Further Study

‣ For a powerful and moving testimony of a father's struggle with the mental illness of his son, and his grappling to find God's faithfulness in the midst of repeated and profound disappointment and loss, see *Souls Are Made of Endurance: Surviving Mental Illness in the Family* (Louisville: Westminster John Knox, 1994).

24 Was Infant Baptism Practiced in the Early Centuries of the Church's Life?

When the debate between believer baptists and paedobaptists turns to the evidence from early church history, we confront a classic example of the proverbial argument about whether the glass of water is half-full or half-empty. Most scholars agree that, beginning shortly after the year 200, we have direct evidence of the baptism of young children unable to confess their own faith. Hippolytus, a church father in the West, writes of this practice in his book *The Apostolic Tradition*, which dates from around 215.[1] He speaks of the practice as part of the apostolic tradition which was always practiced in the church. At about the same time, Tertullian, in North Africa, argues *against* the practice of infant baptism, providing evidence that it was practiced at least by some at that time.[2] The early theologian Origen, in the East, speaks of the practice, and writes as if he himself was baptized as an infant, pushing an attestation of infant baptism back at least to the late second century.

Paedobaptists and believer baptists generally agree about this much. Yet there is much disagreement about the larger picture of infant baptism in the early church. The debate focuses particularly on how extensively or consistently infant baptism was practiced. The debate has been a lively and contentious one in scholarship over the last fifty years. It is a fairly complex debate, and we will not touch upon its details here, but will try to sketch out the broad outlines of the discussion.

1. For the text of this document, as well as extensive commentary, see Paul F. Bradshaw, Maxwell E. Johnson, and L. Edward Phillips, *The Apostolic Tradition: A Commentary*, ed. Harold W. Attridge (Minneapolis: Fortress, 2002).

2. Tertullian argued (mistakenly, in our view) that infants were innocent, and therefore did not need baptism. See his work *De Baptismo*.

We begin with the period of the New Testament itself. Here it is important to remember that the earliest church, as witnessed in the New Testament, was in a missionary situation where the dominant pattern was conversion to the faith. It is thus not surprising that the baptism of those who have come to faith is the norm in the book of Acts, and elsewhere in the New Testament to a significant degree. But this fact tells us nothing about infant baptism in itself.

It is also vital to keep in mind the significance of household baptisms in the New Testament. There is every reason to believe that infant baptism was practiced from the earliest point in the early church, within the context of household baptisms. The ancient world looked at the relationship between the individual and the group very differently from the way western Christians do today, and we need to remember this as we assess the significance of household baptisms in the New Testament.

At the same time we must recognize that we also have an absence of any *direct* evidence of the baptism of small children who are unable to confess their own faith until the evidence we noted at the beginning of this chapter in the late second century, beginning with Hippolytus (around 215), Origen, and Tertullian. Earlier than that, we have no explicit evidence.[3] So there is a gap of approximately a century, in which the sources available to us are silent about infant baptism.

There is also reason to believe that the faith and practice of the early church may not have always been consistent or uniform with respect to baptism in general, and infant baptism in particular. We have already noted Tertullian's objection to infant baptism, early in the third century. Other texts suggest some ambiguity as well. The *Didache,* an early second-century Christian text, seems to presuppose a period of instruction and fasting prior to baptism (7:1, 4). We do not know if or how this instruction

---

3. Joachim Jeremias, a scholar who argues that there is earlier evidence for the practice of infant baptism, points to Jewish proselyte baptism as an earlier parallel and precedent for the baptism of infants. There is evidence in rabbinic sources that when families converted to Judaism, the males were circumcised and the females were ritually bathed, even at a very young age. Jeremias tries to argue that Christian baptism builds on this as a precedent, although he is rather hard pressed to find clear evidence that this practice can be documented in the first century. Jewish proselyte baptism underscores the general sense of household solidarity in religious matters that we find in the ancient world, but provides little in the way of more direct evidence. See his *Infant Baptism in the First Four Centuries* (London: SCM, 1960), pp. 24ff.

may have been interpreted with reference to infants, or whether the *Didache* assumes that infants were baptized at all. Other early Christian texts, such as the *Shepherd of Hermas* (dating from the middle of the second century), voiced a belief that sins committed after baptism could not be forgiven, and held to a notion of a kind of purgatory for unconfessed post-baptismal sin (*Vision 3*, 7.3, 6). Some have argued that it is unlikely that those who held such a belief would baptize infants.[4]

The German theologian Kurt Aland has tried to argue that there was an "age limit" in the second century, below which children were not baptized in the early church. The evidence he cites for this, however, is also indirect, rather than explicit.[5] Jeremias argues that there is no unambiguous evidence of pre-baptismal instruction given to children of believers in the early church.[6] There is much that we simply do not know about the baptism of children in the ancient church.

The debate among scholars continues. As is often the case when evidence is meager, many theories continue to be propounded on all sides of the debate. It seems reasonable to conclude from the conflicted nature of the debate that, while there are good reasons to believe that infants were baptized from the earliest period, there is also evidence which suggests that they may not have been baptized always and everywhere in the earliest church. Both sides have texts to support their positions.

What are we to make of this? First, we should note that, for almost all Protestant Christians, the practice of the early church does not carry the same authority as Scripture itself. The notion of a kind of "purgatory" such as we find in the *Shepherd of Hermas*, for example, was rejected by the Reformation because it lacked attestation in Scripture and contradicted the radical grace of the gospel of Christ. So we must recognize that the practice of the early church is not a final authority. If its practice with respect to infant baptism was not entirely consistent, this tells us little definitively about what the church should do today.

At the same time, it is worth noting that as time progresses through

---

4. See the discussion in Kurt Aland, *Did the Early Church Baptize Infants?* (Philadelphia: Westminster, 1963), pp. 54ff. See also the rejoinder in J. Jeremias, *The Origins of Infant Baptism: A Further Study in Reply to Kurt Aland* (London: SCM, 1963), pp. 38ff.

5. Aland, *Did the Early Church Baptize Infants?*, pp. 53ff.

6. In *Did the Early Church Baptize Infants?*, Aland argues that the *Apology* of Aristides provides such evidence in the second century (see pp. 54ff.), but Jeremias offers strong arguments to the contrary in *The Origins of Infant Baptism*, pp. 43ff.

the third and fourth centuries, the evidence becomes more and more pervasive that infant baptism became the universally accepted practice throughout the church.[7] Why did this happen? One theory advanced by Kurt Aland may help to illumine this puzzle.[8] He notes that it was in the third and fourth centuries that the church was forced to clarify its understanding of human sinfulness. Prior to that time, there were some parts of the church that assumed that infants may not have needed baptism because of their innocence and sinlessness.[9] As the church continued to reflect on the nature of original sin, it came to the conclusion that it was erroneous to attribute sinlessness or innocence to infants, who were also implicated in original sin. This controversy came to its climax in the debate between Augustine and Pelagius in the fourth century, in which the church adopted formally an understanding of original sin that understood infants to be included in the guilt and power of sin we all inherit from Adam.

Once this understanding of the universality of human sinfulness was clearly recognized, it quickly became the universally attested practice of the church *not* to withhold baptism from infants, who need the grace of God as we all do. Augustine's debates with Pelagius also underscored the radical priority of grace, making clear the theological basis for the baptism of infants as well.[10]

These developments in the history of the church raise profound questions about the wisdom of attempting to return to an earlier period when the practice of the church with respect to infant baptism may have been more diverse. In the second century, the church may not always have recognized so clearly the implications of a full doctrine of human sinfulness, and the radicality of divine grace attested within Scripture itself. If this failure consistently to understand these doctrines resulted in a diversity of baptismal practice, such diversity is surely no warrant for continuing this confusion today. Indeed, those who reject infant baptism would do well to reflect on their understanding of human sinfulness, and the implications

7. Curiously, we see for a brief period from about 330-360 a tendency to avoid baptism until very late in life, so as to avoid post-baptismal sins. This reflects the contemporary perspective and practice of neither believer baptists nor paedobaptists. For further discussion, see Jeremias, *Infant Baptism in the First Four Centuries*, pp. 87ff.

8. Aland, *Did the Early Church Baptize Infants?*, pp. 100ff.

9. See, for example, Tertullian, *De Baptismo,* chap. xviii.

10. See the earlier discussion on infant salvation in chapters 19 and 21.

of that understanding for the salvation of infants. One of the important reasons why the Reformed tradition has continued to baptize infants (in addition to the biblical warrants for the practice we have already explored) is because the Reformed tradition has also recognized the radical nature of sin and our radical need — even the need of our infant children — for God's grace. The doctrine of infant baptism affirms unequivocally that God's grace is both needed by and granted to infants. Those who reject the practice of infant baptism run the great risk of losing a clear grasp on this basic and important doctrine. We have learned some important lessons in the history of the church — lessons we do well to retain.

To Sum Up

> The first *direct* evidence of infant baptism in the early church dates from around 200.

> The evidence prior to this period is ambiguous with respect to infant baptism.

> By the latter part of the fourth century, infant baptism is clearly the norm throughout the church.

> There may well be a close link between the church's clarification of its understanding of original sin and the adoption of infant baptism as a more consistent and universal practice.

For Further Reflection and Discussion

> How authoritative is the practice of the church in the first four centuries? How relevant is this debate to your acceptance or rejection of infant baptism?

> How do you assess Kurt Aland's argument that it was the clarification of the church's doctrine of original sin that triggered greater consistency in the practice of infant baptism?

For Further Study

> You may want to read Hippolytus's *Apostolic Tradition,* the first direct evidence of the baptism of small children in the early church. The standard

scholarly translation and commentary is Paul F. Bradshaw, Maxwell E. John-son, and L. Edward Phillips, *The Apostolic Tradition: A Commentary,* ed. Harold W. Attridge (Minneapolis: Fortress, 2002). The text of Hippolytus's work is found online at http://www.bombaxo.com/hippolytus.html. The reference to the baptism of small children unable to confess faith for them-selves is in chapter 21 of that work.

PASTORAL DECISIONS SURROUNDING BAPTISM

Baptism is a very practical matter, which involves a variety of pastoral decisions by church leaders. This last section addresses some of the more common decisions that church leaders confront as they try to be faithful in administering the sacrament of baptism. The focus falls particularly on the kinds of decisions pastors and elders are called upon to make with respect to baptism. Chapter 25 explores "confirmation" or "profession of faith," and its relationship to baptism. These issues involve the pastoral care and nurture of baptized children. Chapter 26 explores several questions that center on decision-making authority in matters pertaining to baptism. Chapter 27 addresses a question that was common in the nineteenth century in America, and continues to come up from time to time, especially in cultures where grandparents play a prominent role. Chapters 28 and 29 address the common and challenging questions of rebaptism and infant dedication. Finally, chapter 30 looks at baptism within the larger context of the life of the church. If baptism is a forward-looking sacrament, as we have argued throughout this book, what comes after baptism?

25   What Is "Confirmation" or "Profession of Faith," and What Is Its Relationship to Baptism?

Scripture itself never speaks of "confirmation" as a Christian practice. There is very little in Scripture that addresses how those who have been born into the faith are to "grow into" their responsibilities and privileges as disciples of Jesus. We therefore must turn to the history of the church, if we are to understand this practice and its contemporary relevance.

In some of the earliest baptismal manuals, dating from the third century, we find that after people were baptized, the bishop would lay hands upon them and pray for them, anointing them with oil as a sign of the gift of the Holy Spirit.[1] Over time, however, this act of the bishop began to become separated in time from the rest of the baptismal rite. Since in some places, baptisms were done in the nude, modesty prevented baptisms from being conducted in public worship. In these cases, the action of the bishop (who, in most cases, was simply the local pastoral leader) may have been the "public" extension of the baptismal rite itself. In other cases at a somewhat later period in church history, when bishops were distinguished from local pastoral leaders, this act done by the bishop was necessarily separated in time from the act of baptism, since each church had to wait for a visit from the bishop. By the time we reach the Middle Ages, "confirmation" had become a distinct sacrament, separate from baptism, focused particularly on anointing with oil, and administered solely by the bishop, in contrast to baptism, which was administered by the local priest. It was numbered among the seven sacraments of the church, and was understood to

---

1. See Tertullian's *De Baptismo*, available online at http://www.tertullian.org/articles/evans_bapt/evans_bapt_text_trans.htm; and the *Apostolic Tradition* of Hippolytus, available online at http://www.bombaxo.com/hippolytus.html.

be a sacrament of "strengthening for the battle," as opposed to baptism, which conferred new birth. From the year 1200 or so onward, this sacrament of confirmation was required before one was permitted to partake of the Lord's Supper.[2]

This medieval practice was justified by appeal to Acts 8:14-17, where Samaritan believers were baptized, and only later received the Holy Spirit at the hands of the apostles (represented in the medieval church by the bishops). During the Reformation, however, both Calvin and Luther insisted that the gift of the Holy Spirit is centrally promised in baptism itself. The Spirit needs no further "confirmation" in order to be at work in the lives of the baptized. Calvin in particular had two complaints about confirmation. First, he found nothing in Scripture which mandated confirmation as a practice distinct from baptism. Both he and Luther particularly rejected the notion that confirmation was a bestowal of the Holy Spirit beyond what was given in baptism itself. Secondly, Calvin worried that the medieval practice of confirmation, and its preoccupation with the oil of anointing, had displaced the biblical centrality of the waters of baptism.

But Calvin also believed that the laying on of hands might be a helpful pastoral gesture of intercessory prayer (though not a sacrament), in conjunction with the catechizing of children and their profession of faith before the church. This idea was widely embraced in the churches of the Reformation, and became part of the regular practice of many churches, though with some noteworthy variations. The churches of the Reformation attempted to develop educational materials and practices which would result in the training of young people to articulate and confess the Christian faith for themselves. In some churches, this "profession of faith" was done before the elders or pastoral leaders of the church; in other churches, the profession of faith was done publicly before the entire congregation. In many Protestant churches, this profession of faith came also to be regarded as the prerequisite for the baptized child to be eligible to receive the Lord's Supper, despite the reformers' earlier rejection of confirmation as a prerequisite for communion. This practice resulted, in some churches, in the distinction between "baptized members" of a church, and

2. For a more complete discussion of this history, see the article on "Confirmation" in *The New Westminster Dictionary of Liturgy and Worship,* ed. Paul Bradshaw (Louisville: Westminster John Knox, 2002).

"communicant members," even though such a distinction cannot be found either in Scripture or in the writings of the Reformation.

In the last few decades, however, many Protestant churches have been moving away from the notion that this "profession of faith" should always be a prerequisite for receiving communion. The key biblical text discussed in this context is 1 Corinthians 11:17-34, in which Paul discusses abuses of the Lord's Supper at Corinth. The Corinthians were celebrating the Lord's Supper before everyone could be present to partake of it, and some were even getting drunk at the celebration. In response, Paul declares,

> Whoever, therefore, eats the bread or drinks the cup of the Lord in an unworthy manner will be answerable for the body and blood of the Lord. Examine yourselves, and only then eat of the bread and drink of the cup. For all who eat and drink without discerning the body, eat and drink judgment against themselves. (11:27-29)

For many Protestants, Paul's injunction not to eat and drink "in an unworthy manner" or "without discerning the body" meant that one's faith should be examined by the pastoral leaders of the church before one partakes of communion. But Paul never says this (he calls for self-examination), and in its context, Paul's words are addressing something a bit more down-to-earth. More recent scholarship has clarified that in this text, "discerning the body" focuses not so much on discerning the presence of Christ in the bread and the wine, but rather, on discerning the *community* as the body of Christ, and hence celebrating the Lord's Supper as a whole community, and not in private groups. Eating and drinking "unworthily" refers to celebrating the Lord's Supper in ways that do not do full justice to the shared life of the body of Christ. The problem in Corinth is not centrally the lack of proper catechesis; it is the lack of mutual concern for the shared life of the community as a whole.

Moreover, there is absolutely nothing in this text (or any other text of Scripture for that matter) about *public* profession of faith as a requirement for partaking of communion. Both baptism and the Lord's Supper are addressed to *faith*, and without faith, the sacraments convey none of their blessings. Yet there is nothing in Scripture which says that the faith that lays hold of the sacrament must necessarily be *publicly professed*. As a result, more Protestant churches are developing strategies for Christian education, both by parents and by the church as a whole, which can assist children in understanding the Lord's Supper. As young children learn about the Lord's Supper, and begin to show faith appropriate to their age and level of understanding, they are encouraged to partake at earlier ages, under the supervision of parents and the pastoral leaders of the church. This process is beginning at an earlier level, and is no longer always tied to public profession of faith, but is oriented instead toward the emerging faith and understanding of children. In many respects, this move is a recovery of the original impetus of the Reformation, to remove the sacrament of confirmation as an unscriptural barrier between baptism and the Lord's Supper.

Of what use, then, is public profession of faith? Some Protestants are not so enthused about disconnecting public profession of faith from communion. They are concerned that if participation in the Lord's Supper is no longer tied to public profession of faith, then the value of public profession will be diminished. The result, they fear, will be baptized children who merely *presume* upon their baptism, rather than taking seriously their own responsibility to publicly confess the faith for themselves. They worry that the privileges of church membership will be regarded as *inherited rights,* rather than as gracious gifts linked to solemn responsibilities, willingly accepted by those who have freely chosen to follow Jesus.

These concerns are understandable. When infant baptism is not accompanied by strong practices of Christian nurture and education, and when it is not supported by the discipline of the church, the result can easily become a kind of complacency in the baptized that falls far short of Jesus' radical call to discipleship. But making public profession a requirement for partaking of the Lord's Supper is no magic cure for this danger. Indeed, in some Protestant churches, even profession of faith, when made a prerequisite for communion, can still become a ritualized "rite of passage" that has little substance and meaning: One simply learns the "correct" answers, and then one is admitted to the table.

What is needed, rather than making public profession of faith a prerequisite to participation in the Lord's Supper, is a deeper and more biblical grasp of what public confession of faith means. To "confess" is to "say the same thing" as others, to agree with others in basic affirmations. To confess one's faith, then, is to stand together with the rest of the church, to say the same thing that Christians have said before you, down through the ages. To confess one's faith is to identify publicly with the faith of God's people, and with the people of God.

This may mean different things for us, depending on our context. For an adolescent, emerging from her family as an individual in her own right, it means claiming the faith for herself, not simply accepting without question her parents' convictions, but taking her own stand in the faith, taking her place, not just in her family, but in the mission and witness of the whole church. For Dietrich Bonhoeffer in Word War II, confessing the faith meant returning to Germany from the safety of New York City, and becoming involved in the dangerous resistance to Hitler's tyranny. For the signers of the Belhar Confession in South Africa, confessing the faith meant standing with the wider church against all attempts by other Christians to justify racial segregation and oppression on Christian principles.

Sometimes confession of faith is not quite so dramatic, but nonetheless significant. A family may feel called by God to adopt four children who have lost their parents. For them, this is what following Jesus means. Why shouldn't they ask the church to gather around them and pray for the strengthening of God's Spirit for such a daunting task? A team of people in a congregation feels called to start a Habitat for Humanity chapter. They too might stand to confess this expression of their faith, and ask for God's grace. An alcoholic has been through AA, and now feels ready to begin a new chapter of his life. He too stands to confess his trust and commitment, and asks for the prayers and support of God's people. An elderly widower has weathered a storm of grief with the loss of his wife of many years, but begins to find a new hope and a new purpose in the midst of his loss, and stands to declare the faithfulness of God in the midst of the congregation.

What all these examples share in common is this: confession is never a one-time event, after which we are finished. It is rather a summons that comes to us at key points in the Christian life. At these points, we are called to take a stand, to find our place in the great cloud of witnesses, confessing our faith precisely at those points where it makes a difference to do so — a difference on which everything depends.

In western culture, one of those "confession points" happens typically during that period of time when adolescents move toward making more of their own decisions, and toward taking more responsibility for their own lives. The church needs to teach and encourage these young people to recognize the need for public confession of their faith, the need to claim the faith not merely as something inherited from their parents, but embraced by themselves as the foundation of their lives. Some churches may also find it expedient to make certain rights of membership contingent upon such public profession — rights such as voting in congregational decision-making, for example.

Does public profession make someone a "member" of the church? There is no biblical evidence to support this claim. One becomes a member of the church through the promises sealed to us in our baptism. Baptized children already are "members" of the church, by virtue of their baptism.[3] Just as one is a citizen of a country before one is a voting member, one can be a member of a church, without necessarily having access to all the rights and responsibilities of adult members of the church. It is well for churches to reflect carefully and sensitively about how children grow to assume the blessings and responsibilities of church membership that are given implicitly in their baptism. Part of that process of discipleship, for Christians of all ages, is the challenge of confessing the faith, precisely at those points where the future direction of our lives is at stake. There may be — indeed there *should be* — multiple times in our lives when we must stand and say what we believe, and ask the community of God's people to surround us, lay their hands upon us, and ask for the power of the Holy Spirit to be poured out upon us, so that we can stand together with all God's people as disciples of Jesus. We should ask this of our children, and we should ask this of ourselves. We make this confession, not so that we can *become* members of the body of Christ. We make this confession because we *are* members of Christ's body, and our confession expresses our discipleship to Jesus Christ.

To Sum Up

> Confirmation emerged in the medieval church as a separate sacrament in which the bishop laid hands on a candidate and anointed the candidate with oil, symbolizing the gift of the Holy Spirit. Confirmation was a prerequisite for partaking of communion.

> The reformers rejected confirmation as a separate sacrament, but developed catechetical materials to prepare people to confess their faith.

---

3. The *Belgic Confession,* Article 34, declares, "Having abolished circumcision, which was done with blood, [Christ] established in its place the sacrament of baptism. By it we are received into God's church and set apart from all other people and alien religions, that we may be dedicated entirely to him, bearing his mark and sign. It also witnesses to us that he will be our God forever, since he is our gracious Father."

➤ This profession of faith — whether public or before the elders — came also to be the basis of admission to the Lord's Table.

➤ There is no scriptural requirement of public profession of faith before receiving communion.

➤ What is needed in the church is the encouragement of public profession of faith at critical points in the life of believers, not as an entry into membership in the church, but as an appropriate expression of discipleship.

For Further Reflection and Discussion

➤ My own denomination, when it calculates membership statistics, has two categories. One of them is "baptized membership." The other category used to be called "communicant membership," but now is called "confessing membership." In light of this chapter, how would you evaluate this terminology?

➤ This chapter suggests that public profession of faith might be used as a prerequisite for voting rights in congregational meetings, but not for admission to the Lord's Table. What do you think of this suggestion?

For Further Study

➤ For an interesting study of one denomination's struggle with clarifying the role and purpose of "confirmation," see "Confirmation and the Reformed Church," available online at http://www.rca.org/aboutus/beliefs/confirmation.html.

26 *Who* Decides If Someone Should Be Baptized, *How* Should That Decision Be Made, and *When* and *Where* Should Baptisms Take Place?

In the life of the church, two things are closely related to each other: The way the church conducts baptisms, and the way the church thinks about itself and understands itself. The way we answer the very practical questions with which this chapter begins, therefore, will be shaped by our *ecclesiology* — the way we think about ourselves as the church of Jesus Christ. We see this linkage emerging already in the New Testament. In Paul's first letter to the Corinthians, for example, he confronts the problem of divisions that are threatening the fellowship in Corinth. Immediately after he finishes with the formalities of his greeting, he plunges directly into this problem:

> Now I appeal to you, brothers and sisters, by the name of our Lord Jesus Christ, that all of you be in agreement and that there be no divisions among you, but that you be united in the same mind and the same purpose. For it has been reported to me by Chloe's people that there are quarrels among you, my brothers and sisters. What I mean is that each of you says, "I belong to Paul," or "I belong to Apollos," or "I belong to Cephas," or "I belong to Christ." Has Christ been divided? Was Paul crucified for you? Or were you baptized in the name of Paul? I thank God that I baptized none of you except Crispus and Gaius, so that no one can say that you were baptized in my name. (I did baptize also the household of Stephanas; beyond that, I do not know whether I baptized anyone else.) For Christ did not send me to baptize but to proclaim the gospel, and not with eloquent wisdom, so that the cross of Christ might not be emptied of its power. (1 Cor. 1:10-17)

As we noted in chapter 12 on baptism "in the name of Jesus," the baptismal formula would have been regarded by Greek-speakers as a statement of ownership. To put something "in the name of" someone is to attribute ownership to the person in whose name something is held. So these quarrels and divisions in Corinth appear to be closely related to their practice of baptism. Apparently, they thought that the person who did the baptizing affected the power or spiritual efficacy of the baptism itself. Or at the very least, they regarded the person who baptized them with particular loyalty and devotion. They spoke of themselves as "belonging" to the person who baptized them, rather than as belonging only to Jesus Christ.

Paul will have none of this approach, and speaks against it passionately. It doesn't matter *who* baptized you, Paul says, because baptism is a sign of union with *Christ,* not of connection to a particular person. This preoccupation with baptism itself, rather than what is signified by baptism, results in spiritual chaos and division. Paul seeks to redirect their attention away from the baptismal rite and the individual performing it to the cross of Christ signified in the rite. This, of course, is where the focus needs to be.

Paul's advice needs to be kept in mind as we move through these practical questions. In baptism, we need to "keep the main thing the main thing." We must keep our focus on what is fundamental and central. Later in 1 Corinthians, Paul makes another comment about baptism that is equally helpful and relevant. He says, in 12:13, "For in the one Spirit we were all baptized into one body — Jews or Greeks, slaves or free — and we were all made to drink of one Spirit." This is the second vital thing to remember in our practice of baptism: *Baptism is not a private event; baptism unites us to the one body of Christ, the church.* There is only "one Lord, one faith, one baptism" (Eph. 4:5).

So who should conduct baptisms? Can anyone do it? Does one need a special power invested at the time of ordination? We know that the apostles, at least, were commanded to baptize (Matt. 28:19). The church has always understood this as a command given not only to the apostles as individuals, but to the whole church, whose vocation is to "make disciples of all nations." I believe this is the starting point for the "who" question: baptism is the responsibility of the whole church. Yet I also believe that the apostles, and the pastoral leaders who follow after them, have a responsibility to oversee the sacrament of baptism, not because they have some special power, but because they are in the unique position of being able to represent and speak for the whole church, and because they speak for the whole church, they also, in a sense, speak for Christ.

It is the failure to understand this truth that lands the Corinthians in such a muddle. They do not see their pastoral leaders as speaking for the whole church and representing Christ, and so they divide up into camps and bicker with each other. Leadership in baptism needs to be conducted on behalf of and with a view to the whole church and to the larger purposes for which Christ instituted baptism.

This means that the decision-making about baptism should be done by those persons who have been invested with leadership responsibility in a local congregation. In the Presbyterian/Reformed structure, that means the elders together with the pastors of the church. Other church structures may work differently, but the underlying principle is the same: those appointed by the church to pastoral leadership should make decisions about baptism on behalf of, and with a view to, the well-being of the whole church. This means that it won't do for just anyone to get up and start baptizing people. If baptism truly ushers us into the body of Christ, then someone who is recognized as representing the body of Christ should authorize and conduct the baptism.

How should pastoral leaders make decisions about who should be baptized? Some Baptist churches give an open invitation for anyone to come forward, make a profession of faith, and be baptized, right on the spot. In those churches, baptism is entirely a decision of the individual seeking baptism. If baptism is simply a public profession of faith, there is a certain logic in this approach. But if, as we have argued, baptism is a sign and seal of God's promise and call, then this open invitation will not be adequate, because then a more focused question emerges: Is there good reason to believe that God is indeed calling this person, individually and personally, to become a disciple of Jesus Christ?

As we have noted in earlier chapters, there are two different ways that congregational leaders discern the answer to this question. They can affirm the reality of God's promise and call, either (1) because they have good reason to believe the parents are believers, and hence God's promise extends to their children, or (2) because they have good reason to believe that the Holy Spirit has brought about repentance and faith in the person seeking baptism.

It is one thing to claim God's promise to the children of believers; we have already explored the ground for this in previous chapters. It is another matter to say that the church has good reason to believe that God is calling a particular person, because we see the Spirit's work in that person's life already. Can we really know whether God is calling someone, based on their testimony of repentance and faith? Is even this a sufficient basis on which to baptize, or must we always have a "hedge" in the back of our minds, assuming that this might, or might not, really work out?

The apostle Paul seemed to think that we could have a sufficiently firm ground for such knowledge. Consider, for example, his words in 1 Thessalonians 1:4-8:

> For we know, brothers and sisters beloved by God, that he has chosen you, because our message of the gospel came to you not in word only, but also in power and in the Holy Spirit and with full conviction; just as you know what kind of persons we proved to be among you for your sake. And you became imitators of us and of the Lord, for in spite of persecution you received the word with joy inspired by the Holy Spirit, so that you became an example to all the believers in Macedonia and in Achaia. For the word of the Lord has sounded forth from you not only in Macedonia and Achaia, but in every place your faith in God has become known, so that we have no need to speak about it.

Paul says that he *knows* that God has chosen the Thessalonian Christians (verse 4). He has this knowledge because they embraced the proclaimed Word, and the Word bore fruit in their lives that other Christians recognized. Here we have in Scripture the kind of "working confidence" that needs to shape the church's decisions about baptism. Where the Word is believed, and the fruit of the Spirit is evident, there people should be baptized as the sign and seal of what God is doing in their lives, and of the promise that the God who began a good work in them will bring it to completion (Phil. 1:6). God's promise and call are not so mysterious that we can know nothing about them; the discernment of such things is part of normal pastoral work.

The corporate focus of baptism as entry into the body of Christ also provides the essential answer to the *when* and *where* questions regarding the baptismal rite: Baptisms should be part of the church's normal worship service, whenever and wherever those services are held. Although some early baptisms were conducted in private because the candidates were baptized in the nude, the church's usual practice, throughout most of its history, has been to conduct baptisms as part of its normal worshipping life. There are very good reasons for this.

First, it is when the church is *gathered* that it is most clearly and fully the church. The very word "church" means literally "assembly." We are most truly the church when we assemble together. If baptism signifies one's entry into the church, it should be done in assembly. Secondly, baptisms in the assembly of the church lend themselves naturally to the beginning of relationships of mutual accountability that are part of the life of discipleship. When I am baptized, I now belong to other Christians, and they belong to me. We have responsibility for each other. It is important to recognize and affirm these truths within a service of baptism, and it is much more difficult to do so in a private baptism.

There are some Christian traditions that tend to emphasize more strongly the necessity of baptism for salvation. In those traditions, there is often pressure, especially in the case of infants who die at or near childbirth, to conduct baptisms outside of normal worship services. As we have explored in previous chapters, however, this pressure is a misguided one. If baptism is indeed based on the promise of God, that promise is in force, even before baptism takes place, and baptism only ratifies and confirms God's promise. Parents who lose a child in childbirth need not be anxious about whether or not the absence of baptism will affect the child's covenant standing before God. At the same time, despite the fact that such private baptisms are not *required* theologically, pastoral leaders at times have conducted baptisms in hospital for such dying infants, as a way of bringing the church, as a loving and supportive community, to the parents and the child, when the family cannot come to the church. This too can be a powerful expression of the unity of the body of Christ.

However, churches would do well to resist agreeing too quickly to other requests for baptism outside of normal worship services. In such cases, it may be fruitful to explore why the person wants to avoid the usual worship service. Is there resistance to taking one's place as part of the body of Christ? Such resistances should be addressed, before baptism is administered. In unusual cases, of course, the pastoral discretion of congregational leaders should be exercised, in a way consistent with the broader understanding of baptism and the church we have explored in this study.

One last point needs to be addressed. In this chapter, we are speaking of what is desirable, and what best contributes to the good order of the church and its mission. We are not speaking of the *minimum* requirements for a valid baptism. Many Christians have been baptized in churches or other contexts that do not share the perspectives outlined in this chapter. I heard recently of one young adult Christian who was baptized by his father (who was not a minister) in the bathtub at age four! Was this a valid baptism? (By "valid" I do not mean "proper" or "desirable." Instead, the question of validity focuses on whether the person should be baptized again or not — whether such an unusual baptism can be recognized as a Christian baptism.) I believe, despite the fact that this is certainly not the way baptism *should* be done, that this may be a valid baptism, if it was done in faith with solemn intent. I believe that any baptism is valid that is done sincerely in the name of the Triune God. The reason for this is simple: the power and efficacy of baptism does not finally depend on the person or community doing the baptism, but only on God's faithfulness. The church should strongly discourage such baptisms outside of the corporate fellowship, since they threaten to undermine the unity and good order of the church. But in the final analysis, the church should recognize any sincere Christian baptism done in faith, and in the name of the Father, Son, and Holy Spirit. Baptism does not belong to us; it belongs to God, and Scripture is full of the mysterious ways in which God sometimes works outside of normal systems and structures to accomplish the divine purposes.

There is only one body of Christ, which manifests itself wherever Christians gather in assembly to worship. It is this one body into which we are baptized. Decisions about who should baptize, who should be baptized, and when and where baptisms should be conducted all flow from this core understanding of baptism as entry into the body of Christ.

To Sum Up

> Our *practice* of baptism needs to affirm what we *believe* about baptism, especially its focus on union with Christ, and its corporate emphasis on entry into the body of Christ.

> Decisions about baptism and leadership in baptismal practice should be in the hands of church leaders, who represent the whole church.

> The discernment of readiness for baptism is a practical matter, involving looking for tangible signs of repentance and faith in the candidate, or in the case of small children, in the parents.

> Baptisms should normally be done in regular worship services.

> While churches should attend carefully to their own good order, they also should *recognize* as valid any baptism done sincerely, in faith, and in the name of the Triune God.

For Further Reflection and Discussion

> Imagine you are a minister meeting with the young person described at the end of this chapter, baptized by his father in a bathtub. What questions would you want to ask? What concerns would you have?

> Under what circumstances, if any, would you be willing to participate in a baptism outside of a normal worship service? Why?

> What unusual sorts of baptisms or requests for baptism have you encountered? How would you evaluate them, in light of the principles outlined in this chapter?

For Further Study

> One interesting ecumenical document that seeks to lay out a consensus understanding of baptism among many denominations, and is very attentive to the question of the unity of the church, is *Baptism, Eucharist and Ministry* (Geneva: World Council of Churches, 1982). It is available online at http://www.wcc-coe.org/wcc/what/faith/bem1.html.

27 Can Grandparents Present Grandchildren for Baptism If the Parents Are Not Confessing Members of the Church? What About the Children of Parents Whose Faith Is Weak, or Whose Church Membership Is Uncertain?

This is a question with a long history behind it in America. When the Puritans settled New England in the seventeenth century, they established churches with a structure and order commonly termed *congregationalist.* They practiced infant baptism on the basis of a theology of God's covenant. However, they made a distinction between this membership by baptism and full membership in the church. Full membership required public testimony of a conversion experience, and the evidence of repentance and faith in one's life. This full membership included both the right to partake of communion, and to vote in congregational meetings. Since in early New England congregations made most of the decisions regarding local governance, full membership also involved the right to participate in decision-making for the community as a whole.

In this context, full church membership did not spring at its core from baptism, but rather from the voluntary "covenant" made by mutual consent among the "saints" — those who had given public testimony of their conversion. The form of the visible church was defined by the *Cambridge Platform,* an early (1648) Congregationalist church order, as "a visible Covenant, Agreement or Consent, whereby [saints] give up themselves unto the Lord, to the observing of the Ordinances of Christ together in the same Society, which is usually call'd The Church Covenant."[1]

This twofold way of thinking about church membership — involving

1. As cited in H. Shelton Smith, Robert T. Handy, Lefferts A. Loetscher, *American Christianity: An Historical Interpretation with Representative Documents* (New York: Charles Scribner's Sons, 1960), p. 132. The *Cambridge Platform* is available online at http://www.pragmatism.org/american/cambridge_platform.htm.

recognition of infant baptism, but with the predominant focus set on voluntary covenant — resulted eventually in controversy. Many of the children of those early Puritans continued, as baptized members, to attend church regularly, but made no public testimony of their own conversion experience. When these children then began to have children of their own, the problems started to arise: What should be done with these grandchildren of saints, born of *baptized* members of the church, but who were not *full* members in the sense of embracing the voluntary covenant on which the church was based? Should the infant children of those baptized members who attended church, but were not themselves full members, be baptized?

The New England churches formulated an answer in 1662, which has often been termed the "Half-Way Covenant." This decision allowed for the baptism of the grandchildren of those who were in full communion with the church, even if the immediate parents of the child had not given public testimony of their own conversion experience, so long as the immediate parents were not involved in scandal and continued in the fellowship of the church. Still later developments in some parts of New England resulted in the admission of these baptized-but-not-publicly professing children and grandchildren to the communion table, in the hopes that communion would nourish the "germ of grace" that was already in them by virtue of their baptism.[2]

Many church historians see the Half-Way Covenant as reflective of a decline in spiritual vitality in New England in this period, part of the eventual collapse of the Puritan movement, despite subsequent attempts at revival, including the "Great Awakening" under the leadership of Jonathan Edwards, a vocal critic of the Half-Way Covenant. The New England experiment in the Half-Way Covenant is thus not a particularly attractive historical example to follow, in seeking to discern which children are appropriate candidates for infant baptism.

But what are we to make of these issues from a biblical and theological perspective? God's covenant with Abraham was a covenant not merely with Abraham and his own immediate children, but with *all* Abraham's subsequent descendants. God says to Abraham (Gen. 17:7): "I will establish

---

2. This practice is attributed in its origin to Solomon Stoddard, grandfather to Jonathan Edwards. Edwards eventually repudiated this practice. See Smith, Handy, and Loetscher, *American Christianity*, p. 220.

my covenant between me and you, and your offspring after you *throughout their generations,* for an everlasting covenant, to be God to you and to your offspring after you." By this reckoning, directly applied to the church, anyone who could trace their lineage back to *any* Christian might be eligible for baptism.[3] Yet as we have seen in chapter 17, this particular covenant with Abraham (which God made with no one else), constituted Israel as a people, and found its culmination in Christ. But this ethnic identity of the people of God has been transcended in the gospel. In the New Covenant, there is no covenant promise of God which applies "throughout the generations" of believers. Rather, as we saw in chapter 18, the focus of God's covenant promise falls on *families* or *households.* God's gracious purpose for the world in the New Covenant begins with the renewal of the foundational unit of society, the household. That is why, as we have noted, there is so much exhortation and instruction devoted in the New Testament to households. The gospel promises not the establishment of religious dynasties, but rather the transformation and renewal of household units — the basic building blocks of a new creation.

It is this New Testament concern for families and households that forms the basic framework within which we must make decisions about candidates for infant baptism. God's promise to be our God and the God of our children is not fulfilled in the abstract, on some spiritual plane divorced from human experience. It is fulfilled in the tangible, day-to-day relationship between parents and their children. Parents pray for their children. Children watch their parents pray. They hear their parents' instruction in the faith. They see how the truths of the gospel take shape in the day-to-day decisions made by believing parents. In these concrete ways, the gospel is communicated, both in words and in deeds. It is this witness that God uses most centrally to awaken faith in the hearts of baptized children and to draw them into the fullness of fellowship with God and with the wider church.

This is the context that must inform decisions the church makes about which infants it should baptize. To put it simply and directly, I believe that the church should baptize only those infants who have at least one parent who is both a believer and a member of the church into which the infant is

---

3. Of course, this logic was never applied in such a sweeping way, even within Judaism. Even among Jews, the mere fact that a distant ancestor might have been Jewish is not sufficient reason for a person to be considered Jewish.

baptized. Several aspects of this assertion require further explanation and elaboration.

First, the church should only baptize infants who have *at least one parent* who is a believer. By "parent," I mean someone who has a recognized and final responsibility for the care and nurture of that child. The question of who counts as such a "parent" may vary, depending on the cultural context. Some cultures have much more extended households where grandparents may exercise a significant role in the lives of children. But even in such cases, I believe the final determinant should be whether that "parent" has a *recognized* and *final* responsibility for the care of the child. The parent of a child is the person on whom this primary and ultimate responsibility rests. If this most basic parental relationship is not infused with the presence of the Spirit emanating from the life of a believer, then the household in which this relationship exists is not a believing household, and the infant born to such a household should not be baptized on the basis of God's covenant promise to believers and their children. This is the essential error of the Half-Way Covenant, which abstracts God's covenant promise from the actual faith life of believing parents.

Secondly, by "believer" I mean *someone who is baptized and whose life and witness show, by charitable judgment, the signs of repentance and faith in the gospel.* Parents must themselves receive the covenant sign, before their children do. But parents also must embrace the gospel for themselves. The baptism of children cannot be done in a way that simply presumes on the baptism of the parents. Rather, pastoral leaders have a responsibility to determine if the parents have embraced the meaning of their baptism in faith, and are bearing the fruits of that faith. If the parents are not speaking and acting as if they belong to God's covenant people, there is little ground to believe that God's covenant promise extends to their children.

Finally, the parent(s) must be *members of the church into which the infant is baptized.* Since baptism ushers an infant into the body of Christ, the parents must also be actively involved with that same expression of the body of Christ, in relationships of mutual accountability in a local congregation. To baptize members of a household that is not actively participating in the body of Christ is to deny the members of that household the regular sustenance they need to be followers of Jesus. The entire Christian community is a means of grace, through which baptized persons are nurtured in their faith and brought to Christian maturity. Pastoral leaders have a responsibility to ensure that baptized infants will receive the nurture from the body of Christ through which God brings them into full discipleship.

All of these judgments are pastoral in nature, and require a delicate balance of wisdom, good judgment, and effective communication, if they are to be implemented effectively and gracefully. Often requests for the baptism of infants can be opportunities for the church to help the parents to take deeper steps in their own Christian walk. These moments ought not to be passed by. Holding clearly to God's central covenant purpose for the renewal of households, and to the necessity of participation in the body of Christ, can assist pastoral leaders in sorting through the maze of decisions that often accompany unusual requests for infant baptism.

However, a bit more should also be said about grandparents. Even though I find no basis in the New Testament for baptizing grandchildren on the basis of the faith of their grandparents (unless grandparents have final parental responsibility for the grandchildren), this does not mean that the witness, faith, and prayers of grandparents for their grandchildren have no importance. In the first of the Ten Commandments, God says, "I the Lord your God am a jealous God, punishing children for the iniquity of parents, to the third and the fourth generation of those who reject me, but showing steadfast love to the thousandth generation of those who love me and keep my commandments" (Exod. 20:5b-6). What is being described here is not the *membership* of subsequent generations in the covenant community. (The children of the disobedient are not removed from the covenant community.) Rather, the focus here is on the negative and positive *impact* of disobedience or obedience on subsequent generations. It does not take any special revelation to see the impact "to the third and fourth generation" of many of our sinful behaviors. Specialists in "family systems" note how many destructive patterns of behavior replicate themselves in following generations. But it is a great hope and encouragement to know that our acts of faithfulness and obedience will also have impact, long after we are gone, even to the thousandth generation! Such impact is not the basis for church membership, but it testifies to the enduring effects brought about by simple lives of faithfulness in those who follow us — an impact that by God's grace often extends far beyond what we ourselves can see.

To Sum Up

> The question of whether children can be baptized on the basis of their grandparents' faith, without having believing parents, is one with a long history in America.

> Because the focus of New Covenant promises centers on *households,* the church should baptize only those infants who have at least one parent who is both a believer and a member of the church into which the infant is baptized.

> Although the faith of grandparents is not a sufficient ground for baptizing children into church membership, there are strong promises in Scripture regarding the positive impact of the faith of parents extending down through generations to come.

For Further Reflection and Discussion

> This restriction of baptism as a covenant sign for households, rather than a sign to be given "throughout your generations" is one difference between baptism and circumcision as covenant signs. Do you think this distinction is justified? Why or why not?

> Can you think of examples where the "final responsibility" for parenting is not entirely clear? How should the principles of this chapter be applied in such instances?

For Further Study

> An Internet search on "Half-Way Covenant" will provide a good bit of additional historical information about this practice in American history.

28 I Don't Remember My Baptism as an Infant, and My Parents Didn't Raise Me as a Christian. Now the Holy Spirit Has Brought Me to Faith in Christ. Should I Be Baptized Again?

There are a number of issues at stake in this question. It may be easier to consider it as a whole if the more specific issues are teased out separately. We can begin by framing the original question this way: was this person's original baptism *valid?* When the question is framed this way, we confront again the division that we have encountered repeatedly in this book: the debate between those who regard baptism as a sacrament and those who regard it as an ordinance (see chapter 4). If baptism is an ordinance that points primarily to our repentance and faith, then the answer might be that the original baptism spoken of here is *not valid,* since it claimed a faith for the child and for the parents that was not present when the child was baptized. At the very least, the parents failed to express with their lives the faith they professed at their child's baptism. And the infant, of course, was incapable of expressing faith when he or she was baptized. So if baptism is an ordinance that points primarily to our faith, then the option of conducting another baptism, in which the person has the opportunity to bear witness to his or her own faith in Christ, might seem appropriate. It would clarify, under this assumption, what was left ambiguous in the first baptism as an infant.

For believer baptists, the same basic answer might be given, even if the parents had attempted to raise the baptized child as a Christian, but the child rejected the faith, only to return later in life to faith in Christ. Here as well, the newly converted adult might feel, since the baptism as an infant did not express the child's own faith, that he or she should be rebaptized. This is the policy of many believer baptist churches: whether a baptized infant is raised as a Christian is irrelevant. Whether baptized infants even wander from the church is irrelevant. Rather, the only valid baptism is one that expresses personal repentance and faith. Any baptism that does not express the repentance and faith of the person being baptized is invalid, and any such person should, when they come to true faith, be baptized again on the basis of their own confession. Strictly speaking, believer baptists do not regard this as *rebaptism;* rather, baptism on the basis of repentance and faith is the *only* true baptism. Christians who have not offered their *own* repentance and faith to God in the ordinance of baptism have not yet been fully obedient to the will of God.

Some believer baptist churches take this line of argument a step further still. Since baptism, they argue, is a sign of repentance and faith, it should be done *whenever* someone experiences a fresh movement of the Spirit, resulting in renewed repentance and faith. In many respects, this is the most consistent application of the interpretation of baptism as a sign of our repentance and faith. Yet the problems become all the more obvious with this approach. Clearly, in the New Testament, baptism is a rite of *initiation.* Nowhere in the New Testament is Christian baptism performed more than once. Everywhere it is spoken of as the *beginning* of the Christian life, not as its *renewal.*

In this book we have rejected this whole line of argument that treats baptism as a sign of faith and repentance, arguing instead that baptism is primarily an expression not of our faith, but of God's promise (see chapters 4, 5). Consequently, this strategy for justifying the rebaptism of someone already baptized as an infant who has only recently been converted to Christianity cannot be accepted.

But the question of the validity of the original baptism looks very different if we understand that baptism expresses not primarily our faith and repentance, but God's promise. Then the question becomes something like this: Did God really make a promise to unite this child to Christ when he or she was baptized as an infant? Some might be inclined to answer No. They might argue that the original baptism did not truly express the divine promise. Since the parents failed to raise the child as a Christian, there was no true faith in the lives of the parents when the infant was baptized. Since the baptized infant initially rejected the gospel as he or she grew older, there was no reason to believe that the Spirit, at that point, was at work in his or her life. Therefore, there was no basis for believing that God's promise extended to the infant, when the baby was baptized. Thus, the person should be baptized again, now that there is firm ground for believing that God's promise extends to this person.

But when we press this argument a little further, it breaks down. How do we *know* that the parents lacked true faith when they brought that infant for baptism? It is challenging enough to discern the presence of true faith when we can sit down with someone, talk to them, and observe their life. Even in such instances, the best the church can do is to make a "charitable judgment," accepting a person's confession of faith unless there are clear reasons for calling it into question. Who are we to say that the parents of this child lacked true faith, even if their parenting abilities were lacking, or even if their own faith weakened and wandered when they were raising the child? Furthermore, how do we *know* that the Spirit was *not* at work in this person, even when he or she was, at the surface level, alienated from the church and from the gospel? Can we know how and where the Spirit is at work so surely? The apostle Paul, after all, said that God had set him apart before he was born (Gal. 1:15), yet in his early life, he was a blasphemer and persecutor of the church (1 Tim. 1:13)!

The more we press on this line of argument, the more it becomes clear that it leads us into a maze from which there is no escape. Ultimately, it makes the validity of God's promise dependent on the relative obedience of the parents and the baptized child. It requires that we act as judges of the past, attempting to discern in the past whether the parents had true faith, and whether the Spirit was at work in the child. But the maze gets even more entangling. Ultimately this line of argument must leave us agnostic about whether *any* baptism expresses God's promise, since we can never *know* for certain if the faith that parents profess, or even the faith that converted adults profess, is genuine. If God's promise is only valid if our faith is sure, we are left with a divine "promise" on which no one can place any trust. Faith finally turns back on itself, since the validity of the promise is entirely dependent on the faith of the one who seeks to claim it. The validity of the promise is then based on our faith, rather than on God's faithfulness. Something is very wrong with this picture!

Here is where a distinction may be helpful. We have already argued that the *fulfillment* of God's promise is conditional, based on faith.[1] We receive the promise in no other way than through faith. But the *validity* of the promise itself is not conditional, nor is the validity of the promise based on the faith of the parents or of the person being baptized. God truly and genuinely offers us promises in baptism, and those promises are valid, regardless of whether we believe and trust in them. God never qualifies or

---

1. See chapter 23.

withdraws the promise to unite us by faith to Jesus Christ and make us heirs of all of Christ's benefits. We may spurn the promise and refuse to trust in it, and therefore fail to receive its blessings, but it is no less *valid* a promise, simply because of our failure to respond. If I promise to give you something, and you never show up at my house to receive it, my promise is no less valid because of your failure to arrive.

So if baptism points primarily to God's promise, and not to our faith, then that promise is still *valid,* even if, for a period of time, it is not yet *fulfilled* in our life, because we have not yet laid hold of it in faith. Ironically, when we return to the question with which this chapter begins, it becomes clear that the conversion of this baptized infant in reality *confirms* the validity of the promise that was originally given in the infant baptism. That promise, given long ago, has proved true, despite the failure of the parents, despite the rebellion and resistance of the person's earlier life. God's promise has proved itself true, despite human failure. This is precisely Paul's line of argument in Romans 3:3-4, when he considers that some Israelites failed to receive God's promise in faith: "What if some were unfaithful? Will their faithlessness nullify the faithfulness of God? By no means! Although everyone is a liar, let God be proved true."

In light of this discussion, it becomes clear how mistaken it is to answer *yes* to the question with which this chapter begins. To baptize such a person again is to confuse matters at a very deep level. Either it sends the message that baptism signifies our faith, rather than God's promise (which violates what Scripture says about baptism), or it calls into question whether God's promise given in baptism can be truly trusted — even though the person's conversion demonstrates the *trustworthiness* of God's original promise and God's faithfulness to the promise!

Sometimes, however, such an answer may be *intellectually* convincing, but still *emotionally* unsatisfying to people who, like the Prodigal Son, have wandered in a far-off country for a long time. They feel, in their own experience, that they were dead, and have come back to life; they were lost, and now have been found. The symbolism of baptism speaks powerfully to them. They know what it is like to be dead in their sins, and they know what it is like to experience the powerful life of Christ surging within them, healing and cleansing them and making them a new creation. They long for some tangible way to express this in the midst of the people of God, and to embrace, this time by their own choice and with their own faith, the covenant promises God has made to them.

But this longing, at its core, is not a longing for baptism — as if God's promise was not yet sure. It is instead a longing to *confess* one's faith — a longing prompted by the Spirit of God. Indeed, to ignore this longing is to ignore the prompting of the Spirit. But the question must be faced squarely: is rebaptism the best way to confess this faith? We must not ignore the ways in which such an act may, quite inadvertently, call into question the validity of *all* baptisms, and indeed may call into question the trustworthiness of the promise of God signified in baptism. It is far better for such persons to stand beside the baptismal font and to confess anew their faith. To locate confession of faith at this place in the sanctuary is to remind both them and the congregation of their baptisms. On the basis of those rich promises, these newly returned prodigal sons and daughters can confess afresh and anew their own faith, laying hold of those promises in faith and hope. Many churches are exploring creative ways to express these renewed commitments with fresh vitality and power in the worship of the church.

But there is also one further reason why the church does well to avoid rebaptisms. It has to do with the unity of the church. Ephesians 4:5 tells us that there is "one Lord, one faith, one baptism." To rebaptize someone is, almost necessarily, to deny the validity of the person's first baptism. It is thus to call into question one's Christian unity with all those who have received a similar baptism. Baptism is not only about us; it is about the body of Christ into which we are incorporated in baptism. We must be very careful, and very cautious, about taking actions through rebaptism that can threaten to divide the church that stands united in Christ.

This was an issue that arose all the way back in the fourth century, in the Donatist controversy. As we noted earlier, in chapter 5, there were some leaders who had denied their faith under persecution. The question then emerged: Were the baptisms done by those ministers valid, or were the baptisms called into question because of the unfaithfulness of the person who conducted them? The church's answer to that question is still relevant to us. The church said that the validity of baptism does not depend on the faith of the person who conducts the baptism, but simply on the truth of the Word of God. For the vast majority of Christian churches, therefore, any baptism which is done in the name of the Triune God is accepted as a valid baptism, regardless of disagreements, or even accusations of sin or failure that might occur between denominations. The core issue here is exactly the one we have been exploring in this chapter. The validity of God's promise does not depend on our faithfulness, but entirely upon God's faithfulness. Every baptism in the name of the Triune God expresses the promise of God. That promise never needs to be repeated or renewed; it stands forever on the faithfulness of God. Likewise no Christian baptism, which attests to this promise, should ever need to be repeated.

To Sum Up

> Some believer baptists practice "rebaptisms" (though they usually don't call the practice "rebaptism"). They do this because they believe that the only valid baptism is one in which people express their own faith. This perspective is not adopted by this book.

> Others might be attracted to rebaptism because of doubts about the sincerity of the faith of parents who brought an infant for the initial baptism. Yet the *validity* of baptism does not depend on the faith of the parents, but on God's faithfulness.

> When baptized infants come to faith later in life, this indicates the truth and validity of the promise of God given to them in their original baptism. Rebaptism can obscure this important truth.

> Because Scripture tells us that we are all one in Christ, and because baptism's validity depends not on us, but on God, local churches should affirm that any baptism which is done in the name of the Triune God is accepted as a valid baptism.

For Further Reflection and Discussion

> Sometimes the question of "rebaptism" involves not only a debate about infant baptism. A person may feel alienated from parents, and may desire to establish an identity separate from the religious identity handed down by parents, even though both parents and children are Christians. How do we best address not only the theological issues in this question, but also the emotional ones?

> Do you accept the statement made in this chapter that "to rebaptize someone is, almost necessarily, to deny the validity of the person's first baptism"? Why or why not?

For Further Study

➤ Arguments over rebaptism were heated during the Reformation, and much persecution was carried out against those who engaged in the practice, who were called (by their opponents) "Anabaptists." An Internet search on "Anabaptist" will turn up a wide variety of sources on this controversy.

29 Some Parents Are Not Persuaded by the Biblical Case for Infant Baptism. Is It Appropriate in Such Cases for Them to Dedicate Their Baby to God in a Public Worship Service?

The dedication of babies to God in public worship services is a fairly recent innovation in the life of the church.[1] In our increasingly mobile society, churches find themselves filled with Christians who have grown up in many different denominational traditions, often with differing approaches to baptism. As these differing traditions engage each other, and as pastors struggle to work with congregations with increasingly diverse expectations and assumptions regarding infant baptism, services of dedication often arise as a kind of compromise measure. They sometimes function as a "dry baptism," which seeks to express some more direct involvement of God in the lives of small children, but which stops short of the affirmations implicit in infant baptism.

There are points where infant dedication grates against *both* the theology of believer baptism and the Reformed theology of infant baptism. Some believer baptists object that it weakens their clear emphasis that a decision for or against the gospel can be made only by an individual; no

---

1. For an erudite, but in my judgment unconvincing, attempt to establish infant dedication as a liturgical church practice in the third and fourth century, see David F. Wright, "Infant Dedication in the Early Church," in *Baptism, the New Testament, and the Church: Historical and Contemporary Studies in Honour of R. E. O. White*, ed. Stanley E. Porter and Anthony R. Cross (Sheffield: Sheffield Academic Press, 1999), pp. 353-78. While Wright demonstrates that the sign of the cross was often placed on the forehead of catechumens well before baptism, he fails to document that this was a regular liturgical practice. Moreover, his central piece of evidence — the early and repeated signation of Augustine by his mother and his baptism later in life — indicates that such signation was not done only by priests or other church leaders. This is a telltale indicator that such marking with the sign of the cross was a pious gesture, and not a liturgical act. This can scarcely be understood to be a precedent for infant dedication as it is practiced today.

one else can make that decision for you. Infant dedication, in this view, threatens to compromise the unique responsibility of the individual to confess faith. No one can "dedicate" someone else to God; we can only dedicate ourselves to God in response to the gospel. Interestingly, the Reformed theological perspective of this book would agree with this argument. Reformed theology also believes that infant baptism has legitimacy only if it is based on God's promise and intent, not on our desires or interests. We can only act on behalf of our children to baptize them if God wills this to be done. From the perspective of Reformed theology, we do not *dedicate* our children in baptism; rather, God *claims and marks* them.

Infant dedication is also problematic for other reasons, from the perspective of Reformed theology. From a Reformed perspective, infant dedication also lacks sufficient grounding in the covenant promise of God. It becomes a merely *human* action, rather than a human *response* to God's promise and claim. But some people may be attracted to infant dedication, precisely *because* they believe that there is a covenant promise that God makes to families. These people may believe in a theology of the covenant, but they may reject the notion that baptism is a sign of the covenant, insisting that baptism must be understood as a sign of repentance and faith. In this view, infant dedication is a mediating position that recognizes and claims the covenant promises of God, but preserves baptism as a sign of repentance and faith.

We have already discussed in chapters 4 and 5 the difference between a sacrament and an ordinance, and have argued that baptism is not centrally a sign of our repentance and faith, but of God's promise and call. We need not rehearse those arguments here, though they argue strongly against the practice of infant dedication as a substitute for baptism. However, we will explore here a more focused question: Can a service of infant dedication be understood as an acceptable means for celebrating and claiming God's covenant promise for the children of believers?

A service of infant dedication can be understood in two different ways, and it will be useful to explore both of these possible meanings attached to infant dedication. One of these dimensions focuses on the child. Here the emphasis falls on offering the child up to God as a gift to God, in response to God's covenant claim upon the child. The other dimension focuses on the parents, who make a commitment to raise the child faithfully, and who ask God for grace to be able to do so. In the first case, we can speak more definitively of *infant* dedication; in the latter, one might describe the practice more precisely as *parent* dedication, since the focus falls on what the parents promise to do.

There are a few biblical passages that are commonly cited in support of infant dedication. One of them is the story of Hannah, the mother of Samuel. When she is unable to bear a child, she prays to God and asks for a male child. She declares that if God will give her a male child, "then I will set him before you as a nazirite until the day of his death. He shall drink neither wine nor intoxicants, and no razor shall touch his head" (1 Sam. 1:11b). The nazirite vow was normally made by someone on his own behalf, but in this instance, as well as in the story of Samson in Judges 13, a barren woman promises to offer the child as a nazirite if she is able to conceive. A nazirite is someone consecrated in a special way to God, beyond the relationship with God experienced by a normal Israelite. In some biblical contexts, such individuals are understood to be endowed with the Spirit of God in a special way. They could touch no alcohol, could not cut their hair as long as they were nazirites, and could not go near any corpse, even if their own parents should die (see Numbers 6).

Clearly, then, the story of Hannah is not talking about a general way in which all parents dedicate their children to God, but something more specific, and less universally applicable. It is worth noting that Hannah actually gave up custody of the child as soon as he was weaned, in fulfillment of her vow, leaving him at the sanctuary (1 Sam. 1:24-28). It is difficult to base a more general practice of infant dedication on this text.

Others appeal to Luke 2:22-24, in which Jesus was presented at the Temple. Here the text reads,

> When the time came for their purification according to the law of Moses, they brought him up to Jerusalem to present him to the Lord (as it is written in the law of the Lord, "Every firstborn male shall be designated as holy to the Lord"), and they offered a sacrifice according to what is stated in the law of the Lord, "a pair of turtledoves or two young pigeons."

Yet neither can this account be understood to function in a way that is parallel to infant dedications today. This trip to the Temple is motivated by two specific requirements of the Old Testament law. On the one hand, Mary comes to offer a sacrifice to purify herself after childbirth, as is required in Leviticus 12:2-8. On the other hand, there is a special sacrifice required to redeem each firstborn male child, as required by Exodus 13:2, 12. Yet neither of these has anything to do with infant dedication as it is practiced in churches today. Infant dedications today are not restricted to firstborn male children, and have nothing to do with the need of mothers to "purify" themselves after childbirth. Both of these requirements were done away with when the sacrificial requirements of the law became fulfilled and set aside in Christ's sacrifice.

Other Christians, recognizing that these texts are not adequate to establish a biblical warrant for Christian dedication of infants, turn instead to broader themes of Scripture. Some turn to the biblical theme of *consecration* as a warrant for infant dedication. Throughout the Bible, people are consecrated, or set apart, to be devoted to God in a special way. Priests are consecrated (e.g., Exod. 28:41), as are prophets (Jer. 1:5), and nazirites (Num. 6). Yet the consecration of priests and prophets never occurs at the initiative of human beings. It is always God who commands that someone be consecrated or set apart as prophet or priest. The nazirite vow is a voluntary vow, but also represents a specific order that is established by divine decree, not by human initiative. In all these instances, it is difficult to see how the biblical theme of consecration can be used to justify a general practice in which all children are "consecrated" to God in a service of infant dedication.

Others turn to the theme of *covenant* as a background for infant dedication. Yet even here, there are significant variations. For some, the dedication of infants is understood as an act of covenant-making before God, in which the parents solemnly promise to raise their children to be Christians, and call upon God to honor their commitment by drawing the child to himself. The problem, however, with understanding infant dedication as covenant-making in this sense, is that in the Bible, covenants always begin not with a human promise but with God's initiative. We do not initiate the covenant-making process with God; we only respond to God's initiative to make covenant with us. Unless God has made covenant promises to us with respect to our children, there is no basis for parents to offer themselves or their children in covenant to God.

But what shall we say to those who believe that God *has* made covenant promises to believing parents regarding their children, but who do not accept that infant baptism is the proper sign of that covenant? Is it appropriate to dedicate infants as a sign of a divinely-initiated covenant? I believe that churches do well to *avoid* this practice. First, there is no scriptural warrant for dedication as a sign of God's covenant. We have seen that the dedication stories of Hannah and Mary do not represent covenant signs relevant to us. Both baptism and circumcision are clearly signs of God's covenant in Scripture, but there is no scriptural precedent for dedication as a covenant sign. Secondly we must ask about the nature of this covenant which is allegedly signified by infant dedication. Is this a covenant that is centered in Jesus Christ? If it is not centered in Christ, then infant dedication cannot be a Christian practice, for all of Christian faith and life flows to and from our union with Christ.

But let us assume that infant dedication signifies a covenant that is centered in Christ. What then is the status of this dedicated child, with respect to Christ? Does this child belong to Jesus Christ? If we do not know that the child belongs to Christ, then we have no business dedicating the child to Christ. We are then imposing our will on God, rather than submitting to God's will. If the child *does* belong to Christ, then all the benefits of belonging to Christ are promised to the child, including new life, cleansing, and the gift of the Holy Spirit (Rom. 8:9; 1 Cor. 15:23; Gal. 3:29; 5:24). In this case, why not baptize the child, since baptism points more clearly and powerfully to these realities than dedication does? But if we do not believe that these benefits of belonging to Christ are promised to the child, then we are left with a covenant devoid of promises, merely an expression of the hopes and wishes of the parents, rather than God's promise.

So it seems that there is no scriptural basis for a general service of infant dedication, at least if such a service focuses specifically on the dedication of the baby to God. We cannot make any decisions for infants that God requires them to make for themselves in relation to God, and we cannot claim or offer to God any status for the child that God has not established and ordained in his Word. Infant dedication also has no warrant as a covenant sign, and even if it is practiced as a covenant sign, it leaves the relationship between the child and Jesus Christ uncertain — a vital and central issue too important to be left unclear.

Sensing these problems, many churches that practice infant dedication do not speak of God's covenant, and place the focus not on the dedication of *infants,* but on the promises that *parents* and the church as a whole make to raise their children in obedience to God's instruction in Scripture. So in many such services, the parents make solemn promises to teach their children the truths of the Christian faith, to pray for them and to teach them to pray, to model for them in a winsome way the path of discipleship, and to challenge them with their need to make a personal decision to follow Jesus. Sometimes extended family members offer their promises to provide support and encouragement to the child, and the church as a whole is engaged in a vow to care for and pray for the child. Curiously, after all these promises are made, the *child* is then dedicated to God. One might suppose that the logic of the ceremony would require that the parents and members of the church would dedicate *themselves*, not the child! They, after all, are the ones who have taken the vow.

But logical consistency is not the only problem with infant dedication, when the emphasis falls on the vows of the parents. The deeper problem has to do with the expectations that such a ceremony sets in place. If parents promise to raise their children to make their own commitment as Christians, and the children subsequently fail to do so, then the seemingly inevitable conclusion is that the parents failed to fulfill their vow. If the parents protest that they have fulfilled their vow, then the finger of blame necessarily turns to the child, who has turned away from the gifts of God. All of this, of course, may well be true: parents do at times fail, and some children do grow up to reject the faith commended to them, despite the best intentions of their parents to raise them differently. What is striking in all of this, however, is the absence of any reference to God's activity. Because infant dedication is unsure of God's promises with respect to the child, the child's salvation becomes dependent on human factors, rather than ultimately upon the Spirit of God. If the salvation of our children is part of a bargain we strike with God — a bargain based ultimately on our keeping of our vow — then we have only ourselves to blame when we fail. Indeed, crying out to God for deliverance in the midst of our own failures is a form of complaining that we have no right to make.

The end result is to lead parents into despair, at precisely the point where they need to be led into a deeper repentance and reliance upon God. If the salvation of our children depends on our faithfulness, there is no sure ground on which to stand. If the salvation of our children depends on God's faithfulness, there is reason to hope, to pray, to work, and to endure in love, even when our best efforts seem to bear no fruit, even when our past failings seem to leave no ground for hope. The promise of God is not to be presumed upon, but it is our last and strongest ground for hope and endurance in the spiritual nurture and care of our children. Infant dedication can offer at best only a pale reflection of that hope, and at worst, can send the message that the salvation of our children depends finally on us, rather than on God. Churches do well to avoid this practice, which has no scriptural warrant and only scanty attestation in the history of the church.

To Sum Up

> As a halfway measure, infant dedication conflicts with the theology underlying both believer baptism and infant baptism.

> There is no meaningful scriptural support for the practice of infant dedication.

> If parents believe that their children are included in God's covenant, then baptism is a more scriptural sign of that covenant than dedication.

> When the emphasis in infant dedication falls on the vows of the parents, the implicit tendency is to blame the parents when children do not profess the faith for themselves, rather than to call parents to deeper trust in and reliance upon God.

> With little precedent in church history, and no clear scriptural warrant, infant dedication should be discouraged.

For Further Reflection and Discussion

> Some people who practice infant dedication defend the practice by saying that, in reality, it is merely a way for the church to pray for and extend its support to parents in the demanding task of raising their children. In light of the discussion in this chapter, how would you respond?

> Is it ever warranted for one person to *dedicate* another to God?

For Further Study

> An Internet search for "baby dedication" or "infant dedication" will turn up numerous suggestions for how churches should bring the practice into public worship. Review a few, and analyze the theology implicit in them in light of the discussion in this chapter.

30 What Happens *After* Baptism?

Baptism marks the beginning of discipleship. In baptism, Jesus Christ marks us as his own, and our union with him is sealed to us as both a present gift and a future calling. Baptism seals to us the promise of the gospel that through faith in Christ we are united with him, cleansed of our sin, given new life, and empowered by the Holy Spirit. All this is promised to us in baptism and received by faith. In baptism, Jesus comes to us, as he came to his disciples long ago beside the Sea of Galilee, and says, "Follow me." We did not deserve this invitation. The invitation did not come because Jesus saw our faith and decided that we would "make the grade." It is not the drama of our decision that is in focus in baptism; it is the graciousness and trustworthiness of God's invitation and promise. The invitation to follow Jesus, as well as the power to say "yes" to that invitation, come to us entirely by God's mercy and by the power of the Spirit. We live our lives, choosing over and over to follow Jesus, because Jesus first chose us, and called us in our baptism.

There is a tendency, among some North American Christians, to regard baptism as the goal and end of the Christian life, rather than as the beginning of discipleship. For some, the temptation is to become so preoccupied with the initial *decision* of faith that we lose sight of the fact that the decision to accept God's call is one which must be made again and again, throughout our lives. Over and over, in deepening ways, we confront the need to respond to Jesus' call to be disciples. In baptism, we are placed on the road of discipleship. Of course, the journey begins with that first step, and this should be celebrated heartily. Yet baptism is only the first step of what is usually a long journey.

For some parents of young children, the baptism of their child sadly becomes a goal and end, rather than a beginning, because it is one of the few occasions on which they will ever gather with Christians for worship. Some regard baptism merely as a "christening," in which the child formally and publicly receives its name. For others, it is simply the first public celebration of the birth of a new child. For still others, it is a gesture to please grandparents, or merely a vague impulse arising from a long dormant faith. There is little awareness or recognition of the claims that baptism will make on them and on their children.

For all these reasons, it is important to think about what comes *after* baptism. In most Christian traditions that practice infant baptism, the baptismal service involves the making of promises. Parents whose children are to be baptized, as well as adult candidates for baptism, are called upon to renounce evil, and to commit themselves to following Jesus within the fellowship of the church. Parents promise to nurture their children in the Christian faith, to pray for them, and to teach them to pray, and to teach them, by word and example, what it means to follow Jesus. The congregation also promises to care for and nurture its newly baptized members. These promises are not what baptism is *about*, at its core. Baptism is centrally about *God's* promise and call. We make promises *because* God makes promises to us in baptism. Given the fickleness of our hearts and the weakness of our wills, God's promise is the only sure ground of confidence in our baptism, the only basis on which we can have the boldness to make promises of our own. But when we make our promises in baptism, it directs our attention forward, to the journey into which our baptism ushers us. What does that journey look like, and how can these promises that we make be fulfilled?

We keep our bearings on the journey, first of all, by remembering that baptism gives us a new *identity*, an identity shaped not by who we have been in the past, but by who we are becoming in union with Christ.[1] Romans 6:11 reminds us that we are to consider ourselves "dead to sin and alive to God in Christ Jesus." This may not be what we always experience day to day, but it is our core identity, our destiny that awaits us in Christ. Baptism looks forward to this destiny by giving us an image of who it is that we are becoming in Christ.

The first and foremost task, after baptism, is therefore to *remember who we are,* by remembering our baptism and what it signifies. Each day,

---

1. We discussed this in more detail in chapter 7.

we do well to remind ourselves of the meaning of our baptism: We have died with Christ, and a new creation is growing within us. We have been cleansed of our sins, joined to our fellow Christians, and gifted by the Holy Spirit. We need to tell this over and over to ourselves, and we need to tell it to our baptized children. There are thousands of voices that we encounter every day which try to tell us who we are and what really matters about us. They tell us that we are Americans, that we are consumers, that we are victims or perpetrators, winners or losers, rich or poor, beautiful or ugly, nameless faces in a crowd, or perfect individuals around whom the whole world revolves. In the midst of so many voices calling out to us, it is hard to remember who we are. We can get sidetracked, distracted, and forget the path on which we are walking. After baptism, we need to work hard to remember the identity given to us in our baptism, and to hold on to that identity, as we are constantly being asked to exchange it for another.

We also need to remember *whom we are following.* We are not the "masters of our fate, the captains of our souls." That place belongs to Jesus Christ, who has called us to follow him. We belong to him, and we bear his mark upon us. We are called to follow him, and to pattern our lives after his. Thousands of other voices each day try to persuade us to follow them, but our baptism invites us continually to listen for the voice of the Good Shepherd, and to ignore the voices of those who would distract us from the path of discipleship.

But *how* do we do this? How do we remember who we are, and whom we are following? We get a start by remembering that the life journey into which baptism ushers us is not one that we take in solitude. Baptism makes us a member of the visible church, the flesh-and-blood gathering of disciples of Jesus who walk together as they follow Jesus. When we ask about what happens after baptism we are asking centrally about the life of the Christian community. Most of what happens after baptism in the Christian life takes place in the context of the relationships that make up the body of Christ.

During the time of the Reformation, there was tremendous upheaval in the church, controversy over what was the true church, and how it could be distinguished from the false church. Calvin and the later Reformed tradition identified three "marks of the church," as indicators of where the church was genuinely present. These marks of the church point us to the central ways in which the shared life of the church helps us to remember our baptism and to keep our bearings on the journey of faith.

First, the true church is known by the preaching of the Word of God. The baptized keep their bearings by constantly returning to Scripture, meditating on its truth, hearing it proclaimed and explained. The Word of God is like oxygen for Christians: take it away, and Christian life quickly withers away. So the first and most central way in which we live out our baptism is by continuing to be regular hearers of the Word, in worship, in small group settings, and in personal reading and study. Our baptized children need to be regularly exposed to the Word of God, so that it sinks into the marrow of their bones and forms their self-understanding. Scripture continually reminds us who we are, and whom we are following. We will not stay focused and clear on these questions without its strength and support.

The second mark of the true church singled out by the reformers was the proper administration of the sacraments. If baptism is the beginning of new life in Christ, the Lord's Supper is the meal that sustains us on the journey. The Lord's Supper conveys to us the same essential truth signified by our baptism: our union with Christ by the power of the Holy Spirit. Although Christians throughout the history of the church have not always agreed on the precise meaning of the words, "This is my body," they have recognized that in the Lord's Supper, Jesus is pointing our attention to a deep and profound way in which Jesus' life is joined to ours. He becomes our food and sustenance, and the life we draw from the Supper is the life of Christ himself. Whether Christians conceive that life as physically present in the bread and the wine or as spiritually present in them, it is still Christ's life which the Supper conveys to us. Without this life, Christian life withers, just as it withers without the constant renewal of the Word of God.

This means that the baptized need to feed regularly at the Lord's Table. Baptized children need to be taught at an early age the meaning of the Supper, and when they are ready to receive the Supper with a faith appropriate to their age level, they should partake, along with adults.

But it is not only through eating and drinking at the Lord's Supper that we are sustained for the journey. We are also sustained by the practices that surround the Lord's Supper. In preparation for the meal, we are exhorted to be reconciled with our brothers and sisters in Christ. We are also encouraged to confess our sins in a fresh and probing way before partaking. In the Eucharistic service, we bring forward our gifts, along with the bread and wine, as the symbolic offering of our whole lives to God. In all these ways, our minds and hearts are focused afresh on our true and deepest identity, and our lives are shaped, more and more, into the image of Christ.

In addition to the Word and the sacraments, the reformers, especially in the later Reformed tradition, identified *discipline* as a third mark of the church as well. By discipline, the reformers meant in part the practice of intervention in the lives of those who are not acting in ways that are true to their baptism. When we are baptized, whether as infants or adults, we become subject to the discipline of the church. We agree that both we and our baptized children are not "on our own," but are part of this body, and amenable to its discipline. But something more positive is also envisioned by the practice of discipline. The true church *orders its life* around practices that help to keep it faithful to Christ, and Christians hold each other accountable to that shared and ordered life. The disciplined life is a life of regular prayer, both individually and with others. It includes practices of generosity, hospitality, and Sabbath-keeping.[2] It is a life that seeks to be shaped by the commandments, the rich wisdom that conveys God's intentions for a redeemed humanity. It is a life that involves the making and keeping of promises, and the wisdom and grace of granting forgiveness, reconciliation, and healing amidst our failures.[3] It is only through such shared disciplines and practices that Jesus' deepest purpose for us can be fulfilled, and that we can begin to be what he has called us to be: the salt of the earth and the light of the world.

When we are united to Christ's life in baptism, that life is lived out concretely in the hearing of the Word, in the celebration of the Lord's Supper, and in the disciplines of the church. These marks of the true church are also the central and indispensable resources that sustain the baptized in the life of discipleship. When we think about baptism, we need always to remember that this is the life into which we are ushered by our baptism. It is this sustaining life that empowers us continually to lay hold of the promise of our baptism in faith, and to endure to the end.

2. When I speak of "Sabbath-keeping," I refer to the regular weekly practice of rest, renewal, and worship. Christians find a variety of ways to incorporate the rhythms of Sabbath into their lives. What matters most is living out the essential principles, rather than whether a specific day is legalistically set aside.

3. For further helpful discussion of these practices that make up the ordering of life after baptism, see *After Baptism: Shaping the Christian Life* by John P. Burgess (Louisville: Westminster John Knox, 2005).

To Sum Up

> Baptism at its core points to God's promise to us, but God's promise calls forth promises from us as well, as we are directed to the path of discipleship that lies before us.

> The central challenge in living out our baptism is to remember *who we are,* and *whom we are following,* as disciples united to Jesus Christ.

> We are sustained in our baptismal identity through the preaching of the Word, through the use of the sacraments, and through discipline and the practices of the church.

For Further Reflection and Discussion

> In many churches, the practice of church discipline and mutual accountability has become rather weak. Where have you seen discipline and mutual accountability working most effectively?

> Which Christian practices have been most helpful to you in assisting you to remember who you are, and whom you are following?

For Further Study

> For an excellent discussion of the subject matter of this chapter, see John P. Burgess, *After Baptism: Shaping the Christian Life* (Louisville: Westminster John Knox, 2005).

A Select Annotated Bibliography on Baptism

Aland, Kurt. *Did the Early Church Baptize Infants?* Philadelphia: Westminster, 1963.

A critical response to the work of Joachim Jeremias listed below *(Infant Baptism in the First Four Centuries)*. Should be read in conjunction with that book.

Armour, Rollin Stely. *Anabaptist Baptism: A Representative Study.* Studies in Anabaptist and Mennonite History, No. 11. Scottdale, Pa.: Herald Press, 1966.

An excellent resource for Anabaptist theology and practice.

Beasley-Murray, George R. *Baptism in the New Testament.* London: Macmillan, 1962.

The most exhaustive biblical study from a believer baptist perspective.

Bromiley, Geoffrey. *Children of Promise: The Case for Baptizing Infants.* Grand Rapids: Eerdmans, 1979.

A concise defense of infant baptism from a Reformed perspective.

Brooks, Oscar S. *The Drama of Decision: Baptism in the New Testament.* Peabody, Mass.: Hendrickson, 1987.

A biblical study from a believer baptist perspective emphasizing baptism as an expression of the decision for faith, rather than as a divine promise.

Burgess, John P. *After Baptism: Shaping the Christian Life.* Louisville: Westminster John Knox, 2005.

An excellent resource for the material covered more briefly in chapter 30 of this book.

Calvin, John. *Institutes of the Christian Religion.* Edited by John T. McNeill and translated by Ford Lewis Battles. Philadelphia: Westminster, 1960.
A classic source for Reformation thinking on the sacraments. On the subject of baptism, see especially Book IV, chapters 14-16.

Green, Michael. *Baptism: Its Purpose, Practice, and Power.* Downers Grove, Ill.: InterVarsity, 1987.
An accessible evangelical Anglican perspective on baptism.

Jeremias, Joachim. *Infant Baptism in the First Four Centuries.* Translated by David Cairns. London: SCM Press, 1960.
An excellent, though perhaps overly ambitious historical study arguing that infant baptism was practiced consistently from the earliest period of the church. Note the critique of Kurt Aland listed above.

————. *The Origins of Infant Baptism: A Further Study in Reply to Kurt Aland.* Translated by Dorothea M. Barton. London: SCM Press, 1963.
Response to the critique of Kurt Aland listed above.

Jewett, Paul K. *Infant Baptism and the Covenant of Grace.* Grand Rapids: Eerdmans, 1978.
The most thoughtful and comprehensive critique of infant baptism from a covenantal, yet believer baptist perspective.

Luther, Martin, "The Babylonian Captivity of the Church." In *Selected Writings of Martin Luther, 1517-1520,* translated by A. T. W. Steinhaeuser and edited by Theodore G. Tappert. Philadelphia: Fortress, 1967. Available online at http://www.ctsfw.edu/etext/luther/babylonian/.
Luther's critique of the seven sacraments of the medieval church was one of the foundational documents of the Reformation.

Marty, Martin. *Baptism.* Philadelphia: Fortress, 1962.
A brief introduction from a Lutheran perspective.

Osmer, Richard Robert. *Confirmation: Presbyterian Practices in Ecumenical Perspective.* Louisville: Geneva, 1996.
Summarizes a wide range of ecumenical conversation surrounding confirmation.

Porter, Stanley E., and Anthony R. Cross, eds. *Baptism, the New Testament, and the Church: Historical and Contemporary Studies in Honour of*

R. E. O. White. JSNTS Supplement Series 171. Sheffield: Sheffield Academic Press, 1999.

A collection of New Testament studies from a believer baptist perspective.

————. *Dimensions of Baptism: Biblical and Theological Studies*. JSNTS Supplement Series 234. Sheffield: Sheffield Academic Press, 2002.

More New Testament studies from a believer baptist perspective.

Riggs, John W. *Baptism in the Reformed Tradition: A Historical and Practical Theology*. Louisville: Westminster John Knox, 2002.

The best overview of baptism in the Reformed tradition from the perspective of historical theology.

Schlink, Edmund. *The Doctrine of Baptism*. Translated by Herbert J. A. Bouman. St. Louis: Concordia Publishing House, 1972.

Contemporary systematic treatment from a Lutheran paedobaptist perspective.

Smedes, Lewis B. *Union with Christ: A Biblical View of the New Life in Jesus Christ*. Grand Rapids: Eerdmans, 1983.

A superb and accessible study of an important theme in baptism.

Strawbridge, Gregg, ed. *The Case for Covenantal Infant Baptism*. Phillipsburg, N.J.: P&R Publishing, 2003.

A somewhat scholastic, but vigorously argued case for infant baptism from a Reformed perspective.

Warfield, B. B. The Polemics of Infant Baptism." 1899. Available online at http://the-highway.com/InfantBaptism_Warfield.html.

A classic defense of infant baptism from the perspective of Reformed scholasticism.

White, James F. *The Sacraments in Protestant Practice and Faith*. Nashville: Abingdon, 1999.

A helpful overview of recent ecumenical conversation about sacraments in general.

Willimon, William H. *Remember Who You Are: Baptism, a Model for Christian Life*. Nashville: Upper Room, 1980.

A very accessible and broad discussion affirming infant baptism.

World Council of Churches. *Baptism, Eucharist and Ministry* (Geneva: WCC,

1982). Available online at http://www.wcc-coe.org/wcc/what/faith/bem1.html.

An important resource indicating areas of ecumenical consensus surrounding baptism.

Index of Scripture References